Praise for *Mystical Stories from the Mahabharata:*

"The *Mahabharata* is a treasury too little known to the West, and these selections can only help to bring it to a wider audience. Highly recommended."
> —*Library Journal*

"Bhakta's careful selection of the poem's most memorable and uplifting tales makes this an entertaining introduction to Hindu literature."
> —*Publishers Weekly*

"A collection of gripping stories of heroes, heroines, devils, and demons, filled with adventure, romance, intrigue, and wisdom."
> —*India Abroad*

"There is nothing trivial or petty about any of these gemlike vignettes from India's ancient past. Expertly rendered by Amal Bhakta, a lifelong devotee of India's Vedic culture, the book's noble characters and amazing tales convincingly enchant, absorb, enlighten, and renew one. No household should be without a copy."
> —Christopher Warden, Director KHQN
> Radio, Spanish Fork, Utah

"Amal Bhakta has mined the *Mahabharata,* one of the great classics of world literature, for jewellike stories of heroes and heroines that sparkle not only with adventure and romance but with deep spiritual meaning. At a time when many find themselves adrift in a sea of perplexity, *Mystical Stories from the Mahabharata* offers a new moral compass that enables us to chart a better course for ourselves, individually and collectively."
> —Michael A. Cremo, Coauthor of
> *Forbidden Archeology*

"A charming and edifying compendium of lesser known stories from the *Mahabharata.* In an age desperately in need of genuine morality and culture, these pearls of the Vedic wisdom tradition will inspire the reader to lead a more noble life."
> —Hrdayananda das Goswami, Ph.D.,
> Cotranslator of *Srimad Bhagavatam*

Mystical Stories from the
BHAGAVATAM
Twenty-six Timeless Lessons in Self-Discovery

Mystical Stories from the
BHAGAVATAM
Twenty-six Timeless Lessons in Self-Discovery

Amal Bhakta

TORCHLIGHT
PUBLISHING

First printing 2001

Cover design Kurma Rupa Dasa.

Interior design Subala Dasa of Ecstatic Creations

Illustrations by Bhavasindhu Dasa (Ben McClintic)

Printed in India by Indira Printers , New Delhi – 110020

Published simultaneously in the United States of America and Canada by Torchlight Publishing, Inc.

Library of Congress Cataloging-in-Publication Data

Bhakta, Amal, 1932–
    Mystical stories from the Bhagavatam / twenty-six timeless lessons in self-discovery / Amal Bhakta
        p. cm.
    ISBN 1-887089-27-6

    1. Puranas. Bhagavatapurana—Paraphrases, English. I. Puranas. Bhagavatapurana. II. Title.

    BL1140.4.B435 B45 2000   294.5'925 — dc21
                                    00-037733

Attention Colleges, Universities, Corporations, Associations, and Professional Organizations: *Mystical Stories from the Bhagavatam* is available at special discounts for bulk purchases for fund-raising or educational use. Special books, booklets, or excerpts can be created to suit your specific needs.

For more information, contact the Publisher:

Torchlight Publishing
PO Box 52, Badger, CA 93603
Telephone: (559) 337-2200, Fax: (559) 337-2354
Email: Torchlight@spiralcomm.net, Web: www.Torchlight.com

DEDICATION

This book is respectfully and lovingly dedicated to my spiritual master, His Divine Grace A. C. Bhaktivedanta Swami Prabhupada. I can never thank him enough for so mercifully and ably translating and commenting on the *Shrimad Bhagavatam,* which has given me the inspiration and impetus to adapt its transcendental stories for this introductory book. By his example and guidance, I have learned the most important and enriching truth in life, namely, to surrender to and take shelter of God continuously, for by this means one can discover one's true self and achieve real fulfillment.

Acknowledgments

For their invaluable assistance to me in producing this book, I wish to thank Lord Krishna for His inconceivable love and mercy; Sally Raleigh, my mother, for her encouragement and support; Alister Taylor, the publisher, for his creative input; Stewart Cannon (Subala Dasa) for his excellent book design; Kurma Rupa Dasa for his fine jacket design; Bhavasindhu Dasa (Ben McClintic) for his well-crafted story illustrations; Jadurani Dasi for her excellent jacket illustration; H.H. Hrdayananda Das Goswami, Ph.D., for his explanations of difficult Sanskrit verses and brief review; Dr. Thomas Hopkins, Ph.D., for his enlightening foreword; Steven Rosen for his suggestion that I contact Dr. Hopkins to write the foreword; Dravida Dasa for his editing of the introduction; Sujana Dasi, my chief editor, for her many helpful suggestions; Charles Daniel for his useful story feedback; Michael A. Cremo for his suggestions and inspiration; H. H. Radhanatha Swami for encouraging me to include the incredible story of King Rantideva; all the devotees of the Los Angeles ISKCON temple who inspire me daily by their devotional love and service to God; and anyone else whom I may have regretfully omitted who enabled me to better appreciate and enjoy these remarkable stories.

TABLE OF CONTENTS

TABLE OF ILLUSTRATIONS

Every culture has traditional stories that help define its values and beliefs. The best-known stories of this sort in the West come from the Hebrew Bible, the New Testament, and the epics and dramas of classical Greece, supplemented by the folk tales and myths of various European, African, Arabian, and Native American peoples. Most of these stories first appeared in specific religious contexts, but they have not been confined to their original setting. Many have been used by several religious traditions, at times to reinforce different doctrines. Stories, it is clear, have the potential to convey different meanings in different contexts, which is why the most powerful stories have been so often borrowed.

If this is true in the West, it is even more true in India, which has, with little doubt, the world's richest story-telling tradition. From this rich tradition came such great epics as the *Ramayana* and *Mahabharata* and a number of scriptures called Puranas (ancient historical texts). The climax of this line of development was the *Bhagavata Purana*, also known as *Shrimad Bhagavatam*. It was the most influential of all the Puranas in affirming Vishnu (a name and form of God) as the proper focus of faith and worship. The text is famous for the biography of Krishna (another name and form of God) that it presents in the tenth of its twelve books, an account with an element of devotion not found in any previous Sanskrit work.

It is not only Krishna to whom the *Bhagavatam* advocates devotion, however, but Vishnu in all of His forms, and much attention is given to those many forms throughout the text. Alongside its definitive telling of Krishna's story, the *Bhagavatam*'s major contribution is its detailed accounts of Vishnu's numerous other incarnations and their related exemplary devotees, all within a theological framework that presents an integrated rationale for devotion. And, as with other great scriptures, much of the credit for this achievement lies in its rich collection of stories that present easily understood examples of what devotion should be.

The twenty-six "mystical stories" chosen for the present book are clearly only a very small sampling of the *Bhagavatam*'s total number, and some whole categories of stories are not represented. There are no stories of Krishna in this collection, for example, even though the *Bhagavatam*'s account of Krishna's life in Book X covers some ninety chapters and several hundred pages of text. Rather than give a short and inadequate sample of this justly famous account, the author has wisely left the Krishna story as a whole for the reader's separate enjoyment—to be published in the future. Instead, he has focused the selections here on the kind of stories and vignettes that typify the rest of the *Bhagavatam*, has chosen his examples well, and has told them in a way that makes them very accessible. Thus, although the stories may be less familiar than the Krishna story, they effectively convey the same message of devotion to Vishnu as the essential means of salvation—and not just devotion to Krishna, but to all of His manifestations.

This devotional message is, of course, magnified many times over by the *Bhagavatam*'s full array of stories, but the twenty-six stories before us help us understand the influence of this Purana over the centuries. The stories told here are quite representative of the larger array. The subjects and basic plots of many of the stories can be found elsewhere in the Vedas, the epics, and other Puranas, but the *Bhagavatam*'s versions are consistently shaped by the devotional theology that characterizes the scripture as a whole. The stories in many other Puranas often seem out of place, as if they had been assembled by different authors or editors with different agendas. The *Bhagavatam*, by contrast, presents a consistent message throughout, and the stories it shares with other texts have all been subsumed under a single agenda to illustrate the power of devotion. Whatever these stories meant elsewhere in other forms or contexts, there is never any doubt what they mean here.

Finally, one must say that these are good stories: interesting, well told, and fun to read or listen to. The *Bhagavatam*'s message may be uniform but it is never bland, and the variety of stories here and in the text as a whole gives its message nuance and broad appeal. It is, of course, the purpose of stories in every scripture to provide an entertaining hook on which to hang a moral, an ethical principle, or a theological doctrine. That is how traditions have always been conveyed, and why the basic stories of a tradition are often called "grandmother stories"—i.e., stories told on a grandmother's knee to successive generations. It takes good stories to serve this purpose, and this collection has some of the *Bhagavatam*'s best.

So read these stories, think about them, learn from them, tell them to others, but first of all, enjoy them as good stories should be enjoyed.

Thomas J. Hopkins, Ph.D.
Emeritus Professor of Religious Studies
Franklin and Marshall College, USA

INTRODUCTION

What is the *Bhagavatam*?

Actually, the book's full name is the *Shrimad Bhagavatam*, and it literally means the beautiful or glorious activities of God. Known also as the *Bhagavat Purana*, it was written by Krishna-Dwaipayana Vyasa, an incarnation of God, about 5,000 years ago in India. Consisting of twelve cantos and eighteen thousand verses, it is considered to be a holy scripture or *Veda* because it contains knowledge that was originally revealed by God. Thus, it is authoritative and transcendental. Although the *Bhagavatam* includes such subjects as philosophy, theology, psychology, sociology, metaphysics, and history, it does so only in connection with spiritual knowledge.

But how is it spiritual?

The *Bhagavatam* tells us who we really are, why we're in this world, where we originally came from, and what the true purpose of life is. Moreover, it explains the basic cause of all our suffering—physical, mental, and emotional—and shows us how to prevent or overcome it forever. But most important, the *Bhagavatam* shows us how to awaken our lost relationship with God and thereby experience continuous peace and joy under all circumstances. It does this by presenting remarkable stories about the Lord and His dealings with powerful gods, terrifying demons, illustrious kings, compassionate saints, and ordinary people.

When we read about God's glorious activities, we, in effect, get a chance to closely associate with Him. This association is highly beneficial, for it enables us to receive His merciful blessings. These help to purify our hearts and minds of painful materialism, destroy our ignorance and illusions with wisdom and truth, and generate within us admiration, attraction, and devotion for the Lord. Thus, to read these divine stories is to engage in a valuable meditation, for not only are the mind and heart affected, but the soul as well. By regularly nourishing the soul with the transcendental food of God's activities, the soul gradually discovers itself and its relationship with the Lord.

But what is self-discovery? And what is its value?

To discover our true self means to know and to experience ourselves as eternal souls instead of as temporary material bodies—and to act in this understanding. When we do, we cannot be affected or disturbed by the difficulties and distresses we encounter in the material world. This is because we know, without the slightest doubt, that nothing can threaten or harm our real, immortal existence. Consequently, we become filled with confidence and determination to fulfill our daily duties and are able to perform them well. This, of course, results in a glorious future or destiny.

However, to discover our real self, it is absolutely essential that we develop transcendental qualities. Such qualities help to detach us from our materialistic entanglements—especially our bad habits—and to attach us to the service of God, which frees us from our various distresses. To assist the reader in developing such qualities, twenty-six amazing stories have been selected from the *Bhagavatam* and included in this book. Each story emphasizes certain ideal qualities and, when we see them in action, we can only become inspired to incorporate them into our lives.

Vyasa narrated the *Bhagavatam* to his son Shukadeva Goswami, and he revealed it to the saintly King Parikshit, as well as to other sages present with him. But what were the mystical circumstances surrounding its revelation? The answer is given in the first story, "King Parikshit Cursed." Had the king not been cursed to die untimely, the world might not have received this great scripture, nor would we have had a chance to observe how serenely the monarch resigned himself to God's will. He remained fully optimistic, considering his tragedy an excellent opportunity to advance spiritually and enter the eternal world. These qualities are indispensable for discovering our selves.

In the story "Hiranyaksha Challenges God," we learn how a goddess, by inducing her husband to have sex with her at an improper time, caused personal as well as worldwide chaos. We thus discover the value of cultivating self-control. In "Lord Narasingha Saves Prahlada," we see the most horrific case of child abuse in history. But because the five-year-old child Prahlada knew how to depend on God for guidance and security, he was miraculously saved from his terrible ordeal. The fourth story is about a goddess who wanted to kill her innocent nephew but who was artfully dissuaded from doing so by her saintly husband.

The story "Churning for Nectar" teaches us that even though the gods had lost their property and positions to demons, by being deliberately patient and enduring, they recovered all their losses. Also, Lord

Shiva shows us the ultimate expression of compassion, performing an astonishing sacrifice that benefited the whole world. However, in "Lord Shiva Beguiled," when he became proud of his power to be unattracted by beautiful women, his pride was embarrassingly smashed by the alluring charms of the Lord's female incarnation. "Lord Vamana's Conquest" shows us how pleased God was when King Bali kept his promise to Him—even at the expense of Bali's losing his vast galactic kingdom.

"King Bharata's Fall and Rise" is a story about an advanced ascetic who became so slavishly attached to his pet deer that he had to helplessly reincarnate as one; this account informs us of the dangers of attachment. In "God's Name Rescues Ajamila," we learn about the amazing power of the Lord's holy name—how it irrevocably changed a man's future. "Dhruva's Incredible Victory" shows us how a five-year-old boy, by his firm, unflinching determination, achieved the ultimate goal of seeing God within and outside his own being. In "Lord Vishnu Tricks Vrika," we see how a demon, by failing to show proper appreciation to the god who gave him a special blessing, met with disaster.

"Bhrigu Discovers Who God Is" reveals how the Lord expressed the highest level of tolerance and humility even when He was strongly offended by His devotee. In "Narada Sees God Everywhere," we observe how a child, out of helplessness, cultivated the habit of always remembering God and thus became one of the greatest saints in existence. The story "Ashvatthama Punished" shows the folly of vengeance and the necessity of forgiveness and kindness. "King Yudhishthira Sees Evil Omens" instructs us in how to overcome the pangs of separation from a loved one and become peaceful again. In "Kali's Evil Challenged," we see how King Parikshit fearlessly stops Kali from infecting his kingdom with immoral and unethical ideas and practices. "King Chitraketu's Awakening" shows us how possessiveness makes our lives extremely miserable.

We learn how important it is to not belittle saintly persons in "Lord Indra Fights Vritra," and how we should rather honor them to gain their blessings. "Pingala the Prostitute" shows us the futility of living only for money and sex and how we can become detached from them. In the account, "King Ambarisha Protected," we observe how the Lord shielded His fully surrendered devotee from an angry yogi who, by his mystic powers, tried to kill him. "Yogi Saubhari's Downfall" reveals how a powerful mystic fell from his spiritual path when he failed to repent for offending one of the Lord's greatest devotees.

In "King Sudyumna's Sex Change," we note how a king learned to tolerate an undesirable change in his life and still live productively. "Urvashi Enchants Pururava" betrays the abysmal misery associated with becoming addicted to sex. In "Daksha Offends Lord Shiva," a falsely proud king learns, at great expense, the importance of modesty and simplicity. "King Rantideva's Mercy" teaches us, by an extreme example, the value of giving up our personal comfort to relieve others of suffering. And in "Gajendra Fights the Crocodile," we observe how an elephant was freed from his terrifying ordeal by praying unceasingly to the Lord.

These stories, originally written in Sanskrit, are not literal translations. Rather, they are dramatic adaptations, so the author has taken the liberty of trying to make them as entertaining, instructive, and enlivening as possible—without changing any of the stories' facts. In a few cases, to better complete the accounts, the author has added material from other scriptures written by Vyasa. The stories are based on actual historical events that occurred over an extremely long period—most of them on Earth and some on other planets. They have not been arranged in any particular order—variety and novelty dictate their overall sequence—although in several instances certain stories have been intentionally placed after others because they naturally follow or result from them.

Many prayers and explanations of the original text have been either omitted or abridged, not because they are unimportant, but only because their length and complexity make them unsuitable for this introductory presentation. In certain cases, only the names Vishnu and Krishna have been used in place of the epithets in the original text; this was done to prevent the confusion that often arises in readers who may be unfamiliar with the epithets. A glossary has been provided in the Appendix that clearly defines and explains the various Vedic names and terms used in this book.

For whom have these fascinating *Bhagavatam* stories been written?

For anyone sincerely interested in advancing in spiritual life—especially persons who are new to it and who are searching for absolute answers to life's unfathomable mysteries. These stories may also be useful to persons who teach or lecture on spiritual subjects, as they can be used to clearly and colorfully illustrate certain philosophical or psychological points. This book can also be used by persons who have in the past read the *Shrimad Bhagavatam* but who stopped reading it due to no longer having enough time; however, each of the stories contained herein takes only several minutes to read and can thus assist the reader in resuming his or her spiritual progress.

At the end of many of the stories, various spiritual and material benefits are promised to the reader. The author can personally attest to having obtained many of them, and in due course of time—if the reader hasn't already acquired them—he or she also will. If, after reading this volume, the reader's interest and curiosity about its underlying philosophy have been strongly provoked, the author urges the reader to peruse the complete, unabridged *Shrimad Bhagavatam*. The version recommended is the one on which this book was almost exclusively based, namely, the eighteen-volume edition clearly translated and elaborately commented on by His Divine Grace A. C. Bhaktivedanta Swami Prabhupada and his disciples (published by the Bhaktivedanta Book Trust, USA/India). Any questions the reader may have about improving his or her spiritual life will surely be answered in that definitive, invaluable masterpiece. It is a veritable cornucopia—if not an encyclopedia—of transcendental knowledge!

Amal Bhakta

King Parikshit punishes the sage Shamika

CHAPTER ONE

KING PARIKSHIT CURSED

When the king learned about his forthcoming tragedy, he regarded it as God's will and thus welcomed it as an opportunity to advance spiritually. If we wish to discover ourselves, it is very useful to remain optimistic when we are confronted by reverses and adversities.

Riding on his horse-drawn chariot, King Parikshit was extremely hungry and thirsty. He halted the car near a footpath, alighted from it, and slogged through the dense, leafy forest. "I must find some water," he said to himself wearily. "I can hardly walk." With his bow and arrows, the king had been vigorously hunting and trailing stags all day. But now he felt exhausted and faint. He looked here and there for a pond or a puddle. But he found nothing—only trees and bushes and flowers and bowers and—

Then he saw something in the distance. No, it wasn't a stream or a pool. It was the hermitage of the famous sage Shamika. Surely, he would have some water and food to supply him. As he drew closer, the king imagined the recluse pouring him a cup of refreshing water and the uncomfortable dryness in his throat pleasantly disappearing.

Parikshit shambled towards the open door of the thatched hut and kicked off his sandals. Feeling dizzy and breathing heavily, he exclaimed, "Water! I need water!" in a parched voice. He lumbered up the three steps and stumbled into the hermitage. At the opposite end of the room, he saw the sage sitting cross-legged on a straw mat on the floor.

Shamika's eyes were closed, his black hair and beard were long and matted, his arms were outstretched, and the backs of his hands rested on his knees—his thumbs touching his forefingers. Wearing nothing over his trim torso and a cloth over his loins, Shamika was deeply meditating. Scarcely breathing, the sage was blissfully absorbed in the spiritual realm. Thus, he could not hear or see anything external.

At that moment, a few young boys came to the door, stopped, and curiously watched the king.

"I need some water!" said the king desperately to the sage.

But Shamika remained motionless.

"I said I need some water!"

Still, no response.

Perhaps he didn't hear me, thought Parikshit. So he shuffled closer to Shamika. "I need water!" the king shouted. "Water!"

Again, no answer.

This greatly angered the king. "Why are you ignoring me? Open your eyes! It's your king! And I'm thirsty! So take care of me—as you should!"

When the sage failed to reply, the king exclaimed, "Why are you pretending to not hear me? Have I ever wronged you? Never! All I've ever done is protect the Brahmins—so they can live a tranquil life. Is this how you show your gratitude? Or do you think you're better than me—because I'm a warrior and you're a holy man? Is that it? Well, if you're so high, why are you so unmannerly? Even the worst of persons knows to give the king a seat, some water, and nice words. But look at you—pretending you're so deep in meditation that you can't even hear me!"

The boys outside were surprised to see the king speaking so disrespectfully to the sage.

Extremely incensed, Parikshit's energy was now stirred. Thus, he wheeled around and stomped toward the door.

The boys stepped back several feet.

The king's thirst, hunger, and fatigue were somehow more tolerable now. As he reached the doorway and glanced at the side of the steps, he noticed a dead snake lying in the dry grass. Approaching it, he picked it up on the end of his bow, re-entered the ashram, and contemptuously draped the snake over the recluse's shoulder. "This is what you deserve!"

The boys outside were aghast. They hastened away, talking animatedly to each other.

Parikshit abruptly turned and angrily stalked out the door.

As the king, on his chariot, was returning to his palace in Hastinapura, he began to have second thoughts about what he had said and done to the sage. *Why did I suspect him of pretending to not hear me? He's a sage, so he had no reason to pretend. He was probably too deeply absorbed in meditation. How foolish of me! How offensive! I've never in my whole life spoken or acted like that.*

The king considered the possible reasons. *Was it my thirst, hunger, and fatigue that made me act that way? But—how could that be? All my life I've practiced disciplines and austerities. I've gone for days without food, water, and sleep. And never once have I yielded to anger and revenge. But today—I acted totally out of character. It was as if...as if...* He was reluctant to think it because it was not his tendency to blame God. *And yet*, he continued, *it was as if He had totally taken over my thinking, feeling, willing, and speaking. But—why would He do that? What purpose would it serve?*

Parikshit was known as an exemplary king. He ruled the entire world with righteousness and enlightenment. So there was virtually no crime, corruption, poverty, disaster, disease, or pestilence anywhere. His subjects performed their duties skillfully and gladly, and they loved Parikshit immensely. This was because he had established policies— economic, political, social, and religious—that resulted in the people's material happiness and spiritual fulfillment.

The king had been raised by his close relatives—the famous Pandavas—who were personal companions of Lord Krishna (God). He had not only been taught what he should and should not do—according to the Vedic scriptures—but in his life he had always practiced those rules. And above this, he was a self-realized, God-realized soul who, when he was still in his mother's womb, had seen Lord Vishnu save him from death. So there was rarely a moment when Parikshit was unaware of God and of his personal relationship with Him. Thus, he performed his executive duties as loving devotional service to the Lord.

Considering his body, mind, feelings, and speech as belonging to God, the king always begged the Lord to use those faculties as instruments to fulfill the divine will. And the Lord always did. But if God was totally in control of the king, why had He caused him to act as he had— so offensively—towards the sage? Was there some greater plan the Lord had in which Parikshit, as His surrendered servant, would play a significant part? The king could not, at this time, come to any conclusion. But he would soon realize that God did have a plan—and that He had used the king to initiate it. It was an awesome plan—one that would serve to benefit all of humanity for millennia to come.

The boys who had seen the king offend Shamika hastened to the bank of the Kaushika River, where their playmates had gathered. One of their friends, Shringi, was the holy man's son. After Shringi heard how the king had affronted his father, he became furious. "How sinful! What right did he have to enter my father's house?"

"None!" answered one of the boys.

"Can watchdogs enter their master's house and demand to eat with him on the same plate?" asked Shringi sarcastically.

"Never!" said the friend.

"Since Lord Krishna left this world, we Brahmins really have no protector."

"That's right," a few of the boys answered.

"Therefore, I will punish the king myself!" Shringi angrily exclaimed.

"How?"

"Just see my power!" bragged Shringi, his eyes narrowed into slits. For purification, he touched the water of the river and then uttered a curse: "O wretched king, you have violated the rules of etiquette by insulting my father. Therefore, on the seventh day from today, a snake-bird will bite and kill you!"

Since the boy possessed mystical power by birth and training, his deadly curse would be effective and inescapable.

Shringi then hurried home. Along the way, he realized he had acted improperly by cursing the king. Feeling intense guilt and remorse, he began to sob. And when he entered the ashram and saw the snake hanging over his father's shoulder, he sobbed even louder.

Returning to normal consciousness, Shamika heard his son's piercing cries. He opened his eyes, noticed the dead snake hanging over his shoulder, and nonchalantly threw it aside. Then he asked, "Why are you crying?"

In a halting voice, Shringi explained what had happened and what he had done to punish the king.

"What?!" His father was surprised and alarmed.

"I'm sorry, Father."

"The king's offense was insignificant!"

"But it seemed so wrong."

"No!"

"Father, I—"

"What a terrible misuse of your power!"

Shringi bowed his head contritely.

"Do you have any idea of how great King Parikshit is?"

The boy looked up curiously.

"He's like the Supreme Lord. He protects everyone from harm, generates prosperity, and has the character of a saint. That's why people are so happy in this kingdom."

Shringi nodded faintly.

"Without a king like Parikshit, the world becomes filled with thieves. And that leads to social disruptions. People are injured and killed. Animals and women are stolen. The Vedic injunctions are disregarded. Sense gratification is increased. Unwanted children multiply like dogs and monkeys. And we will be responsible for all these sins."

The boy looked down, deeply regretful.

Shamika was overwhelmed with remorse and shame for his son. Dropping to his knees, he clasped his hands, looked up, and prayed, "O Lord, please pardon my son for this great sin—of cursing a sinless king. My boy is still very young and not very intelligent. Please be merciful to him."

In his private chamber, the king was greatly distressed. He felt that his offense against the faultless holy man was wicked and barbaric. He therefore expected some calamity to overcome him in the near future. "Let it come now," he declared. "Then I can be freed from my sin and never commit it again. Yes, let my kingdom, power, and wealth be burned immediately by the Brahmin's anger."

There was a knock on the door.

Parikshit opened it. "Yes?" he said to one of his ministers, who looked very gloomy.

"I have some ill news to bring you, my lord."

"Oh? What is it?"

"Please brace yourself."

"I'm braced. Now what is it?"

The minister paused. "The sage Shamika regrets to inform you that his son Shringi—" He could hardly say it.

"Yes?"

"He foolishly cursed you—to die by a snake bite in seven days."

Although the minister was about to cry, Parikshit smiled, accepting this as good news. He felt it would allow him to become justifiably indifferent to worldly concerns and now concentrate his mind completely on spiritual matters. Albeit the king was spiritually powerful enough to neutralize Shringi's curse, he refused to; he considered the curse to represent God's will, as a means of enabling him to quickly enter the blissful, eternal world and glorify the Lord everlastingly. Thus he welcomed, rather than feared, death.

Parikshit wanted to go to Shamika to apologize and beg pardon for his offense. However, he decided against this because he knew that the sage was feeling profound grief and remorse for his son's imprecation. To visit the holy man, he felt, would only shame him further.

The king explained the situation to his son Janamejaya and bestowed the kingdom on him. Then, accepting the vows of a sage and freeing himself from all kinds of mundane associations and attachments, Parikshit unhesitatingly left the palace and headed for the bank of the holy Ganges River. *Anyone who is about to die*, he thought, *should take shelter of this auspicious river. It is mixed with the dust of Lord Vishnu's lotus feet and thus sanctifies the lower, middle, and upper worlds.*

The king sat down on the riverbank, and soon after, the news of his impending death spread throughout the universe. Thus, numerous sages, gods, and kings, who could understand the value of the occasion, arrived there to meet Parikshit. He received them properly, humbly bowing his head to the ground. When everyone was comfortably seated, he stood up, folded his palms prayerfully, and said, "O saints, sages, and gods, I have decided to stay here and fast to death. Already, I have taken the Lord's lotus feet into my heart. So let the snake-bird bite me immediately. My only desire is that you continue singing about the glorious exploits of Lord Vishnu."

The congregation smiled and nodded admiringly.

"I pray that if I should be reborn in the material world, I'll become totally attached to Lord Vishnu, associate with His devotees, and have friendly relations with all living beings." He then sat down on a straw seat and faced north.

All the gods of the higher planets lauded the king's actions, joyfully scattered flowers over the earth, and vigorously beat drums. The sages were equally pleased and exclaimed, "Very good!" Then one of them said, "It is not astonishing that you have renounced your throne to attain the Lord's eternal association. Thus, we will all stay here till you have achieved this."

"Thank you," said the king. "I would appreciate if you would now tell me — what is the duty of a person who is about to die?"

At that moment, the son of the illustrious sage Vyasa, Shukadeva Goswami, who was only sixteen years of age, arrived there. Among the greatest of sages, he had been traveling over the earth, disinterested in the world and satisfied within himself. Blackish in complexion, he wore no clothes, had curly, tousled hair, appeared to be crazy, and was being followed by curious women and children. He had delicately formed limbs, long arms, attractively wide eyes, a highly raised nose, and a beautifully shaped face and neck. Although he looked unassuming, the great sages there, who were expert in reading faces, honored him by respectfully standing up. Then they sat down again.

King Parikshit bowed his head to receive the young sage. All the women and children who had been following him were surprised and amazed by the youth's prestige, so they quickly left the area. Shukadeva Goswami then sat down on an exalted seat, facing the assembly. Parikshit approached him, bowed down before him, rose, and then said, "O sage, by your mercy, you have sanctified us. You are the spiritual master of great saints and devotees of God. Therefore, I am entreating you to show us the way of perfection, especially when a person is about to die. What should such a person hear, chant, remember, and worship? And what should he not do?"

Shukadeva Goswami answered, "Whoever desires to be free from all miseries must hear about, glorify, and remember the Supreme Lord. He is the Supersoul within the heart, the controller of everyone and everything, and the deliverer from all miseries."

Parikshit nodded in agreement.

"The highest perfection of human life," continued Shukadeva Goswami, "is to remember the Supreme Lord at the end of life. I shall now recite the *Shrimad Bhagavatam*, which my venerable father, Vyasa, taught me, because you are the most sincere devotee of Lord Vishnu. Whoever listens attentively to this work attains unwavering faith in God, the giver of salvation. And whoever constantly chants the Lord's holy name will attain success—in both material and spiritual pursuits."

Shukadeva Goswami then proceeded, for the next seven days, to instruct King Parikshit in many spiritual matters. Some of the subjects included the nature of the soul and the Supersoul; the Lord's incarnations and holy name; the creation, maintenance, and destruction of the world; spiritual salvation, heaven, and hell; and the eternal planets and pure love of God. Everyone present was enrapt and enlivened by his captivating, authoritative discourse. In fact, many of the congregants memorized the eighteen thousand verses Shukadeva Goswami spoke and would later broadcast them to their disciples, who in turn would disseminate them to their students. Thus, this illuminating, liberating knowledge—despite the harmful, enslaving evils of *Kali*-yuga—would be preserved and accessible to all sincere seekers of the truth down through the ages.

This was one of the confidential reasons that the Lord caused the king to commit his offense against the sage Shamika and then be cursed by his son Shringi. The curse would serve as the perfect catalyst for Shukadeva Goswami to come there and narrate the *Shrimad Bhagavatam*, as well as for all the sages and gods to gather, hear, and be benefited by it. The benefit, of course, was that the listeners would be freed from all karmic reactions and reincarnations and thereby ultimately return to the pure planets of the spiritual world. And although the king knew the answers to many of the questions he asked, he asked them anyway so that future truth-seekers would be benefited by Shukadeva Goswami's authoritative answers.

Parikshit then humbly bowed his head at the feet of the young sage, rose, and folded his hands in prayer. "By your mercy, I have now achieved my life's purpose. Because you have revealed God to me, I do not fear death, or repeated births and deaths, in the least."

Shukadeva nodded gladly.

"Please allow me to resign my speech and my senses to the Lord. Permit me to sink my mind in Him and to surrender my life to Him. You have shown me that which is most blessed—the personal feature of God. Now I am firm in spiritual knowledge and self-realization, and whatever ignorance I had has been dispelled."

Shukadeva gave the king his permission.

Along with the sages, Parikshit worshiped the young saint, who afterwards departed. The monarch, free from material attachments and doubts, proceeded to meditate deeply on the Supreme Lord. Soon his life air ceased to move and he became as immobile as a tree.

The snake-bird, Takshaka, was now traveling towards the king to kill him. However, along the way, he met the sage Kashyapa, who was expert in counteracting poison and who wanted to protect the king. But the snake-bird flattered Kashyapa by presenting him valuable offerings and thereby diverted the sage's attention. Able to assume any form he wished, Takshaka disguised himself as a Brahmin. He then approached the king and bit him. Instantly, the snake's poison, like a roaring fire, burned the king's body to ashes.

A terrible cry of sorrow arose in all directions—on the earth and in the heavens—and many gods, demons, human beings, and other creatures were amazed. Then the gods showered flowers, spoke praises, and beat kettledrums while the Gandharvas and Apsaras sang jubilantly. Since the king had returned to the spiritual world, it was certainly a cause for celebration.

When King Parikshit's son, Janamejaya, heard that his father had been bitten by Takshaka, he became furious. Capturing all the snakes in the world, he had the Brahmins perform an awesome sacrifice in which the reptiles were offered in the fire. When Takshaka noted that even the most powerful snakes were being slaughtered, he was overcome with dread. Therefore, he approached Lord Indra, leader of the gods, for succor.

When King Janamejaya did not perceive Takshaka entering the sacrificial fire, he asked the Brahmins, "Why isn't the snake-bird also burning?"

A Brahmin replied, "Because Indra is now protecting him by holding him back from falling into the fire."

"Then why not make Takshaka and Indra both fall into the fire?"

The priests then chanted the mantra for accomplishing this.

Lord Indra, on his airplane with Takshaka, was suddenly thrown from his position and became very upset.

Brihaspati, the preceptor of the gods, saw Indra and Takshaka in the airplane, falling from the sky. He therefore approached King Janamejaya and said, "O King, it's not right for you to kill Takshaka. In the past, when he drank the gods' nectar, he was promised virtual immortality—to be free from old age and death arising from ordinary circumstances. He killed your father as a result of the Lord's will— not from hatred. Therefore, he doesn't deserve to die. So please stop this sacrifice. You have killed many innocent snakes."

Respecting Brihaspati's authority, Janamejaya bowed his head and said, "All right." He then halted the sacrifice and worshiped the sage.

Some of the stories that Shukadeva Goswami narrated to King Parikshit during the seven-day period will now follow. Whoever reads them with faith and devotion will be blessed in the various ways mentioned at the ends of many of the stories.

Lord Boar fights King Hiranyaksha

CHAPTER TWO

HIRANYAKSHA CHALLENGES GOD

Because Diti knowingly induced her husband to have sexual relations with her at an improper time, she caused grave conse-quences for the entire world. Unless we cultivate self-control, we may create serious problems for ourselves and others that seriously prevent us from discovering ourselves.

As the sun sank behind the verdant hills on one of the heavenly planets, Diti, a beautiful goddess, intensely desired to have sex with her handsome husband, Kashyapa. An extremely learned and enlightened man, he was known as a great sage. Having just completed his evening oblations—pouring grains and clarified butter into a sacri-ficial fire—he was now sitting cross-legged on a *kusha* grass mat and facing a silently moving river. His grave eyes were closed and his firm body still as he meditated deeply on the Divine.

Diti gazed at him longingly. She noted his handsome face—with its black beard and mustache—his flowing shoulder-length hair, his bare manly chest, and his sturdy legs beneath his thin white dhoti. She wanted to tell him how aroused she was. But she hesitated, unwilling to disturb his deep meditation. After all, was her desire to have sex more important than his desire to commune with God? Of course not. And yet—she found herself unable to suppress this surging, overpowering force any longer.

As she began walking towards Kashyapa, she sensed a fragrant breeze on her face and body, saw a pair of green flirting parrots flying nearby, and heard a medley of crowing peacocks in the distance. Sitting down before her still husband, she looked at him helplessly and then said loudly, "I'm sorry to bother you, but—"

He opened his eyes curiously.

"But I'm very agitated."

"Agitated?"

11

"Yes—sexually."

He stared at her pleading eyes.

"Please satisfy me—so that I can have a son."

"Of course. But let's wait awhile, so that—"

"I don't want to wait. All my co-wives have sons—but you haven't given me any."

"Just be patient and—"

"I've been just as faithful to you as they—haven't I?"

"Of course."

"Then please bless me with sons—now!"

"I think we should wait a few seconds. Otherwise, people will criticize me."

"Why?"

"Lord Shiva will be passing by in a few moments—with his devotees."

"So?"

"So it would be very disrespectful if we engaged in sex now."

Diti was losing her patience.

He reminded her, "Lord Shiva is extremely powerful—and very easily offended."

She wondered whether Lord Shiva might punish her for such an offense.

"Therefore, let's wait till after he passes."

But Diti couldn't wait a second longer. Losing all reason and control, she clutched at her husband's dhoti and, like a shameless prostitute, dragged him to a secluded bush. Her lust was so overwhelming that it equally engulfed and submerged Kashyapa. Yielding to its irresistible force, he lay down with his wife and fully gratified her desire.

Several minutes later, Kashyapa left his wife's side and entered the river to bathe. Then he meditated on the eternal effulgence and recited the Gayatri mantra.

Diti was now feeling ashamed of herself. Why had she become so demanding and impetuous? Why hadn't she waited, as her wise husband had advised? Wondering whether Lord Shiva would punish her, she anxiously waded into the river and halted beside Kashyapa. She didn't want to interrupt his meditation, but now she felt so guilty and worried that she had to. "My lord," she said loudly.

He opened his eyes and looked at her inquisitively.

"I'm worried. Lord Shiva, out of anger, might kill my embryo."

Kashyapa considered the possibility.

"But you could stop him—by praying to him. Since you're a great devotee of his, he would listen to you."

Trembling with fear, Diti then offered prayers of glorification and repentance to Lord Shiva. After this, she felt regretful that she had again interrupted her husband's evening prayers. But what could she do, since more than anything else she wanted to be a mother?

Kashyapa peered into the future to ascertain the fate of their offspring.

"Will Lord Shiva kill our child?" Diti asked anxiously.

"No."

"No? Then he's forgiven me?"

"Not exactly."

"What do you mean?"

"You will give birth to two monstrous demons."

"Oh, no!"

"Yes. And they will wreak havoc all over the universe."

Diti felt devastated, utterly heartbroken. Since she was a goddess, and since people at that time lived for many thousands of years, she suppressed the delivery of her babies for one hundred years. However, the two demons in her womb, by their sinister influence, began to affect the whole cosmos: the light of the sun and moon became diminished and darkness began to pervade the universe. This caused anxiety to many of the gods, as they became hindered in their administrative work of creating weather, vegetation, minerals, jewels, etc.

Unable to dispel the darkness, the disturbed gods traveled for guidance to the planet of Lord Brahma, the four-headed, four-armed chief god, who creates the universe under Lord Vishnu's direction. They first offered him respectful obeisances and suitable prayers. Then they disclosed their sad plight and prayed to be able to resume their regular duties. But Lord Brahma explained to them the deeper under-lying cause of the darkness. In essence, he told them…

Just prior to Diti and Kashyapa engaging in their inauspicious sex act, something had happened in the eternal world. Far beyond the material universes, that world is inhabited by only exalted, pure-hearted souls. Their entire lives revolve around glorifying and serving the Supreme Lord, Vishnu, continuously. That domain is called Vaikuntha, or the realm of no anxiety. Since the residents there live in their original spiritual bodies—which are composed of eternal substance—they never die. Thus, they dwell there fearlessly and lovingly, always thinking of how they may enhance God's never-ending pleasure.

As a result of their pure, selfless lifestyle, they experience an ever-increasing amount of spiritual bliss and happiness at almost every moment. This is true not only of those beings occupying humanlike bodies, but also of those inhabiting animal, plant, fruit, and bird bodies. All beings there are spiritually intelligent and equally conscious, and each person renders service to God in his or her own special way. In Vaikuntha, there is no need for sexual intercourse as it is known in the material world; for the quality and intensity of pleasure derived from loving devotional service to the Lord is infinitely greater.

Persons in the material world who have attained spiritual perfection—pure love for God—are promoted to Vaikuntha when they leave their physical bodies. Such persons have no selfish motivations, such as the desire to be beautiful, wealthy, powerful, knowledgeable, or famous. Moreover, they possess all good qualities, such as kindness, affection, humility, gravity, and friendliness, and are fully satisfied by just serving and glorifying God. Lord Brahma's mind-born sons, the four Kumaras—Sanaka, Sanatana, Sanandana, and Sanat-kumara—were such persons.

They were Brahma's first offspring. Although they were the oldest and among the wisest persons in the material world, they chose to appear as naked five-year-old children. Self-realized and God-realized, the Kumaras, by their mystic powers, traveled throughout the material and spiritual universes, instantly appearing (or disappearing from) wherever they chose. One day they desired to visit the Supreme Lord, Vishnu, in Vaikuntha. Although in meditation they had experienced His eternal effulgence as well as His attractive form, they had never actually met Him personally. Thus, they were extremely eager to do so now.

The four sages were highly famous in both the material and spiritual worlds. When they arrived at the entrance of Vaikuntha, they had to pass through seven gold-and-diamond gates before they could enter the Lord's opulent palace. Quickly recognizing them, the guards at each of the first six gates gladly granted them admittance. However, when the Kumaras approached the seventh gate, the two guards there, Jaya and Vijaya, did not recognize them. Considering them to be trespassers, the guards, with their large clubs, blocked them from entering.

Anxious to see the Lord, the Kumaras stared at the guards angrily. The resplendent, youthful watchmen were handsome, four-armed, blue-complexioned, flower-garlanded, and adorned with valuable jewelry. In fact, they closely resembled in face and body the supremely attractive Lord Vishnu (as did all the male humanlike inhabitants there). The Kumaras knew that the Lord was always ready and eager to welcome his pure devotees into His domain, so they were quite peeved by the disdainful treatment they had just received. Therefore, they began to discuss this among themselves.

"This is completely improper," said Sanandana.

"It is," replied Sanaka. "These guards are supposed to have the same nice qualities as the Lord."

"But they don't," added Sanat-kumara. "They're acting just like envious materialists."

"Yes, they are," concurred Sanaka.

"I don't think they belong here," stressed Sanandana.

"Neither do I," replied Sanaka. "Actually, I think they're impostors."

"They must be. And they probably think we are, too," responded Sanatana.

"Then we should punish them. And right now," said Sanaka.

"Yes. Let's send them to the material world—where they belong," Sanatana emphasized.

Then the Kumaras, as a single body, cursed the guards accordingly.

The gatekeepers suddenly realized, from the authoritative and powerful manner of the Kumaras, that they were not at all mischievous children but were great sages. Overwhelmed with fear, the watchmen threw themselves at the Kumaras' feet and begged for mercy. Jaya said, "You have justly punished us for disrespecting you. We should not have acted that way."

"But please," added Vijaya, "when we fall to the material world—please don't let us forget the Lord." The gatekeepers, despite their offense, were great devotees of God, and they never wanted to forget Him, no matter where they went.

At that moment, the Supreme Lord, accompanied by His beautiful wife, the Goddess Lakshmi, and fanned by His attendants with yak-tail whisks, appeared there. He had already heard from His servants about the guards' insult to the Kumaras.

When the four sages saw the Lord, they were intensely captivated by His exquisite beauty. Indeed, He was even more beautiful than His stunning wife. As He rested one of His four hands on the shoulder of His eagle carrier, Garuda, and twirled a lotus flower in another hand, His affectionate smile and glance deeply touched the Kumaras' hearts. They gazed with thirsty eyes at His blackish countenance, bejeweled golden crown, broad chest, yellow garments, charming necklace, and garland of flowers. Their eyes unsated, they blissfully bowed their heads at His lotuslike feet.

As a gentle breeze blew the fragrance of the Tulasi leaves from the toes of the Lord's feet to the Kumaras' eager nostrils, the sages became overwhelmed with bliss and happiness—far more than they had ever experienced in their meditation on the Lord's infinite light. It was a truly transformational experience! Drinking in God's personal sweetness, beauty, and goodness, they wanted only to serve and glorify Him forever. Thus, devotional prayers, pregnant with humility and gratitude, flowed sweetly from their pure mouths. And the more they lauded Him, the more ecstatic they felt.

Lord Vishnu congratulated them for their sweet words and then said, "My guards, Jaya and Vijaya, have greatly offended you. Therefore, I approve of your punishment for them. Since they are My attendants, their offense has become My offense."

"No, Lord," protested Sanandana.

"Yes, it has. I thus seek your forgiveness. It pains Me to see devotees like you offended." The Lord glanced at the gatekeepers and then back to the Kumaras. "Since these guards have rendered fine service to Me, I would appreciate if you would do me a favor."

"Anything, Lord," said Sanat-kumara.

"After they've suffered in the material world, would you please allow them to return here soon?"

"Surely," said Sanaka. "However, it seems to me now that we've cursed two faultless persons."

"Yes," added Sanandana, "for anyone serving You here is incapable of committing any fault."

"That's true," smiled the Lord. "Actually, this situation was completely prearranged by Me."

"Prearranged?" asked the Kumaras, puzzled.

"Yes."

"But—why? Why would you want your devotees to fall to the material world?" asked Sanaka.

The Lord smiled affectionately at them. "In due course of time, you will all understand this mystery."

The Kumaras, out of respect, joined their palms prayerfully, circled Him three times reverently, offered Him obeisances, and then departed from Vaikuntha.

The Lord turned to Jaya and Vijaya. "You should leave for the material world now. But you need not fear. Actually, I could have nullified the sages' curse, but I didn't because it's part of a larger plan that I have."

"Larger?"

"Yes. And both of you are in it."

The guards looked baffled.

"You'll understand later—when you return here. Now go."

Leaving the eternal world, Jaya and Vijaya became morose, and their beauty and luster diminished. As they fell towards the material world, the Kumaras again approached them. "After you take birth three times," said Sanaka, "our curse will end. At that time, you'll return to Vaikuntha."

As Jaya and Vijaya entered the material atmosphere, they were flooded with ignorance and passion. This meant that when they would take birth, they would have no recollection whatsoever of their life in the eternal world as God's servants. Instead, they would become fully preoccupied with acquiring pleasure and power—or trying to become God.

Lord Brahma concluded his explanation to the gods. "The souls of those two gatekeepers have been in Diti's womb for the past one hundred years. You're disturbed because their power—in the form of darkness—has minimized yours."

"True, but isn't there something we can do to overcome it?" asked one of the gods.

"No," said Lord Brahma. "Because it's something desired by God. Therefore, He will rescue us when He wants to."

Understanding the situation, yet feeling heartened and confident, the gods offered their thanks and respects to Lord Brahma and returned to their respective planets.

When Diti finally gave birth to the two demons, many fearsome and wondrous disturbances occurred in nature. There were earthquakes, hurricanes, fires, lightning, and thunder. Unfavorable planets, like Saturn, appeared brightly, while comets and meteors fell swiftly.

Masses of dense clouds hid the luminaries and thick darkness reigned everywhere. The ocean, with its giant waves, wailed loudly, and in the villages, jackals howled ominously. Dogs barked, asses brayed, owls hooted, birds shrieked, and trees fell. Terrified cows yielded blood instead of milk, and temple deities shed profuse tears. Everyone everywhere was horrified and terrified, for they thought that the world was about to end.

Kashyapa named his younger son Hiranyaksha and the older one Hiranyakashipu. The two demons grew up rapidly. Their steellike bodies became so tall that the crests of their golden crowns seemed to kiss the sky. They sported golden anklets, shining bracelets, colorful garlands, and beautiful sashes. Resting their huge clubs on their shoulders, they stomped along angrily, shaking the earth with their every step.

Hiranyaksha was always ready to please his older brother by his deeds. Thus, by his mystic powers, this blond-haired demon with small tusks wandered all over the cosmos in a fighting spirit. Tremendously powerful both physically and mentally, Hiranyaksha was extremely proud. When he challenged the mighty gods to a fight, they fled in panic and disappeared. Believing he was invincible, the demon roared loudly with delight.

After Hiranyaksha returned from the heavenly realm, for the sake of sport, he angrily dived into the deep ocean. There, he roared so terrifyingly that all the aquatics, dreadfully alarmed, swam far away from him. The demon played in the ocean for many, many years, repeatedly smiting gigantic waves with his iron mace.

Finally, he reached Vibhavari, the watery home of the god Varuna, lord of the aquatic creatures and guardian of the lower regions of the universe.

Hiranyaksha first offered him his respects. Then, desiring to prove his supremacy, he smiled and mocked him. "O great lord, you're a famous warrior. You've conquered all the gods and demons. You've performed big sacrifices. Now— fight with me!"

Perceiving that the demon's vanity knew no bounds, Varuna became angry; nonetheless, he managed to restrain his wrath and diplomatically said, "O dear one, I've grown too old for warfare. Thus, I've stopped fighting."

"Stopped?" Hiranyaksha was surprised.

"Yes. But you're so skilled that I think only Lord Vishnu could satisfy you. So why don't you challenge Him?"

"Lord Vishnu?"

"Yes. He's much more your match."

"All right, then I will!"

Learning from the sage Narada where Lord Vishnu was, Hiranyaksha hastened to the Garbhodaka Ocean, at the bottom of the universe.

Now it so happened that while Hiranyaksha had been terrorizing the universe, he had excavated and stolen, for his own selfish purposes, all the gold that existed in the earth. This caused an ecological imbalance, dislocating the earth from its orbit. The earth then fell through space, splashed into the Garbhodaka Ocean and sunk to the bottom. When Lord Brahma learned of this, he became very concerned. Many human beings and animals would have to be born on earth, but its watery environment now made it uninhabitable for them. He therefore spent much time pondering how to lift it out of the ocean.

Hoping that the Supreme Lord would direct him, Lord Brahma, surrounded by some of his enlightened sons, suddenly noticed something very strange. A tiny boar, no larger than the upper portion of a thumb, flew out of one of his nostrils. The boar then rose into the sky and grew to the size of an elephant. Brahma was astonished. Looking at his sons, he asked, "Is he some great person pretending to be a boar? Just look at him: one moment he's tiny and the next, he's huge! Could he be—the Supreme Lord, Vishnu?"

As Lord Brahma discussed this with his sons, the boar tumultuously roared once, then again, His uncommon voice echoing in all directions. Recognizing the auspicious sound to be that of Lord Vishnu—known in this form as Lord Varaha [Boar]—the sages began to chant Vedic hymns in praise of Him. In reply to their prayers, the Lord roared again and flew into the sky. His hard hairs quivering, He waved His tail about and, with His hooves and glittering white tusks, scattered the clouds in the sky. After He glanced over His supplicating devotees, who felt transcendental pleasure in seeing Him, the Lord dove into the ocean and tried to find the earth by smell.

After swimming to the bottom, the Lord saw the earth resting there. He then easily set it on His tusks and swam with it up to the surface. Indeed, He looked magnificent!

At that moment, wearing stunning golden armor and a wealth of ornaments, Hiranyaksha arrived. Seeing the Lord and envying His splendor, the demon laughed, "Ha! An amphibious beast!" Then he looked sternly at Lord Varaha and shouted, "This earth belongs to us—the demons. So don't think You can take it while I'm here!"

But the Lord disregarded him.

"You rascal!" bellowed the demon. "Today I will smash Your head with My club—and kill You!"

Tolerating this verbal abuse, the Lord noted that Mother Earth was frightened. Thus, He rose out of the water and placed the earth on the surface, empowering her to float. As He did, the demon thought the Lord was trying to flee from him. So he chased Him, roaring thunderously and yelling, "Look at You! Running away from battle! Aren't You ashamed?"

"Well," replied the Lord sarcastically, "I'm a jungle beast and I'm looking for hunting dogs like you. So give up all your boastful talk and try to kill Me. Come on—just try!"

Angry and agitated, Hiranyaksha moved like a challenged cobra. Hissing indignantly, the demon quickly sprang towards the Lord and tried to hit Him in the chest with his powerful club. But the Lord skillfully dodged the violent blow, just as an adept yogi eludes death. As Lord Varaha expressed His anger and rushed towards Hiranyaksha, the latter bit his lip and repeatedly brandished his club. Then the Lord, with His mace, struck Hiranyaksha on his right temple. However, the demon, with his own club, protected himself. Thus Diti's son and Varaha, enraged and seeking victory, pounded each other with their huge maces.

The rivalry between the combatants was terrific. Each bore injuries on his body from the blows of the other's pointed club, and each grew more furious due to the smell of his own blood. Both eager to win, they performed various dexterous maneuvers, looking like two horrendous bulls contesting for a cow.

Lord Brahma then approached the Lord and pleaded, "Dear Lord, this monster has proved to be a threat to the gods, the holy men, the cows, and the innocent. He has unnecessarily harassed them and become quite fearsome. He wanders all over the world searching for someone to fight with."

" Yes, I know."

"He's arrogant, independent, and wicked—and very skilled in trickery. The easiest time to kill him is during the day. But daytime is almost over. If you wait till nighttime, it will be harder—for demons are stronger then. Therefore, please kill him immediately."

The Lord laughed heartily and, accepting Brahma's pure entreaty, glanced at him affectionately. Then Varaha aimed His mace at Hiranyaksha's chin. But the demon struck first, causing the Lord's blazing club to fall from His hand and whirl. However, Hiranyaksha did not try to take advantage of this, preferring fair combat. The Lord then invoked His blazing discus and it began revolving in His hand.

Watching the fight from the sky, the gods and the celestials cried to the Lord, "Victory! Kill him! Stop playing with him!"

Feeling resentment, Lord Varaha bit his lip and then hissed like a serpent at Hiranyaksha, who gazed at Him hotly. The titan then jumped into the air, aimed his club at the Lord, and flung it forcefully. But the Lord knocked it down with His left foot. "Pick up your weapon and try again," He urged. Feeling challenged, Hiranyaksha recovered his mace, roared loudly, and again threw it. But the Lord caught it with the same ease that His eagle carrier, Garuda, seizes a snake. He then offered Hiranyaksha his club, but feeling frustrated and humiliated, the demon refused it.

Instead, Diti's son grabbed a fiery trident and, with all his strength, angrily hurled it. But the Lord threw His flaming discus and smashed it, the trident scattering into pieces. Enraged and bellowing, Hiranyaksha attacked the Lord, beating his hard fists against Varaha's broad chest. But the Lord felt no more pain than an elephant does when struck by a wreath of flowers. Then, without warning, Hiranyaksha mystically vanished. However, a few moments later, he conjured up an array of horrifying apparitions.

When the celestials saw them, they were terrified, thinking that the end of the world was near. Fierce winds blew from all directions. Darkness spread everywhere, and dust and hail abounded. Stones flew from all corners. Thick black clouds manifested lightning and thunder. The sky rained pus, hair, blood, feces, urine, and bones. Mountains discharged weapons. Naked demonesses—their hair wildly disheveled—appeared, holding tridents. Ruffian Yakshas and Rakshasas—marching on foot or riding on horses, elephants, or chariots—shouted cruel and savage slogans.

Lord Varaha released His whirling discus at the apparitions and they instantly disappeared. Then the titan reappeared, but he was now so enraged, so furious that he tried to embrace and crush the Lord. But as he squeezed mightily—much to his amazement—he saw the Lord standing outside the circle of his arms. Hiranyaksha then began to pummel the Lord with his hard fists, but Varaha indifferently slapped him at the root of his ear. But even though the slap was indifferent, it was so horrendously powerful that Hiranyaksha's body wheeled, his eyeballs bulged out of their sockets, his arms and legs broke, and the hair on his head scattered about. Completely dazed—and like a gigantic tree uprooted by a hurricane—he collapsed and died in the water.

At that very moment, although far away, a shudder ran threw the heart of Diti, his mother. As she recalled the prophecy of her husband, Kashyapa, blood flowed from her breasts.

Lord Brahma and the other gods approached the scene, and they saw the demon lying on the water, biting his lips. There was still a faint glow on his face, and Lord Brahma admiringly said, "What a blessed death—to be killed by the Supreme Lord Himself! The Lord struck him with His forefoot, and the demon died gazing at the Lord's face. How fortunate!"

Then one of the gods gratefully prayed, "Our dear Lord, we offer You our humble obeisances. This demon was a torment to all the worlds. Fortunately for us, You killed him. Now we can live in peace, perform our duties, and offer our devotion at Your lotuslike feet."

After all the other gods offered their prayers, the Lord returned to His abode in Vaikuntha.

It has been said by great saints that if one hears, recites, or takes pleasure in this pastime of Lord Varaha—fighting and defeating Hiranyaksha—one is immediately relieved of the painful results, due to occur, of all one's past sinful activities, even the killing of a Brahmin [considered to be the most sinful]. Moreover, one gains extraordinary spiritual merit, wealth, fame, longevity, and one's desired objects. And at the last moment of one's life, one is transferred to the Lord's eternal, transcendental world.

CHAPTER THREE

LORD NARASINGHA SAVES PRAHLADA

Prince Prahlada always depended on the Lord for guidance and security. If we wish to discover ourselves, we should try to depend on God, who can give us the perfect guidance and security for this purpose.

When Hiranyakashipu, residing on one of the heavenly planets, heard that Lord Vishnu had killed his younger brother, he was outraged. Standing outside his palace before many demon assistants, he bit his lips angrily and gazed upwards. The intense heat of his glance made the sky smoky. Then, baring his teeth, knitting his brows, and grabbing his trident, he glared at the assembly. "Oh demons," he shouted, "listen to me carefully! Lord Vishnu, the Supreme Person, is supposed to treat the gods and the demons equally. But just because the gods begged Him for help, He killed my brother! Therefore, to avenge my brother's death, I will cut off Vishnu's head with my trident! And when He's dead, my brother's spirit will be delighted and I'll feel peaceful."

"How would you like us to help you, my lord?" asked one assistant.

"While I'm dealing with Vishnu, I want you to descend to the planet Earth. The Brahmins there are practicing austerities, offering sacrifices, studying the scriptures, observing vows, and giving charity. You must destroy them all! Every one of them!"

"But—how will that help your cause, my lord?" asked another.

"When the Brahmins are killed, no one will exist to encourage the kings to perform sacrifices. Without sacrifices, there will be no offerings for the gods. And without offerings, the gods will die."

Everyone in the assembly glanced at one another and nodded gladly.

"Therefore," continued Hiranyakashipu, "go immediately! Destroy the Brahmins, the farmers, their homes, gardens, trees, cow barns, the mines, and the government buildings. Burn them all down!"

Lord Narasingha protects Prahlada

The demon assistants, who delighted in destructive activities, saluted Hiranyakashipu and left. Taking his instructions to heart, they carried them out perfectly—till there was not a shred of Vedic culture left on Earth. Receiving no sacrificial offerings, the gods descended to the earth to inquire about the situation.

Meanwhile, Hiranyakashipu performed his brother's funeral rites. Then he pacified his grieving mother and relatives with philosophical words about the temporary and illusory nature of material life. Although very learned, he himself was unable to apply his knowledge for his own true benefit. Seething with anger, Hiranyakashipu hastened to Lord Vishnu's residence, desiring to slay Him. When he saw the Lord, he raised his trident and rushed madly towards Him. The demon looked like death personified.

Seeing Hiranyakashipu coming, the Lord thought, *Anywhere I go, Hiranyakashipu will follow Me. But if I enter his heart—since he can only see externally—he won't be able to see Me.* The Lord raced away from the demon, who furiously followed Him, and then suddenly disappeared, assuming a subtle invisible form. In that body, the Lord, unbeknown to Hiranyakashipu, entered one of the demon's nostrils as he inhaled. Seeing that Lord Vishnu's abode was vacant, Hiranyakashipu bellowed loudly and searched everywhere for Him— on the earth, in the oceans and caves, and in the upper planets. But nowhere could he find Him.

He therefore abandoned his search. However, he continued to burn with vengeance and hatred for the Lord. More than anything, he wanted to slay Him. But Lord Vishnu was extremely powerful—so much so that to defeat Him, Hiranyakashipu believed he would have to become invincible and immortal. He therefore embarked on a rigorous course of austerity that he hoped would help him achieve these, as well as other materialistic, goals. In other words, he wanted to be Lord of the universe!

The demon thus went to Mount Mandarachala and began standing on the tip of his toes, his arms upraised and his gaze focused on the sky. It was exceedingly difficult to hold this pose steadily, but due to his intense hatred for the Lord, he forced himself to master it.

At this time, since Hiranyakashipu was not guarding his kingdom, the gods mobilized their forces and severely attacked it. Although the demon warriors tried to defend themselves, the gods were so furious and skillful that they killed numerous demon leaders. After awhile, all the demon warriors fled in various directions, leaving their properties and families behind. The victorious gods plundered Hiranyakashipu's palace, destroying everything inside. Then Indra, king of the gods, arrested Hiranyakashipu's queen, who happened to be pregnant. As he led her away, she sobbed like a fearful kurari bird captured by a vulture.

However, quite mystically, the enlightened sage Narada suddenly appeared there. "Release her!" he ordered. "She is sinless and chaste— and another man's wife."

"I'm aware of that, O sage. But Hiranyakashipu's seed is in this woman."

"So?"

"Well, if she gives birth to a boy, he'll probably be as demonic as his father. And that will be a great curse on the world."

Narada began to smile.

"Therefore, we would like to take custody of her."

"For what purpose?"

"So that after her baby is born, we may destroy it."

"Destroy it?" Narada asked doubtfully.

"Yes. Then we'll return her to her kingdom."

"Indra, the boy in this woman's womb is a pure devotee of God."

"A devotee?" Indra was very surprised.

"Yes. So you won't be able to kill him. He's protected by the Lord Himself."

Respecting the sage's words, Indra said, "Oh. All right." He then released the queen. Moreover, because she was carrying the Lord's pure devotee, he and his assistants respectfully circumambulated her. Then all the gods returned to their celestial kingdom. Narada brought the queen to his retreat and assured her of complete protection. He advised her to remain there until her husband completed his austerities and returned to the palace.

The queen, desiring the safety of her unborn baby, decided to deliver it after her husband returned. She stayed at the sage's retreat and rendered devotional service to him with great reverence. While the queen stayed there, Narada gave her instructions on religion and transcendental knowledge. And simultaneously, the boy within her womb listened intently to each priceless word—words that he would never forget.

Meanwhile, as Hiranyakashipu stood on his toes with his arms upraised, his concentration was so intense that a glowing effulgence—as brilliant as the sun at the time of the cosmic dissolution—emanated from his head. Then fire shot out of his skull and smoke spread all over the sky, filling the upper and lower planets and making them extremely hot. Rivers and oceans became agitated, the Earth's plains, mountains, and islands trembled, stars and planets fell, and fire blazed everywhere. The gods were being scorched and disturbed by the heat coming from the demon's head. Unable to dispel it, they traveled to Lord Brahma's planet and respectfully explained the situation to him. One of the gods begged, "O lord, if you think it proper, please stop these disturbances."

Another god added, "If you don't stop it, everything will be destroyed."

"All your obedient subjects will be killed," said another.

"Hiranyakashipu wants to become as powerful as you—and obtain your position."

"If he gains your post, all good in the world will be lost."

After carefully considering the matter, Lord Brahma, along with the gods and several great sages, journeyed to the spot where Hiranyakashipu was practicing his harsh austerities. When Lord Brahma's swan airplane hovered over the area, he at first could not discern where the demon was. All he could see was a big anthill covered by grass and bamboo sticks. But when he looked closer, he realized that because Hiranyakashipu had been there for a long time, the ants had totally devoured his skin, fat, flesh, and blood. And yet, by the sheer strength of his determination, he had been able to remain on his tiptoes with arms upraised—as a mere skeleton!

Struck with wonder, Lord Brahma smiled and said, "O son of Kashyapa, you have achieved perfection in your austerities. I'm astonished to see your endurance. Despite being bitten and eaten by ants, you're still keeping your life force circulating in your bones. Amazing! And you've sustained your life without drinking any water for a hundred celestial years! Even great saintly individuals can't do this. Well, you've certainly won my admiration. So I'm prepared to give you whatever blessings you want."

From his waterpot, Lord Brahma sprinkled rejuvenating water on Hiranyakashipu's skeleton—and suddenly, it was miraculously transformed. The titan now possessed incalculable physical strength and bodily luster. He thus emerged from the anthill as fire emerges from wood—a renewed, young man!

Seeing Lord Brahma hovering on his swan airplane, Hiranyakashipu was very pleased. He at once offered him obeisances, lying flat on the ground. Overcome with joy, tears flowed from his eyes and his body trembled with ecstasy. He rose to his knees and placed his palms together prayerfully. In a humble mood and faltering voice, Hiranyakashipu glorified Lord Brahma's exalted position. Then he said, "O my lord, please don't let me be killed by any beings created or not created by you—inside or outside any residence, during the day or night, on the ground or in the sky, or by any weapon, human being, or animal. Please don't let me be killed by any living or nonliving entity, by any god or demon, nor by any big snake from the lower planets. Please don't let me have any rival. I want to rule over all living beings and chief gods, and I want all the glories that go with that position. I also want all the mystic powers one attains by engaging in austerities for a long time."

Lord Brahma replied, "The blessings you've asked me for are difficult to attain and unavailable to most men. Nevertheless, I now grant them to you." Worshiped by the demon and praised by the saints and sages, the creator of the universe departed.

Continually remembering his brother's death, Hiranyakashipu conquered all the rulers on all the planets—the entire universe—and usurped their power and influence. He resided in the heavenly realm at the palace of Lord Indra, the chief god. Constructed by Vishvakarma, the architect of the gods, the palace was so beautifully wrought that it seemed as if the goddess of fortune herself lived there. The walls, floors, canopies, and beds were decorated with precious jewels, crystals, and stones. Seeing their glamorous reflections in the gems, gorgeous women walked about, their ankle bells tinkling melodiously.

The gods were compelled to bow down and offer respects to Hiranyakashipu, who very severely and for no reason chastised them. Indeed, the demon controlled everyone! Constantly drunk on strong-smelling wines and liquors, the titan's coppery eyes were always rolling. And to please him, all—except Lords Brahma, Vishnu, and Shiva—personally worshiped, glorified, and offered him gifts. He never shared with the gods the oblations offered to him but instead kept them for himself. The earth produced plenty of food grains and the cows supplied an abundance of milk. The various oceans—salt, sugarcane, milk, wine, etc.—provided gems and jewels for Hiranyakashipu's use. The valleys became the demon's pleasure fields, and all the trees and plants produced a plenitude of fruits and flowers in every season. Taking no help from the gods, Hiranyakashipu even generated rain, wind, and fire.

And yet—despite the demon's power to control everyone and everything, and despite his superabundance of sense enjoyment—he was dissatisfied. This was because he was controlled by his senses. Nonetheless, Hiranyakashipu spent a long period of time taking pride in his riches and pleasures, as well as violating the laws and regulations established in the authoritative scriptures.

Just about everyone, including the gods, was exceedingly troubled, for the demon had inflicted severe and steady punishment on them. Afraid and distressed, and incapable of finding any refuge, they finally and fully surrendered themselves to the Supreme Lord, Vishnu. Offering their respectful obeisances to Him, they prayed for necessary relief. In response, they heard a transcendental voice whose source was invisible to materialistic eyes. Grave as a rumbling cloud and dispelling all fear, it was the voice of God. He told them exactly what they had to do to become free from the menace Hiranyakashipu. Thus encouraged and reassured, they proceeded confidently to implement His instructions.

Hiranyakashipu had four wonderful and well-qualified sons. The best of them was named Prahlada, whose mother had taken shelter of the sage Narada after the gods had attacked her husband's kingdom. Although born in a demon family, and despite being only five years of age, Prahlada was a reservoir of divine qualities and a pure devotee of God. He was like the Supersoul—being kind to, and the best friend of, everyone. He had unflinching faith in Lord Vishnu as his savior and unalloyed devotion to Him. This was due to Prahlada's devotional service to the Lord in a previous lifetime. And when his mother had been pregnant with him and Saint Narada had recited the scriptures to her, Prahlada had also heard and understood them. He therefore had been educated in transcendental knowledge, so his love for Lord Vishnu—whom his father hated—had naturally awakened.

Prahlada was always absorbed in thoughts of the Lord. Because of this spiritual practice, the child sometimes cried, laughed, exulted, sang, or danced. Fully ecstatic, he felt oneness in heart with God and sometimes imitated the Lord's glorious activities. During such times, the boy's hairs stood up and tears glided down his cheeks.

Now it so happened that the chief priest of the demons was Shukracharya, and he performed various ritualistic ceremonies for them. His sons, Sanda and Amarka, dwelled near Hiranyakashipu's palace. Prahlada's father sent him to their school to be educated with other demon children. The boy heard and recited political and economic topics taught by his teachers. But he did not like the philosophy underlying them, because it meant considering someone a friend and someone else an enemy. However, Prahlada saw no such distinctions and related to all persons equally.

After some time, Hiranyakashipu summoned the teachers to bring his son to his chamber. After they arrived, the demon, sitting on his throne, very affectionately sat Prahlada on his lap and said, "My dear son, what is the best of all the subjects you've studied from your teachers?"

Prahlada replied, "O king of the demons, my spiritual master [Narada] taught me that anyone who has accepted a temporary body and a temporary household life is always full of anxieties. It is like falling into a dark well where there is no water but only suffering. One should therefore give up this position, go to a sacred forest, take shelter of Lord Vishnu, and worship Him."

Hiranyakashipu could scarcely believe this—his own son speaking about devotional service to Lord Vishnu—his sworn enemy! Nonetheless, since Prahlada was only a child, his father did not take him very seriously. Instead, he laughingly said to himself, "This is the way the enemy spoils children's intelligence." Then the demon looked at Prahlada's teachers admonishingly. "At your school, I want you to protect my son completely. His intelligence must not be allowed to be influenced by Vishnu's devotees—who may be going to your school in disguise."

The teachers brought Prahlada back to the school, and Sanda gently said, "Dear Prahlada, may you be blessed with peace and good fortune. Now please tell us the truth: how did you gain that knowledge you expressed to your father? Who spoiled your intelligence in that way?"

Amarka added, "None of the other boys here are speaking like you—in such a deviant way."

"Did our enemies pollute your intelligence or—did you do something to cause it?"

After Prahlada respectfully bowed down to the Lord, he rose and said to his teachers, "I heard from a sage that the material energy deludes people's intelligence—by creating such differences as 'my friend' and 'my enemy.' Now I'm actually seeing this happen."

"What are you talking about?" asked Sanda.

"This: when the Lord is pleased by our devotional service, He blesses us with spiritual knowledge. Then we don't make distinctions between enemies, friends, and ourselves. Instead, we understand that we're all related, we're all one family, and we're all eternal servants of God."

"You're speaking nonsense, Prahlada," said Amarka, irritated.

"No, I'm not. Persons who always think in terms of 'enemy' and 'friend' are unable to sense the Lord within themselves. But I do, and He's given me the intelligence to take the side of your so-called enemy."

"How dare you speak so disrespectfully!" exclaimed Sanda.

Ignoring him, Prahlada emphasized, "Just as iron is attracted to a magnet, my consciousness is attracted to Lord Vishnu. It has completely surrendered to Him."

"Amarka, bring me a stick! This Prahlada is damaging our reputation. He needs to be corrected!"

The teachers rebuked and threatened Prahlada by various means, and then began educating him in the ways of religion, economic development, and sense gratification. After some time, they believed that Prahlada was sufficiently knowledgeable in the four kinds of governance—negotiating, flattering, dividing and ruling, and punishing. Feeling confident about their charge, the instructors one day brought Prahlada to the king's chambers and presented him before his father.

Prahlada offered his respects at the king's feet. Impressed by his son's humility, Hiranyakashipu showered him with blessings and embraced him with both arms. Extremely happy, the demon sat down on his throne, seated Prahlada on his lap, and affectionately smelled his head. Tears coursed down Hiranyakashipu's cheeks and moistened his son's smiling face. Then he said, "My dear son, you've been learning things from your teachers for some time. Now please tell me what you think is the best of that knowledge."

"I think that hearing and chanting about the glories of Lord Vishnu, as well as remembering them, serving the Lord's lotuslike feet, worshiping Him, praying to Him, serving Him, considering Him to be our best friend, and surrendering our body, mind, and words to Him— is the best of that knowledge. And whoever dedicates his life to serving Lord Vishnu by these nine methods is the most learned person."

Hiranyakashipu was stunned. Was he hearing right? His own son again praising "the enemy?" With trembling lips, he glared at Sanda and said, "You unqualified, wicked son of a Brahmin! You've disobeyed my order. You've sympathized with my enemies."

"No, my lord, I haven't! I—"

"Yes, you have! You've taught my son about devotional service to Vishnu!"

"No!"

"You're an impostor!"

"I never taught Prahlada those things. No one did. It—it developed naturally in him."

"Naturally?" The demon was puzzled.

"Yes. So please abandon your anger and stop accusing us."

Hiranyakashipu then looked scornfully at Prahlada. "You rascal! Who taught you all those things?"

Instead of answering his father's question, he compassionately preached to him. "People should not waste their time in temporary sense pleasures, for these only lead to miseries—from the body and mind, from other living beings, and from the attacks of nature. Rather, they should engage in the devotional service of Lord Vishnu, become free from—"

"What?!" the king glowered.

"—from materialistic contamination, and then happily return to the eternal world. This is the only way to be happy."

Blinded by fury, Hiranyakashipu pushed his son off his lap onto the marble floor and gazed at the teachers. "Take this rascal away—and kill him! He's given up his own family to serve my enemy!"

"Yes, my lord."

"Thus, he's become my enemy."

"True."

"Therefore, he must be killed—and now!"

Hiranyakashipu summoned several formidable servants. They had fearsome faces, sharp teeth, and coppery beards and hair. With their sharp tridents, they repeatedly struck Prahlada's tender body and shouted, "Chop him up! Chop him up!"

But Prahlada merely sat there, silently, meditating on Lord Vishnu. Trusting in the Lord's judgment, he was completely resigned to accept whatever pains God might heap on him. Notwithstanding this, the Lord prevented the demons from either killing or even paining Prahlada. In fact, He protected His devotee the way a loving mother protects her helpless child.

When Hiranyakashipu perceived this, he devised many other schemes to kill his "traitorous" son. He had him thrown beneath the feet of huge elephants; lowered into a pit of many poisonous snakes; hurled from the top of a mountain to the ground; attacked with destructive spells; poisoned and starved; exposed to icy cold, blistering heat, biting winds, and drowning water. He even had him pounded by heavy, crushing boulders. But in every attempt, he failed to kill or even injure Prahlada. This made Hiranyakashipu extremely anxious and morose.

The demon was amazed by Prahlada's invulnerability and fearlessness. Believing that his son might be immortal, he wondered what to do next. Then Sanda and Amarka approached him, and the latter said, "There's no need to worry about Prahlada. After all, he's only a child. What harm can he do?"

Sanda remarked, "I think he's going through a phase. As time goes on, I'm sure he'll change."

"But for the time being," added Amarka, "just leave him to us and we'll train him properly."

"You must teach him all about the duties of a warrior," insisted the king.

"Of course we will, my lord," said Sanda.

"Yes, we'll make a fine warrior out of him yet."

The two teachers, with Prahlada in tow, returned to their school. They then proceeded again to systematically and unceasingly instruct the boy—who was very submissive and humble—in worldly religion, economic development, and sense gratification. But Prahlada, being above such teachings, abhorred them. For he knew they were based on the duality of worldly affairs—heat and cold, success and failure, loss and gain, etc.—and led to the miseries of birth, disease, old age, and death, lifetime after lifetime.

When the teachers went into their houses to attend to some household matter, Prahlada's schoolmates called him for fun and games. But instead of joining in, he sweetly asked them to gather around him. Dropping their playthings, the boys did so and listened to him in great earnestness. They sensed that he desired their welfare. He then began teaching them about the futility of materialistic life and the glories of devotional service to the Lord. "We should begin such service when we're children," he said. "Then it'll be easy to continue when we're older. Most older people can't do it because they've become too materialistic."

Prahlada taught his schoolmates that they were not their physical bodies but were immortal souls; and that the soul had an eternal relationship with the Lord. He said the real business of the soul was to develop that relationship through devotional service to Him—and not to try to become, or act like, God. He emphasized that engaging in sense pleasure and economic development caused more attachment to the material world (family, home, friends, business, possessions, etc.). And that such attachment led not only to much suffering and bewilderment, but also to the soul being born and dying repeatedly in various species of life.

Prahlada declared that real happiness—which is experienced in the soul and characterized by unceasing transcendental peace and bliss—is attainable only by serving the Lord unconditionally, lovingly, and selflessly. Therefore, he concluded, that even though they were young children, they should not waste their time in frivolous, enslaving pleasures, as death could come to them unexpectedly at any moment.

Prahlada imparted these transcendental teachings daily to his schoolmates. The boys, in turn, appreciated them and took them very seriously. They therefore rejected the materialistic teachings of Sanda and Amarka.

When the teachers noted that their students, under Prahlada's influence, were becoming devotees of Lord Vishnu, they became fearful. Consequently, they took Prahlada to the king's palace and entered the filled assembly hall. Respectfully approaching Hiranyakashipu, they described what had "unfortunately" occurred. Feeling greatly insulted and hissing like a snake trampled underfoot, Hiranyakashipu became furious. His whole body trembled with rage and he decided that he would kill Prahlada personally.

The boy stood before the demon with folded hands—peaceful, mild, and gentle. Based on his age and behavior, it was not proper for his father to chastise him. But Hiranyakashipu could not contain his surging hatred. Glaring at his son with crooked eyes, the demon harshly shouted, "You stubborn, disobedient fool! Today I will kill you! When I'm angry, all the planets and their rulers shake. By whose power have you become so bold and fearless—so as to overstep my power to rule you? By whose power?"

"The source of my power," explained Prahlada, "is the same as yours. Indeed, there's only one source of all power—the Supreme Lord."

"No!"

"Yes."

"*I'm* the most powerful!"

"No, Lord Vishnu is!"

"Wrong!"

"Father, please stop acting like a demon."

"Shut up!" raged the king, pointing his index finger, like a dagger, at Prahlada.

"Stop distinguishing between enemies and friends—"

"I said shut up!"

"—and become equal-minded towards all living beings."

"Did you hear me?!"

"You have no enemy in this world—except your misguided, uncontrolled mind."

"What did you say?!" Hiranyakashipu was shocked.

"Father, if you conquer your mind, you won't have any enemies!"

"You rascal! You think you're better than me, eh? Is that what you think?"

"No, Father."

"Only people who are about to die think like you!

"Father, please—"

"Let's see your Lord Vishnu save you now."

"Please—"

"Where do you think He is now, eh?"

"He's everywhere."

"Everywhere?"

"Yes! The Lord is everywhere."

"Everywhere? Is he in this pillar?" Hiranyakashipu challenged, pointing to one nearby.

"Yes."

"Fool! Idiot!" Enraged, he rose, stepped down from his throne, and smashed his fist loudly against the marble pillar. "Then where is He? Show me! Where?"

"He's there, Father."

Then, from inside the column came a frightening sound. It was horrendous and tumultuous—so much so that it frightened all the other demons in the assembly hall. Suddenly, a most amazing being, roaring and raging, burst out of the pillar, the marble shattering all about. It was neither a man nor a lion, but a combination of both. It was Lord Vishnu's incarnation of—Lord Narasingha!

Hiranyakashipu was amazed. *What kind of creature is this?* he wondered.

Lord Narasingha looked awesome and formidable. His eyes were angry, His teeth were deadly, His mane was shining, and his razor-sharp tongue swiveled about like a dueling sword. His nostrils and gaping mouth looked like mountain caves, and He held a conch shell, disc, club, lotus, and various weapons in His many hands.

He thinks he can kill me, thought Hiranyakashipu. *Never*! The demon grabbed his club and attacked the Lord as a lion might attack an elephant. Enveloped by the Lord's effulgence, the angry demon began beating the Lord furiously with his club. However, Lord Narasingha captured him, just as the eagle Garuda easily captures a snake. But then the Lord deliberately allowed Hiranyakashipu to slip from His hands, as a cat plays with a mouse.

Watching from the sky, the gods became perturbed. *What would the demon do now?* they wondered.

Escaping from the Lord's hands, Hiranyakashipu thought, *See! He's afraid of me!* Prahlada's father, slightly fatigued, decided to rest for a few minutes. But as soon as he felt refreshed, he grabbed his sword and shield and attacked the Lord with tremendous power. Sometimes Hiranyakashipu fought in the air, and at other times he fought on the ground. He was completely unpredictable.

Lord Narasingha laughed loudly. Then he easily yet forcefully captured the demon, whose limbs wriggled about helplessly. Next, in the assembly-hall doorway, the Lord placed Prahlada's father on His lap and tore the demon to pieces with His sharp nails. It was a ghastly sight—the Lord's mouth and mane sprinkled with drops of blood, His ferocious eyes blazing with anger, His neck decorated with the demon's intestines, and one of His hands holding the king's heart. Licking the edge of His mouth with His tongue, He tossed Hiranyakashipu's mangled body aside.

Lord Brahma had given the king several blessings, which appeared to make the demon invincible and immortal. But the omniscient Lord, without violating any of Brahma's promises, counteracted them all. For example, Hiranyakashipu could not be killed on the land or in the sky; so the Lord killed him on His lap. He could not be destroyed either inside or outside; so the Lord destroyed him in a doorway. Nor could he be slain during the day or night; so the Lord slew him at dusk. And he could not be executed by any weapon or by any person; thus the Lord appeared as a half-man, half-lion and executed him with His sharp nails.

Seeing their leader dead, thousands of the demon's loyal warriors, with raised weapons, fiercely attacked Lord Narasingha. But the Lord, roaring thunderously, destroyed them all with the ends of His sharp nails. Then He sat down on the king's opulent throne, and the heavenly goddesses showered flowers on Him. The gods in the sky began beating drums and kettledrums triumphantly, the female angels began dancing rhapsodically, and the Gandharvas started singing sweetly. Then all the chief gods and angels offered their obeisances and prayers to the Lord—glorifying, praising, and thanking Him for His mercy. Now they could fearlessly return to their individual planets and resume their former administrative duties to the world.

Despite the gods' beautiful prayers, Lord Narasingha remained extremely angry at Hiranyakashipu for having so callously abused Prahlada. Thus, none of the celestials dared to approach Him now. They therefore asked Prahlada to go forth and try to pacify Him.

The boy approached the feet of the Lord and, with folded hands, prostrated himself before Him. Lord Narasingha became ecstatically affectionate towards Prahlada and placed His hand on His devotee's head, blessing him. In response, the child's heart overflowed with love, his eyes streamed with tears, and blissful symptoms manifested throughout his small body. He then offered the Lord his most heartfelt prayers, repeatedly lauding the glories of loving devotional service as the end-all and be-all of true happiness.

Prahlada's prayers pacified the Lord completely, and He said, "My dear Prahlada, I am very much pleased with you. Kindly ask Me for any blessing you would like."

"O Lord," replied Prahlada, "all I want is to have no materialistic desires in my heart."

"A devotee like you never desires anything materialistic—in this life or in the next. Nonetheless, I order you to enjoy the wealth of your dynasty and become its king for a long while. At the same time, as you perform your duties, you should always think of Me, serve Me, and worship Me. Then you will not become attached to such wealth and will remain My devotee."

"My father committed many offenses against You and me. I beg that You please excuse him for all those offenses."

The Lord assured him, "Because you were born in his family, not only has your father Hiranyakashipu been purified, but the twenty-one previous fathers you had in your past lifetimes have also been purified; in fact, your entire dynasty has been cleansed. And those who follow your example will naturally become My devotees. You are the best example, so others should follow in your footsteps."

Prahlada lowered his head modestly and thanked the Lord in his heart.

The Lord then looked directly at Lord Brahma and said, "Just as it is dangerous to feed milk to a poisonous snake, it is equally dangerous to give blessings to demons. They are by nature savage and envious. Therefore, I warn you to not give such blessings to them again."

Lord Brahma, appreciating the Lord's guidance, worshiped Him. Then Lord Narasingha disappeared.

After Prahlada performed his father's funeral ceremony, he was installed by the Brahmins as the king of the demon race. The gods then offered the boy their best blessings and returned to their respective planets.

But now it may be asked, why had the Supreme Lord preordained that His devoted servants Jaya and Vijaya be cursed by the four Kumaras and transferred from the spiritual realm to the material world?

It was because the Lord sometimes desires to fight—not out of envy or hatred but out of pure sport. When He yearns to do battle with someone, He has to find a qualified opponent. But in the Vaikuntha world there are no foes, because everyone there is lovingly engaged in service to Him. Therefore, He has to descend to the material world where there are envious, belligerent souls. However, the Lord performs His intimate pastimes—including fighting—only with His devotees. Therefore, He purposely selected Jaya and Vijaya to become His enemies and fight with Him in the material world. And since they were completely surrendered to Him and desired only to serve His pleasure—whatever it might be—they did not protest their transfer to this world and their transformation into demons. They knew that after some time they would be freed from their hatred and return to their eternal service in Vaikuntha.

Moreover, the Lord showed that He personally protects His devotees from harm and ultimately annihilates demoniac persons. This serves fair warning to anyone and everyone to never violate His commandments or try to falsely assume His powerful position, for the result can only be disastrous.

Whoever hears or recites this narration about the omnipotence of the Supreme Lord Narasingha and the activities of His glorious devotee Prahlada will not only be liberated from materialistic miseries, but will surely ascend to Vaikuntha, the realm of no anxiety.

Indra tries to foil Diti's plan

CHAPTER FOUR

DITI VOWS TO KILL INDRA

Although petitioned, Kashyapa refused to help his wife kill an
innocent person. Similarly, if we want to discover our true selves,
we should not kill anyone unnecessarily, for God considers this
highly offensive and punishable.

"I won't rest until Indra is dead!" thought Diti, glancing angrily through the ashram's open window. "For he's the one who instigated Lord Vishnu to kill my sons, Hiranyaksha and Hiranyakashipu." The gentle breeze blowing from the forest into the thatched hut and onto her face did not soothe her. Rather, it stirred her with seething vengeance. "Though Indra is king of the gods, he's cruel, hardhearted, and sinful. I must kill him—even if he is my nephew!"

Diti began pacing the small room and dwelling on how she could slay Indra. Then an idea flashed. "If I could have a powerful son, that would solve my problem." She next considered how she could get one. She knew that her husband, Kashyapa, could help her, for he was cognizant of the mystical secrets of producing a mighty son. But she also knew that if she disclosed her sordid purpose to him, he would refuse to cooperate. Therefore, she had no choice. She would have to cleverly manipulate him into helping her. *But how*, she wondered. *How?*

Then she smiled mischievously and nodded. She knew exactly how!

From that moment on, Diti was a source of constant pleasure to Kashyapa. She executed his orders very faithfully. By serving him affectionately and humbly, by speaking sweetly and warmly, by smiling winsomely and glancing at him coyly, Diti gradually captured and controlled her husband's mind.

Learned as he was, he could not discern her true intention. Then one day, in the sitting room, he felt a strong obligation to please her and said, "My dear beautiful wife, you've made me very happy." He drank

41

in her lovely form with intense delight. "And your body—it's so beautiful, with such a thin waist. And the way you've been treating me—as if I were God Himself."

Diti lowered her head and eyes with false modesty, as if she were unworthy of his praises.

"I'm going to reward you for this," he assured her.

That was just what she wanted to hear.

"Ask me," he smiled, "for whatever blessing you would like."

"Anything?" she asked sheepishly.

"Anything."

"All right. It grieves me that I don't have any sons now."

"Oh?"

"Yes. So I'd like one now—one that's immortal."

"Immortal?" Kashyapa was surprised.

"One who can kill Indra!"

Now he was even more surprised.

"He had Lord Vishnu kill our two sons. So he—"

"But our sons were demonic, so he had to."

"No, he didn't." She glared at Kashyapa. "Are you reneging on your promise now?"

Saddened, he considered the implications of it.

"Are you?!"

"Alas!" he exclaimed. "It's evil to kill Indra. Evil."

"I said are you?!"

Kashyapa turned away. He walked towards the window and looked out at the forest. Musing on all of Diti's recent wiles, he now realized she had conquered him by her insincere charm and concern. *What a fool I've been,* he thought. *I should have known better. Curses on me! All because I couldn't control my senses!*

"Are you going to answer my question?" she probed.

"I'll answer you when I'm ready!"

Diti looked worried and disappointed.

As Kashyapa looked out the window, he philosophically thought, *A woman's face is so attractive—like a lotus flower during autumn. And her words—they give such pleasure to the ear. But her heart—it can sometimes be as sharp as a razor blade. One moment, she can deal with a man as if he were everything to her; and the next moment—as if he were nothing! She cares only for herself. She can even kill her own husband or sons or brothers—or have someone else kill them—just to satisfy some fancy.*

Kashyapa prayerfully recited the Lord's name several times. Then he thought, *I promised her a blessing, so I can't renege. If I do, I'll be a liar. But*—he shook his head helplessly—*Indra doesn't deserve to be killed. If I help her, I'll be implicating myself.* He wondered what to do so that no one would be hurt.

Diti was anxious. She had never anticipated that her husband might break his promise. He was a great Brahmin sage. He had a high reputation to maintain. He was aware that she could ruin it by advertising his broken promise. The whole world would then scorn and disregard him. *Was he willing to risk such ignominy—just to protect cruel Indra?* she wondered.

"Diti," said Kashyapa.

"Yes?"

He turned towards her. "I will grant your wish."

Diti's eyes opened wide and she restrained a smile of victory.

"If you vow to follow my instructions daily for one year, you'll definitely get a son who'll be able to kill Indra."

"For sure?"

"For sure. But are you willing to take such a vow?"

"Yes, of course!" Diti said ecstatically.

"But should you break it," warned Kashyapa, "you'll then get a son who'll be friendly to Indra."

"Friendly?"

Kashyapa nodded.

"Then please tell me everything I have to do—and not do."

"All right. But listen carefully. It's called the Pumsavana rite and it's very purifying. Here is what you shouldn't do. Don't be violent or harm anyone. Don't curse anyone. And don't tell lies. Don't cut your nails and hair, and don't touch impure things like skulls and bones. Don't enter water while bathing, don't be angry, and don't even talk to or associate with evil persons. Don't wear clothes that haven't been properly washed, and don't wear a garland that's already been worn."

"I won't," Diti promised.

"And don't eat leftover food or food that was offered to Goddess Kali or anything polluted by meat or fish. Don't eat anything brought or touched by a low-class person (a Shudra), nor anything a woman in her menstrual period has seen. And don't drink water by joining your palms. After eating, don't go out on the street unless you first wash your mouth, hands, and feet."

"All right," agreed Diti.

"And don't go out in the evening or with your hair loose or without ornaments and unless you're very serious and covered sufficiently. Don't lie down without having washed both of your feet, or without being purified, or with wet feet, or with your head pointed west or north. And don't lie naked, or with other women, or during the sunrise or sunset."

He paused for a few moments.

"And what are the things I'm supposed to do?"

"The following: Before breakfast—put on washed clothing, be pure, adorn yourself with turmeric, sandalwood, and other favorable items, and worship the cows, the Brahmins, the goddess of fortune, and the Supreme Lord." He then gave her a series of prayers to recite to Lord Vishnu daily. "With flower garlands, sandalwood pulp, ornaments, and other paraphernalia, worship women who have sons and whose husbands are living. Worship me and offer me prayers. And meditate on me, thinking I'm in your womb."

"All right. Anything else?"

"No," he said with finality.

"Thank you. I'll follow everything exactly."

As she walked out of the room, Kashyapa smiled to himself. Yes, Diti, by her feminine artfulness, had tricked him into giving her the blessing she desired. But little did she know that he had just tricked her—and she would be quite surprised by the final result.

In due course, Diti happily became pregnant and began following the vow faithfully.

With a humble, devotional attitude, she prayed daily, "My dear Lord Vishnu, You possess the six attractions in full—beauty, wealth, knowledge, strength, fame, and detachment. But I do not entreat You for these attractions. I offer my humble obeisances to You, the master of all mystic powers. You are the husband and master of Lakshmi, the goddess of fortune, who has all the attractions. O my Lord, since You possess unconditional mercy, all attractions, all abilities, all glories, and divine attributes, You are the Supreme Lord, the master of all."

Diti offered Lord Vishnu and His wife Lakshmi other prayers also, and worshiped Them with various paraphernalia—water, garments, a sacred thread, ornaments, scents, flowers, incense, and fire.

When Lord Indra learned that his aunt Diti had undertaken a vow that would enable her to have a child who could kill him, he became extremely alarmed. This meant that at some point in the future he would lose his high position as king of the gods and administrator of the rainfall. And this he did not want. He therefore concocted a scheme that would enable him to stop her—provided he could detect some flaw in the way she practiced her vow.

To accomplish his plan, he one day cordially visited Diti. Noticing that she was practicing austerities, Indra asked if he could lighten her burden by serving her. Since she believed he was unaware of why she was performing them—and of course, she would never dare tell him why—she accepted his offer. Nonetheless, she thought it quite ironic that he would be assisting her in her plan to kill him.

Every day, Indra collected flowers, fruits, roots, and wood from the forest and brought them for her sacrifices. He also delivered *kusha* grass, leaves, sprouts, earth, and water to her at exactly the proper time. Serving Diti faithfully and carefully, Indra never once intimated that he knew about her scheme or that he himself had a preemptive plan. But he watched her vigilantly and hoped that she would soon break her vow. For unless she did, there was no way he could succeed. However, Diti was so determined to achieve her goal that she never deviated even once. This made Indra extremely anxious.

Nonetheless, in the latter months of her pregnancy, Indra noticed a subtle change in his aunt's demeanor. Although Diti had been keeping her vengeance well concealed under a veneer of affability, he had still been able to see it lurking subtly in her various expressions. However, now he could scarcely detect it at all. He wondered whether he was losing his perspicacity or whether his aunt had merely become a better actress. Indeed, this change was quite strange and baffling.

Then one day, just what he was waiting for—happened!

Diti had grown weak and thin. Somewhat distracted and forgetful, she failed to wash her mouth, feet, and hands after eating, and she went to sleep during the twilight. Thus, she broke two conditions of her vow, which now made her vulnerable to Indra's plan. Not wasting a moment, Indra exercised his mystic power—*anima*—and shrunk his body to an extremely tiny size. Then, while Diti was sleeping deeply, he entered her womb and saw the fetus that was supposed to kill him. It was glowing like gold.

He raised his thunderbolt weapon and cut the fetus into seven parts, hoping it was now dead. But it wasn't. Quite miraculously, the seven parts became seven new fetuses! And all of them were crying!

Amazed, Indra said to them, "Stop crying!" Then, with his thunder-bolt, he slashed each of the seven fetuses into seven parts. And quite astonishingly, the seven parts became forty-nine fetuses! Indra was struck with wonder that he could not kill them.

The babies folded their palms and cried out, "Dear Indra, we are your brothers—the Maruts [storm gods]. Why are you trying to kill us?"

Since Indra and the Maruts both had the same father, Kashyapa, they indeed were brothers. Amazed, Indra replied, "Well, then you don't have to be afraid of me anymore." Realizing why he could not kill them, he desisted from further attempts. He had no doubt now—each of the Maruts was a god, just as he was. Since there was no longer any reason for them to remain in Diti's womb, they all exited. Indra then restored his body to normal size.

When Diti awoke, she saw Indra and the forty-nine Maruts, brilliant as fire, standing before her. Indra told her that they were her sons. Seeing that they were friendly with Indra, Diti was pleased. She no longer felt the hatred she had formally harbored towards him. Rather, she felt a sense of affection, relationship, and unity. This was because she had been worshiping Lord Vishnu continually for almost a year, which had completely purified her heart and dissolved her hostility. But she now wondered, "My dear nephew, how have I gotten forty-nine sons?"

Indra explained what he had done while he had been in her womb. "I'm such a fool!" he lamented. "Please excuse me for my offenses. Although I tried to kill your baby, I couldn't succeed. This was because of your great devotional service to Lord Vishnu. Out of love for you, He fully protected them."

Seeing that his aunt was satisfied by his repentant behavior, Indra offered obeisances to her. Then, with Diti's permission, he left with the Maruts for the heavenly planets.

Diti then realized that just as she had tricked her husband into granting her a vicious boon, he had tricked her into changing her attitude towards the person she had wanted to kill. Thus, instead of committing a grave offense, she became a serious devotee of Lord Vishnu on the path of self–discovery. Feeling great happiness and fulfillment, Diti had no doubt that her husband, who had helped her transform her hostility into love, was certainly a great sage.

CHAPTER FIVE

CHURNING FOR NECTAR

By being extremely patient and enduring, the gods recovered their captured property and positions. Similarly, if we want to discover our true identity, we need to cultivate infinite patience and endurance. Otherwise, we may lose our hard-earned spiritual gains and find ourselves functioning on a lower level of consciousness.

At one time Lord Indra, king of the gods, had so much false pride that he didn't even know he had offended the powerful Yogi Durvasa. But the yogi knew it and was firmly determined to teach Indra a painful lesson for his offense. Thus Durvasa cursed Indra in a way that he would never forget!

What had happened was that while the yogi was strolling along a road, he saw Indra riding on the back of his elephant. Wearing a flower garland on his neck, Durvasa was pleased to remove it and respectfully offer it to Indra. Since Indra thought he was certainly worthy of it—and of much more—he proudly accepted the wreath. But instead of appreciatively placing it over his own neck, he just hung it on the trunk of his elephant.

Being only an animal, the elephant could not understand the value or significance of the garland. Consequently, he threw the wreath between his legs and then stomped on it. The yogi construed this to mean that Indra did not consider the garland valuable enough for himself to wear and thus gave it to his ignorant pachyderm. This, of course, was highly offensive to Durvasa. Therefore, he bellowed, "I curse you, Indra, to lose all your opulence and become poverty-stricken!"

In due course of time, Indra, along with all the gods, lost his wealth. Moreover, in a big battle against the demons, many of the gods were killed. Thus, the gods became bereft of all their power and influence.

But who were the gods and the demons?

Mohini-murti beheads the demon Rahu

The gods were Aditi's sons and the demons were Diti's and Danu's, all three women being married to the sage Kashyapa. The gods were often referred to as the Adityas, and they had been entrusted by the Supreme Lord, Vishnu, with managing the universe. Thus they were responsible for the activities of the sun, moon, wind, water, rain, etc., but under God's direction. They never considered themselves independent of Him and, except for occasional lapses, they were generally obedient and submissive. Always devoted to the service of the Lord, they were considered His devotees.

The demons, being sons of Diti and Danu, were known as Daityas and Danavas respectively. But collectively, they were called *asuras* or demons. This was because they were generally opposed to obeying God's laws and rules and preferred to live independently of Him. Filled with lust, anger, greed, pride, and envy, they often tried to establish their own divinity or power over the universe. This they did by acquiring superhuman powers, which they usually used for aggrandizing and domineering purposes. As a result, they frequently clashed with their half-brothers, the gods, and became their bitter enemies, sometimes even declaring war on them.

Since the gods were now in a deplorable condition, they asked Lord Brahma, their grandfather and the first created being, for guidance. Brahma suggested that they visit and take shelter of Lord Vishnu, for He had always been very kind and dear to them. Thus the gods, as a group, traveled to the Polestar. There, they went to an island called Shvetadvipa that was situated in the ocean of milk. Although they did not see the Lord there, they knew it was His abode. Lord Brahma worshiped Him with beautiful prayers that extolled His omnipotence, omniscience, and omnipresence. He also glorified Him as the source of all creation and the cause of all causes, and begged that He be pleased with them.

Satisfied by their prayers, the Lord suddenly appeared before them. His bodily effulgence resembled thousands of suns; thus, the gods were temporarily blinded. However, after awhile their eyes adjusted to the illumination and they were able to see Him. Gazing at His gorgeous form was like drinking the sweetest of nectar. He had a blackish body, reddish eyes, four mighty arms, and an attractive smiling face. He was decorated with jewels, earrings, armlets, and bangles, as well as belts, garlands, necklaces, and ankle bells. He held a disc in one hand, a club in a second hand, a lotus in a third, and a conch-shell in a fourth.

Overwhelmed by His compelling appearance, the gods prostrated themselves at His lotuslike feet in a mood of total surrender. Again, Lord Brahma offered Him the best of prayers and begged for His precious mercy. Then the gods stood up with folded palms and humbly awaited the Lord's response. In a deep voice that resembled rumbling clouds, the Lord said, "O gods, please listen to Me carefully. Since you are not flourishing, you should make a truce with the demons. That will be in your best interest." Then He suggested a project that they could cooperatively engage in with the demons but which would ultimately benefit the gods. "With patience and serenity everything can be accomplished. But if you become easily angered and disturbed, you will not achieve your goal."

"What should we do to keep things peaceful?" asked one of the gods.

"Agree to whatever the demons propose."

The Lord then disappeared.

All the gods then went to Tripura, the abode of King Bali, the demon leader. Since Bali had conquered the universe, his palace was extraordinarily opulent. The gods approached his throne in a peaceful manner, offering him proper respects. But his assistants suspected them of mischief. "What do you want here?" said one, angrily.

"We've come on a peace mission," said Indra.

"Peace? Oh, sure!" said another demon sarcastically.

"They've come to spy on us!" said a third. "Don't trust them!"

"Please believe us," pleaded Indra.

"I say we kill them!" said the second demon.

"Yes, let's kill them!" roared several other demons.

But Bali lifted his arms and silenced them. "Let's first hear their proposal." He turned to Indra, offered him a seat near him, and suspiciously said, "Proceed."

"We would like you to help us churn the ocean of milk."

"For what purpose?" asked Bali.

"To obtain nectar from it—and become immortal."

"Nectar?" cried all the demons, their eyes widening greedily.

"Yes."

"What makes you so sure it's there?" Bali asked.

"Because Lord Vishnu told me it is."

Bali nodded and considered this. "So why do you need our help?"

"Because a tremendous amount of manpower will be needed."

"All right. But then who will keep the nectar?"

"We'll share it," said Indra.

Bali looked at his assistants for their response.

"That sounds fair," they said, nodding reluctantly.

"Then let's do it," said Bali.

The rival parties then declared an armistice and cooperatively proceeded towards the ocean of milk.

Following the instructions the Lord had given to Indra, all the gods and demons gathered around the base of the golden Mount Mandara. They were strongly built and were ready to use their superhuman might. When the leaders gave the signal, they all tried to dislodge the mountain from its deep foundation. Succeeding, they lifted it off the ground. As they strained to carry it towards the ocean, they moaned and groaned loudly. It was so heavy that everyone became quickly fatigued. Consequently, they lost their grip and the mountain fell down with a thundering crash. Many of the warriors were crushed to death. Others' arms, thighs, and shoulders were broken. Frustrated and disheartened, they lamented loudly.

Knowing what had happened, the Lord instantly appeared there on the back of His eagle carrier, Garuda. He dismounted and compassionately glanced over the dead and wounded bodies, fully reviving them.

As the resuscitated men looked about and climbed to their feet, they were incredulous. Those who had died pinched themselves to make sure they were alive. And those who had been disabled stretched their limbs to be sure those parts were again useable. They looked at each other and laughed loudly, hardly able to believe the miracle. The gods raised their arms high with clenched fists and shouted, "Glory to Lord Vishnu!" repeatedly.

The Lord easily raised the mountain with one hand and placed it securely on Garuda's back.

The gods and demons were astounded. They cheered and roared, quite certain now that they would secure the coveted nectar. The gods continued chanting, "Glory to Vishnu!" again and again.

Next, the Lord mounted Garuda and directed him to the ocean of milk, the gods and demons eagerly following. Arriving there, Garuda lowered the mountain into the milk. The Lord then asked Garuda to leave the area.

The gods and demons summoned the giant thousand-headed serpent Vasuki from the nether world, promising to give him a fair share of the nectar if he participated. When he agreed, they coiled him around the mountain and would soon use him as a churning rope. The Lord and the gods clasped the head portion of the snake, expecting the demons to grab the rear end. But the demon leaders were averse to this arrangement. "We don't want to hold that part—it brings bad luck. We want to hold the front end."

"The front?"

"Yes, the good-luck part."

The Lord smiled and said, "All right. We'll switch positions."

So the demons held the head and the gods and Lord Vishnu held the tail. Then they began to vigorously churn Mount Mandara with all the energy they could summon. Their rhythmic shouts of "Heave ho" greatly inspired each other. However, because the mountain had no base on which to rest securely, it fell splashing into the milk. Deeply disappointed, the men let out a mournful cry and their faces shriveled in disgust. It seemed as if all their hard work had come to naught.

Noting the hopeless situation, the Lord assumed the form of a giant tortoise, known as Kurma, and dove into the milk. The gods and demons waited eagerly to see why He had done this. Then the peak of Mount Mandara began to slowly rise above the milky surface. Soon more and more of it appeared—till most of the mountain became visible. Enlivened and encouraged, the men shouted joyously. Now they could understand that Lord Kurma had swum under the mountain and somehow had lifted it upright onto His massive shell.

The gods and demons reassumed their positions and, with renewed hope, began to churn the mountain energetically. As Mount Mandara rotated back and forth on Kurma's shell, the Lord felt the pleasurable sensation one feels when one's itchy back is vigorously scratched. He also continued to infuse the men with an ever-increasing quantity of strength. Then, atop the swiveling mountain, He manifested another incredible form—this one with thousands of arms—and sat there cross-legged, keeping Mandara firmly balanced with one of His hands. Thus, the Lord assisted them from both above and below. Seeing this, the appreciative chief gods replicated their bodies and, from above, showered countless flowers on Him.

The ocean of milk was so intensely agitated that all the creatures living in it—alligators, fishes, sharks, tortoises, whales, etc.—became fearfully perturbed. But the gods and demons, ignoring them, continued churning the milk. Nothing could stop them now from producing the nectar—except one thing: the blazing fire and choking smoke that emitted from Vasuki's thousands of mouths. Gradually, it afflicted them and diminished their strength. The smoke blackened their faces, garments, and weapons, and they soon looked like a sorry lot. No longer able to continue churning, they merely stood there, stooped over, hopeless and lusterless.

Seeing their pathetic condition, the Lord immediately produced in the sky billows of rain clouds. Then torrents of rain fell and gusty winds swirled about. This brought the men instant relief. But when the Lord saw that after so much endeavor the nectar still had not come, He decided to personally help. Grabbing Vasuki, He began churning the milk vigorously. As He worked steadily, He Himself looked like a magnificent mountain.

But then something terrible happened.

The first substance that rose to the surface of the ocean was not nectar at all: it was poison, and it spread all over the sea. Called *halahala*, it was extremely dangerous. If it were not quickly eliminated, it would endanger everyone in the universe. Therefore, before any further churning could be done, the poison would have to be removed. Of course, the Lord, being omnipotent, could have easily accomplished this Himself. But because He often enjoys giving glory to His great devotees, He suggested that they all beg Lord Shiva to help solve the problem.

They promptly flew to the snow-capped Mount Kailash, where Lord Shiva was sitting under a bael tree with his lovely wife, Bhavani. Great saintly persons desiring liberation were worshiping him.

Lord Shiva had a handsome face and a peaceful smile. His hair was long, matted and brownish, and Ganges water spouted from a swirl of hair atop his head. On his forehead, he had an ornamental half-moon and three white clay-painted parallel lines above each other. He wore Rudraksha beads and a live cobra around his neck and similar but smaller snakes around his biceps. A loincloth covered his waist and thighs, and a damaru drum hung from one side of his waist. The handle of his trident was stuck in the earth and a flower garland hung over one of the three upended prongs.

Seeking his shelter, the gods offered him their humble obeisances and reverential prayers. Then they entreated him to help them eliminate the poison from the ocean.

Lord Shiva said to his wife, "My dear Bhavani, when one performs kindly acts for others, the Supreme Lord is very pleased."

"Yes, that's true," she replied.

"And when the Lord is pleased, I'm also pleased, along with everyone else."

"Yes, I know," she said affectionately.

"So—would it bother you if I try to help them?"

Bhavani considered this. Knowing Lord Shiva's supernatural capabilities, she assented. Then they all happily departed for the ocean of milk.

Lord Shiva kneeled on the shore while some cobras, scorpions, and animals gathered about him. Then, by his mystic power, he caused the poison to rise from the ocean and, like an undulating snake, slither towards his outstretched palm. As it fell into his hand, he compressed it into several drops and quickly drank it. This caused a bluish line to appear across Lord Shiva's neck, which everyone there regarded as an ornament. While he was drinking, the creatures near his knees drank the tiny drops of poison that fell from his hand. Lord Shiva's drinking the poison was his way of worshiping the Supreme Lord, so all the gods highly praised his singular devotion.

As soon as the ocean became free of the poison, the happy gods and demons resumed churning the milk with renewed alacrity. After awhile, various items were stirred to the ocean's surface: a cow (*surabhi*), a white horse (Uchchaihshrava), a white elephant (Airavata), eight male and eight female elephants, and sparkling jewels (Kaustubha and Padmaraga).

But where was the nectar? they wondered.

As they continued churning, other items rose to the ocean's surface: fragrant flowers (Parijata), dancing ladies (Apsaras), and Goddess Lakshmi and Goddess Varuni. These items were divided fairly between the gods and the demons, but Lakshmi and the jewels were allotted to Lord Vishnu.

But what about the nectar? Where was it?

Then suddenly, Dhanvantari, a partial incarnation of the Lord acting as a god, rose to the surface. Especially conversant in medical science, he was handsome, well built, strong, adorned, and well dressed. In one of his hands, he was carrying a vase.

Everyone wondered—*what was in the vase?*

And Dhanvantari answered, "Nectar!"

The gods and demons roared with delight, some raising their arms victoriously, others clapping feverishly.

But some of the demons became intensely greedy. One of them forcefully snatched the vase from Dhanvantari's hand and eagerly hastened away to the shore. The other demons joyfully followed him. They were absolutely thrilled, for now they could have all the nectar for themselves. Now they could become virtually immortal—and no god would ever dare challenge or fight with them again. They would rule the universe forever, they thought, and the gods would have to serve them as fawning menials. They cheered and praised their good fortune, feeling the heady pleasure of a great conquest.

But what about the gods? They weren't at all happy. In fact, they were quite morose. Since they were not powerful enough now to fight and defeat the demons, they thus sought shelter at the feet of Lord Vishnu. The Lord said, "Don't be sad. I have a plan to help you."

The gods wondered what it was. Would they ever get the nectar? It seemed practically impossible now.

Then something strange happened. One demon said to the others, "I want to drink the nectar first!"

But another demon challenged, "No, I want the first drink!"

"Why you?" said a third. "I want it!"

"No, I want it!" said a fourth.

"No, give it to me!" said a fifth.

They continued bickering in this way for awhile till one of the weaker demons exclaimed, "The gods worked just as hard as we, so they should also get some."

"Never!" said one of the stronger demons.

"Why not?"

"Because they don't deserve any!"

"That's not true!"

"Yes, it is!"

"No, it's not! We should give them some!"

"Over my dead body, we will!"

One demon grabbed the nectar vase from the one who had snatched it from Dhanvantari. But the first demon wrested it back. Then another demon seized it. And still another jerked it from him. The dispute was just about to become a melee when suddenly their attention was irresistibly captured: a young, gorgeous woman was strolling towards them. She was so ravishing that the demons completely forgot their disagreement. As she gradually drew closer, they just gazed at her seductive gait with lustful absorption.

She had a dark complexion, raised nose, restless eyes, and a lustrous face. Wearing an attractive red sari, she glided like a swan towards them. Her shiny black hair was braided and adorned with scented flowers, her body was perfectly symmetrical—with large breasts and a slim waist—and she wore glittering bangles on her smooth arms and alluring ankle bells around her shapely legs. And her fragrance—it was extremely intoxicating—so much so that the demons became entranced!

When she glanced at them in a coy manner, each demon could think of only one thing: "I must have her—and make her mine!" They began conversing about her. "Who is she?" asked one demon.

"I don't know," said another.

"I've never seen such beauty," said a third.

"Neither have I," said a fourth.

"Let's find out about her," said the second.

They hurried over to her, and the first demon said, "O beautiful one—who are you?"

But she just smiled flirtatiously at them, arousing them even more.

"Please tell us your name," asked the first demon eagerly.

"My name is—Mohini-murti."

"What a lovely name," said the second demon. "And where are you from?"

"That's not really important," she smiled.

"But—what's a pretty lady like you doing here?" the third demon asked.

"Nothing in particular," she answered coquettishly.

"And who's your father?" the fourth demon asked.

"Does it really matter?"

The demons glanced at each other, surprised by her indifferent answer.

"You're obviously not married," guessed the second demon.

"That's true."

The demons' eyes opened wider and some of them began licking their lips.

"Are you—looking for a husband?" the first demon asked, hopefully.

But Mohini-murti just smiled shyly at them. They construed that to mean that she was. Desiring to involve her in their lives so that they could get closer to her, the demon holding the nectar said, "We were just having a little dispute—about this nectar."

"Nectar?" she asked.

"Yes. I was wondering if you might be interested in settling it for us."

"What's your dispute about?"

The first demon explained everything to her.

Mohini-murti smiled at them. "But I'm only a prostitute—so how can I help you settle this?"

The demons' eyebrows jumped up in surprise. Why would a woman so beautiful, who could virtually have any great man in the world as her husband, be a prostitute? Her statement made no sense to them; thus, they refused to believe it.

"Why do you have so much faith in me?" she further asked. "A learned person never puts his faith in a woman."

The demons nodded and chuckled, thinking she was jesting.

"Independent women like me seek new friends daily. You can never have a permanent relationship with a woman like me."

But the demons were so strongly enamored of her that they felt she would never betray them. Confident of her sincerity, the demon holding the nectar handed her the vase. "Please distribute this fairly—between us and the gods."

She looked at the nectar for a few moments, then back at the demons. "I will do so on one condition only."

"And what's that?" several demons asked.

"That you accept whatever I do—whether it's honest or dishonest."

But believing she could never be dishonest, they optimistically said, "Yes, of course we accept."

The moment was nearing when the gods and demons would receive their share of the nectar. Since it was an auspicious occasion, they fasted, bathed, and gave charity. Next, they performed ritualistic ceremonies under the directions of learned Brahmins. They then dressed themselves with new clothes and adorned their bodies with attractive ornaments. Finally, they entered an ornate pavilion that had a reflective marble floor and colorful silks strung across the ceiling. The arena was further enhanced by surrounding golden arches that looked out upon the blue sky and the ocean of milk. The scent of flower garlands, ghee lamps, and incense smoke pervaded the air. Standing about, the gods and demons wondered when Mohini-murti would arrive to distribute the nectar.

Then they heard a tinkling of ankle bells coming from the

entranceway. It was she. Holding the nectar in her hands and wearing an exquisite-looking sari, she ambled across the smooth floor. The men could not help gazing at her ample shaking breasts, at her full swaying hips, and at her lovely adorned face. When she charmingly glanced and smiled at them, they were completely enchanted. In fact, they could scarcely even think of the nectar now—so beguiling was she.

Mohini-murti had the demons sit down in a line, on kusha-grass mats, according to their rank. Then she led the gods to a spot some distance away from the demons and had them also sit in a line on the same type of mats. Returning to the demons, she flashed them a winsome smile that surely made their hearts skip a beat. Then she said, "All of you look so handsome now."

The demons smiled with feigned modesty.

"I've never seen such powerful-looking men."

Some of the demons tensed their muscles just to confirm her statement.

Then she changed the subject: "I was just talking with the gods and—"

The demons became anxiously curious.

"—and I think they're very miserly."

They laughed in agreement. What a smart lady!

"They kept saying to me, 'Please let us drink the nectar first.' They were so nervous."

The demons smiled contemptuously at them.

"They weren't at all like you—so peaceful and patient. So you know what I think?"

"What?" asked the demons.

"Since you're so much more mature than they, why not let them drink the nectar first?"

"First?" asked a few demons apprehensively.

"Yes. That will show them how superior you are to them."

The demons nodded smugly, relishing her every word. Feeling that she liked them more than the gods, they believed she would give the gods only a few drops of the nectar—and reserve the lion's share for them! They couldn't wait to start drinking it and receiving its amazing vivifying benefits—no disease, no old age, and no death (except when it was time for the world to end).

But there was one demon there who did not trust Mohini-murti as much as his brothers did. His name was Rahu, and he wanted to be certain that he got his share of the nectar. Thus, as Mohini-murti continued praising the demons, Rahu left his sitting place and entered an adjoining room. There, he removed his demon uniform and replaced it with a god outfit. Resembling the gods now, Rahu returned to the main hall. But instead of sitting with the demons, he inconspicuously sat down among the gods. And no one there seemed to even notice him because all eyes were riveted on Mohini-murti.

She waved to the demons amiably and then strolled over to the gods. "Time for the nectar," she said.

Each god clutched his goblet. When she came before the chief god, he extended his arm and she poured a goodly amount into his glass. He tasted it with gusto and sighed with delight. Never before had he drunk such a delicious beverage.

The demons, trying not to look obvious, kept glancing over at Mohini-murti. They were concerned about how much nectar she was giving to the gods, and whether there would be enough left for them.

Would there be? some thought. *Of course there would! She herself had indicated that she favored them over the gods. Hadn't she said that the demons were superior to them? Definitely. Thus, there was nothing to worry about.*

Or was there?

Mohini-murti went from one god to the next, filling up goblet after goblet.

As she did, the demons became increasingly anxious. When she tilted the vase to pour the nectar, they noticed that soon it was only half-filled; then one-quarter filled; then one-eighth filled; then—almost nothing left! *How could she do that?* they wondered. She had told them how much more she cared for them than for the gods, and now— They could scarcely believe it! Thus, they began discussing the matter quietly among themselves.

"She's favored the gods!" said one demon angrily.

"That's not fair!" said a second demon.

"Nobody betrays us without suffering!" a third demon said.

"But what can we do?" said a fourth. "We promised that we would accept whatever she would do—whether it was honest or dishonest."

The others nodded slowly, pensively.

"If we break our promise," continued the fourth, "she'll get angry at us."

"Right," said the second. "And I don't know about you, but I'd like to keep our relationship friendly with her."

Although disappointed and glum, the others agreed. There was something mystically charming about having a woman as gorgeous as Mohini-murti friendly to them. It somehow made them feel bigger than they actually were. And who knows, they thought, she might even want to marry one of them. Anything was possible. Therefore, they remained patiently silent.

Meanwhile, as Mohini-murti filled up Rahu's goblet, the sun god and the moon god, his old enemies, noticed something strange about him. As they studied him more closely, the sun god pointed and shouted, "Hey, that's Rahu!"

All the gods turned and stared at him with surprise.

"Yes," agreed the moon god, "he is Rahu!"

"He's stealing the nectar!" said the sun god.

Rahu, to protect himself from a possible attack, took a big drink of the nectar. However, before it could glide down his throat, Lord Vishnu's whirling disc suddenly appeared and cut off his head. Since the nectar had entered his mouth, his head became immortal, while his body died. Thus, his head became one of the planets. And since he was an eternal enemy of the sun and the moon, he would thereafter attack them in the form of eclipses. In this way, he would diminish their splendor and make them inauspicious at that time.

Because one of their brothers had just been decapitated, the demons were enraged and ready to fight. But as they got up, raised their weapons, and headed toward the gods, something quite astonishing occurred.

Mohini-murti smiled at them as they drew closer. And then—in an instant—she was no longer a woman: She was the Supreme Lord, Vishnu! The demons halted, their eyes and mouths wide open in surprise and shock. "He tricked us!" some of them said. Seeing Lord Vishnu's whirling disc and knowing that it was the most powerful weapon in existence, they refrained from attacking Him. But they would not allow the gods to escape their wrath. Never! So they sallied forth and assailed them, the battle moving outside and onto the beach.

Lord Vishnu summoned His carrier, Garuda, mounted him, and ordered the eagle to fly Him to His own abode.

On the beach, the warriors fought on elephants, horses, chariots, and foot; others fought on vultures, hawks, buffaloes, jackals, boars, and bulls, etc. The shouts and cries, along with the sounds of conch shells, bugles, drums, and kettledrums, were tumultuous. The vehicles were decorated with canopies, flags, umbrellas, and fans. As the soldiers' upper and lower garments fluttered in the wind, their shields, ornaments, and weapons glittered in the sunshine. The two hostile parties—with Lord Indra leading the gods and King Bali leading the demons—looked spectacularly beautiful. They appeared like two massive oceans about to engulf one another.

The fighting became fierce and furious, both sides filled with the taste for victory. The warriors, fighting in pairs, scorned each other with hateful words that pierced their hearts and agitated their minds. Many of the soldiers' heads, arms, thighs, and legs were severed from their bodies, and their flags, bows, armor, and ornaments were torn apart. Numerous elephants, horses, chariots, charioteers, and foot soldiers were slashed to pieces. In the course of the fight, the beach became strewn with separated heads, arms, thighs, and calves, along with helmets, earrings, necklaces, and armlets.

Then the main battle began—between Indra and Bali. Indra was situated on his flying elephant, Airavata, and Bali was stationed on his magic airplane. Bali shot ten arrows at Indra, three arrows at his elephant, four at the four horseman guarding Airavata's legs, and one at the elephant driver. But before those arrows could reach Indra, he smiled and repelled them with other arrows that were extremely sharp. This angered Bali intensely, so he grabbed his Shakti weapon, which blazed like a torch. But before he could even release it, Indra cut it to pieces. Then Bali tried to launch a series of other deadly weapons, but Indra destroyed them also.

Becoming desperate, Bali vanished and resorted to magical illusions. He caused a giant mountain to appear above the heads of the gods. And from it fell fiery trees, pointed chips of stone, scorpions, poisonous snakes, and animals, as well as lions, tigers, boar, and elephants—smashing and crushing many of the gods.

Then suddenly, hundreds of totally naked carnivorous male and female demons, holding sharp tridents, appeared and shouted, "Cut them to pieces! Pierce them!"

Next, savage clouds, blown by blustery winds, thundered loudly and dropped hot coals.

Then a devastating fire, accompanied by blasting winds, engulfed some of the gods and horribly burned them. After this, whirlpools and sea waves, stirred by strong surges of wind, appeared everywhere in a raging flood.

Overwhelmed by all this magic and unable to check it, the gods became morose. Thus, they helplessly meditated on the Supreme Lord and begged for His mercy. Lord Vishnu, riding on Garuda, immediately appeared before the gods in His eight-armed form. And instantly, by His insuperable prowess, Bali's magical illusions disappeared. When the demon Kalanemi, who was riding on a lion, saw this, he flung his trident at Garuda's head. However, the Lord caught the weapon in His hand and flung it back at Kalanemi, killing both him and his carrier. Then several other demons angrily attacked the Lord and Garuda, but Lord Vishnu released His sharp, whirling disc and beheaded them all.

The Lord then revived all the gods who lay unconscious. Enlivened, they jumped to their feet, grabbed their weapons, and began to intensely beat the same demons who had previously defeated them. Indra, filled with anger, seized his thunderbolt weapon, which had hundreds of sharp edges, to kill King Bali. Seeing this, all the demons began to wail, "Oh, no! No!" As Bali confronted Indra, awaiting the weapon, Indra shouted, "You cheater! You rascal! Trying to use magic on us! Well, have a look at my magic thunderbolt—as it severs your head!"

Bali calmly replied, "We're all under the influence of time or destiny. We all reap what we have sown. We are simply getting the fruits of our past deeds, and you are only the instrument to give them to us. Only a fool rejoices over his victory—because he's ignorant of the real cause." He then shot more arrows at Indra, further chastising him with other words. But since Indra saw the truth in them, he did not become sorry or disturbed.

Then Indra hurled his infallible thunderbolt at Bali, intending to kill him. As soon as it hit the demon king, he and his airplane fell and smashed into the ground.

Seeing this, Bali's friend Jambhasura, carried by a lion, hastened to Indra and struck him with his club on the shoulder; he also hit Indra's elephant. This confused and pained Airavata, making him drop to his knees and fall unconscious. Then Matali, Indra's chariot driver, brought Indra's chariot, drawn by a thousand horses. Dismounting from his elephant, Indra climbed up onto his car. Jambhasura threw his trident, blazing with fire, at Matali, greatly paining him. Nonetheless, the charioteer tolerated this with admirable patience. Extremely angry at Jambhasura, Indra flung his thunderbolt and decapitated him.

The great sage Narada suddenly appeared in the area and informed Jambhasura's friends and relatives that Indra had killed the demon. Immediately, three demons—Namuchi, Bala, and Paka—hastened to the battlefield and assaulted Indra with coarse, vicious words. Then they pelted him with a shower of arrows. Bala shot one thousand arrows at Indra's one thousand horses, greatly distressing them. And Paka released two hundred arrows simultaneously at Indra's chariot and charioteer. Then Namuchi fired fifteen golden-feathered arrows that roared and tore into Indra. Other demons also covered Indra and Matali with showers of arrows.

The gods, overwhelmed by the demons and unable to see Indra on the battlefield, became apprehensive. Feeling leaderless, they began to sorrow like traders on a shipwreck in the middle of the ocean. However, Indra, along with his driver, chariot, horses, and flag, managed to escape from the incessant flow of arrows. Shining brightly like the rising sun, he saw the demons heavily attacking his soldiers. Enraged, he hurled his thunderbolt at Bala and Paka and beheaded them.

When Namuchi saw this, he became filled with grief and vengeance. Roaring like a lion, he grabbed his decorated steel spear and hurled it at Indra, crying out, "You're dead!" But Indra cut it to pieces with his arrows and then hurled his thunderbolt to decapitate the demon. However, as powerful as it was, the weapon could not even penetrate Namuchi's skin, and thus it returned to Indra. This amazed and frightened Indra, since it meant the demon might have some superior power. Indeed, that very thunderbolt had killed demons who were much more powerful than Namuchi. *So why had it now become useless?* Indra wondered. He considered discarding it now.

As Indra bemoaned his situation, a disembodied voice boomed at him from the sky, "O Indra, I blessed Namuchi that he could never be killed by any dry or moist weapon. Therefore, you have to think of a different way to kill him." Indra then considered how to slay the demon...*How?*...*How?*...Then, in a flash, he knew exactly what he had to do. Summoning a foam weapon—which was neither dry nor moist—Indra discharged it at Namuchi and it instantly lopped off his head. Various sages, who were watching Indra from the sky, showered a multitude of blossoms on him. The chief Gandharvas sang ecstatically, some of the gods began beating their kettledrums, and the sexy Apsaras danced rhapsodically.

Then the gods Vayu, Agni, Varuna, and others began to kill numerous demons, just as lions kill impotent deer in the forest. Seeing that the demons might be totally annihilated, Lord Brahma sent a message through Saint Narada, who said to the gods, "Lord Vishnu has protected you, and by His mercy, you have gotten the nectar. Therefore, you should stop your fighting now."

Submitting to Narada's order, the gods relinquished their anger and desisted from combat. Their followers praised and cheered them, "Glories to the gods! Victory to the gods!" Satisfied with their win, the gods joyously returned to their heavenly planets and quickly recovered their lost prosperity.

Narada ordered the remaining demons to carry King Bali's body to Astagiri Hill. There, the great mystic Shukracharya uttered the Sanjivani mantra and revived him, as well as all the dead demons who had not lost their heads, trunks, or limbs. When King Bali recovered his senses and memory, he could clearly understand everything that had happened. Thus, although he had been vanquished, he did not sorrow. For to Bali, the war was not really over. Only the first act was.

He would be back—more determined than ever—to win!

Whoever hears or describes this narration of the churning of the ocean of milk helps to eradicate all sufferings in the material world.

CHAPTER SIX

LORD SHIVA BEGUILED

Lord Shiva was proud of his power of being unattracted or unaffected by the fair sex—until he met the exquisite, irresistible Mohini-murti. If we are aspiring to discover ourselves, and have acquired some measure of self-control, we should not be vain about this—else God may withdraw this power and turn us into helpless victims of lust.

When Lord Shiva saw the young, beautiful woman bouncing her ball along the forest path, all he could think was that she was absolutely ravishing! There were no words that could adequately describe her quintessential beauty. And the more Lord Shiva stared at her, the more enamored he became. All he wanted to do now was savor her loveliness.

She was about twenty-five yards away. Glancing at him, she smiled bashfully.

Lord Shiva gulped. "She's interested in me," he thought. "Otherwise, why is she looking at me?"

Then the unthinkable happened.

The ball she was bouncing suddenly hit some surface and bounced away. As she hastened after it, a gust of wind blew her loosened sari off her body. Stark naked, she ran after her garment, but the wind kept blowing it here and there. She looked back helplessly at Lord Shiva, as if he might help her recover it. But he was so preoccupied with scrutinizing every curve and mound of her seductive body that he could not have cared less. All he wanted to do now was enjoy her. And nothing, he felt, was going to stop him.

Impelled by her intoxicating fragrance, Lord Shiva hurried towards her.

She modestly hid behind some wild bushes and flowers, smiling shyly at him.

When he drew near, she bounded away.

Mohini-murti repulses Lord Shiva's advances

Lord Shiva raced after her, bubbles of sweat glistening on his forehead.

But she dodged in and out of scattered flower groves, looking back at him momentarily.

He ran faster, strongly determined to catch her. Glimpsing fragments of her nudity, he fervently thought, *She's not getting away! Never!*

As he drew closer and closer, she turned and smiled at him teasingly.

That smile practically drove him mad. It was now or never!

But how could this have happened? In the entire universe, Lord Shiva was the most self-controlled yogi. In fact, he was the king of yogis. More than that, he was one of the chief gods, just slightly less powerful than the supreme Lord Vishnu. It was also a known and proven fact that no woman in the world could attract and enamor him. And yet—it was happening. The very god who could meditate on Lord Vishnu for days on end, who could look at a nude woman (or women) and remain totally unaffected, who was always filled with inner peace and bliss, who could discriminate between reality and illusion perfectly, who was the personification of renunciation—had now become a victim of lust! Theoretically, this was impossible; and yet—it was happening.

Why?

It had all begun shortly after the gods had defeated the demons. Lord Shiva had heard about Lord Vishnu's astounding Mohini-murti incarnation. He was amazed at how, by Her exquisite beauty, She had cunningly beguiled the demons, causing them to surrender the nectar to Her so that she could distribute all of it to the gods. *How was this possible?* he had wondered. *Could She have been so beautiful that She could mesmerize every single demon?* Since the demons themselves had gorgeous wives, the idea seemed highly unlikely. And yet—it had happened. Mohini-murti had captivated every last one of them.

How beautiful could she be? Lord Shiva wondered. His own wife, Goddess Bhavani, was a paragon of beauty and yet she could never control him by her charms. In fact, the opposite was true. He, by his detachment, godliness, and power, attracted her. The more Lord Shiva thought about Mohini-murti, the more he wanted to see Her. When his curiosity became obsessive, he explained this to Bhavani and suggested they visit Lord Vishnu. Hopefully, He would grace them with a sight of that incredible form. Since Bhavani was quite convinced of her husband's superlative sense-control, she was unconcerned about him becoming unfaithful. Having one wife was more than enough for his dispassionate nature!

Thus Lord Shiva, his wife, his bull carrier, and his ghostly companions all left Mount Kailash to visit Lord Vishnu at His palatial residence. There, Lord Vishnu welcomed Lord Shiva and Bhavani with great respect and offered them comfortable seats. Then Lord Shiva worshiped Lord Vishnu, offering Him the most exalted prayers. He emphasized how Lord Vishnu's position was supreme, how He was the indisputable cause of all causes, and how He was the means to attain permanent liberation from this world by the process of loving devotional service. Pleased by these prayers, the Lord smilingly asked Shiva why he had come.

"I'd like to see just how beautiful your Mohini-murti form is."

Lord Vishnu laughed. "It might be dangerous for you," the Lord joked.

"I doubt it," Shiva chuckled.

"What makes you so sure?"

"Well, the gods weren't captivated, so—why should I be?"

"You're right. And you've got much more self-control than they."

"I would hope so."

"But don't blame Me if—" The Lord paused meaningfully.

"Don't worry. Nothing is going to happen."

"All right. Would you like to see that form now?"

"Yes."

"Then come and look for it."

At that moment, Lord Vishnu vanished.

Lord Shiva and Bhavani then went out searching for Him. They entered the forest and ambled along a serpentine path that was dappled with sunlight. Amid the chirping and crying of colorful birds, Shiva and Bhavani began looking here and there. Unable to find Him, they puzzled over where He might have gone. As they continued searching, they suddenly saw a young woman in the distance—about seventy-five yards away. "Maybe that's Him," Lord Shiva said. They quickened their steps until they were about fifty yards from Her.

"Yes, that must be Him," said Shiva. He and Bhavani just stood there, watching Mohini-murti playfully bouncing a ball. She was wearing a glistening red sari that was ornamented with a golden belt. As She moved, Her face glowed, Her smile radiated, Her earrings swung, Her ankle bells tinkled, and Her bangles clinked. She wore Her soft black hair in a single braid over Her back, although some strands hung loosely along the sides of Her lustrous cheeks and dangled over Her ample breasts.

Lord Shiva gazed at Her with rapt attention, admitting to himself that he had never before seen such a gorgeous woman. He could now understand why the demons had been so captivated. In fact, he himself was beginning to feel attracted. But catching himself, he smiled. All he had to do was either close his eyes or look in another direction. And the attraction would be gone.

Or would it?

When he shut his eyes, he saw Her just as clearly in his mind and found himself unable to dismiss Her from it. And when he looked away, he felt so exceedingly curious that he could not help looking back at Her. *This is ridiculous*, he thought. *There is no woman in the world who can capture me.* But the more he tried to resist gazing at Her exciting charms, the more he felt magnetically drawn to Her—even with his lovely wife at his side. He just could not withdraw his gaze from that stunning face and body—as hard as he tried. So he decided to stop resisting. Instead, he just gazed at Her sensual frolicking.

As Mohini-murti bounced Her ball, Her breasts shook, Her garland swayed, and Her waist looked tiny. Soft and reddish like coral, Her feet moved this way and that way. As She slapped the ball, Her sari began to loosen and more of Her hair began to scatter over Her face. So, with Her left hand, She tried to bind Her hair, and with Her right, she continued hitting the ball. It was then that She saw, and smiled bashfully at, Lord Shiva.

That smile was like a sharp arrow that stuck deeply in Lord Shiva's heart—so deeply that he became completely enthralled by Her. He even forgot that his dearly beloved wife was standing nearby. In fact, he totally forgot himself. All he knew now was one thing: Mohini-murti! And when the wind blew Her sari away and he saw Her lovely naked form, he no longer wanted to just see it. He wanted to have it, enjoy it, and make it his own! Feverishly, he began running after Her.

Seeing him coming, Mohini-murti raced away. But Lord Shiva stayed right behind Her. She ran beside the flowing rivers and quiet lakes, near the verdant hills and high mountains, through the flowery glades and leafy forests. She also ran across a beautiful garden where some sages were living austerely. When they saw Lord Shiva chasing the lovely woman, they wondered how that was possible. He was above such attractions. But then they realized that no man, including themselves, was free from the enticement of a beautiful woman. Thus, they regarded the incident as a cautionary lesson and quickly abandoned their pride in their sense control.

As Lord Shiva continued chasing Mohini-murti, he began to feel very frustrated. Therefore, with all the resolve he could muster, he increased his speed considerably. Slowly but surely, he began to get closer to Her...and closer...closer... till he was just behind Her. Sweating profusely and breathing rapidly, he reached out and grabbed Her swinging braid. "Ow!" She said, halting. When She turned around, he dropped Her braid and threw his strong arms around Her soft back. Her skin was smooth and satiny, and Her fragrance was overwhelmingly hypnotic.

As he pulled Her closer, She tried to push him away. He moved his face nearer to Hers, but She turned Her head abruptly. Then She suddenly jerked Her body to the side and spun around, breaking the bonds of his firm grip. Next, She bounded away like a gazelle and Lord Shiva charged after her like a hungry lion. He would not let Her escape. Never! He had to have Her—and now! He felt so aroused, so passionate, so—

And then the unexpected happened.

Watching Her shaking breasts, bouncing buttocks, and moving thighs, he ejaculated. As his semen spurted, he had to stop running, his body stunned by spasms of pleasure. When his discharge ended, he heard himself breathing heavily and rapidly. After a few minutes, his breathing normalized and his mind became grave and dispassionate, as often happens to men immediately after ejaculation. Sitting down on a rock and staring at the ground, Lord Shiva wondered how all this had happened. He had always been free of sex desire and attraction. This was because he was always so blissful from his spiritual practices that he had no need for temporary delights.

Then why had he become so enamored of Mohini-murti?

As he wrestled with the question, Mohini-murti suddenly appeared there.

Lord Shiva looked up at Her. He felt no sexual longing for Her now. In fact, he knew quite clearly that She was Lord Vishnu, and he could only feel great awe and reverence for Her. Now he could better appreciate how amazingly powerful the Lord was and could be. For He alone could stimulate Lord Shiva's sexual appetite—no one else. But he wanted to better understand how the Lord had done this.

Mohini-murti immediately changed Her form into that of Lord Vishnu. "So you thought you were free of sex desire," grinned the Lord.

"Yes, I thought," said Lord Shiva, smiling cynically.

"Actually, you *are* free from it. No woman in the world can tempt you."

"Then why was I tempted by You?"

"You know why."

"No, I don't."

"Well, because I'm the Supreme Controller."

"The controller."

"Yes. So I controlled you sexually."

"You sure did!"

"I'm sorry if I disturbed you. I didn't mean to—"

"No," Lord Shiva interrupted. "It was a wonderful lesson. I admire You even more now."

"Thank you. But rest assured that won't happen again."

"Is that a promise?" Lord Shiva smiled hopefully.

"Yes—unless, of course, I see you becoming proud over your self-control."

"Please accept my obeisance." Lord Shiva bowed his head to the ground, then stood up, joined his palms, and circled around the Lord respectfully three times.

"May you be blessed with good fortune," said Lord Vishnu cheerfully.

"Thank You for Your mercy, O Lord." Then, after a brief pause, Lord Shiva asked, "Would it be all right if I, and my companions, return to Mount Kailash now?"

"Certainly. It was a pleasure seeing you."

"Likewise."

As Lord Shiva and his wife and friends were flying through the sky, he said to Bhavani, "When I finished performing mystic yoga for one thousand years, you asked me who I was meditating on. Well, you've just met Him. Time can never touch Him and the Vedic scriptures can only intimate of Him. He's absolutely incredible!"

Lord Vamana arrests King Bali

CHAPTER SEVEN

LORD VAMANA'S CONQUEST

King Bali preferred to keep his promise to God even if it meant that he would become seriously disadvantaged. Similarly, if we wish to discover ourselves, we have to learn to keep our promises—as if they were made directly to the Lord. Such truthfulness easily attracts God's grace and expedites our progress.

King Bali, although sorely defeated by the gods, was determined to regain his position as ruler of the world. But how could he achieve this—unless he had some special, invincible power? And how could he obtain that power—unless he had the blessings of highly empowered Brahmins?

Then he remembered: Shukracharya! He was the Brahmin who had resuscitated him and his subordinates from death. *So,* Bali reasoned, *if Shukracharya, the son of the great sage Bhrigu, had that amount of power, he could surely help him conquer the gods and acquire their wealth.*

But would he?

Bali decided that the only way he could gain the sympathy and interest of the Brahmin was by humbly serving him. And that is exactly what he did. First, he was spiritually initiated by Shukracharya, and then he affectionately ministered to his needs. Submitting himself to the sage with great faith, he offered him everything he had. There was no sacrifice Bali would not make to please him. He considered his body, mind, and speech as belonging to Shukracharya. Thus, everything he did was for his preceptor's satisfaction and glorification.

Not only was Shukracharya pleased with King Bali's exemplary conduct, but all the Brahmins who were Bhrigu's descendants also were. Thus, to help the king achieve his goal, those Brahmins, after purifying him and properly bathing him, engaged him in a very special ceremony called Vishvajit. As it was conducted, one of the priests ladled ghee into the sacrificial fire. The crackling fire rose up and something extraordinary began to emerge from it: a gold-coated, silk-covered, celestial chariot, like Indra's, tethered to yellow horses and bearing a flag that displayed a lion's image.

Bali was certainly impressed.

Next, a gilded bow, two invincible arrows, and celestial armor rose from the fire, and Bali gratefully accepted them. Then King Prahlada, Bali's grandfather, gave him a garland of flowers that would never wilt. And Shukracharya gave him a conch shell he could blow before and during battle. After Bali decorated himself with the garland, he placed protective armor over his chest (but beneath the wreath), set his quiver of arrows over his shoulder, and grabbed his sword. He then clambered onto the chariot and sat down. His ears adorned with sapphire earrings and his arms decorated with golden bangles, Bali glowed like a formidable fire.

The demon king next assembled his warriors and officers, who equaled him in strength, opulence, and beauty. They looked powerful enough to swallow the sky in one gulp and to burn all the directions with their blazing glances. After all arrangements were made, King Bali departed with his troops on space ships headed for Indra's prosperous capital, Amaravati. As they left, the entire surface of the world seemed to tremble, for Bali was fiercely determined to win this battle!

King Indra's city, constructed by the god Vishvakarma, was indeed beautiful. There were attractive orchards and gardens, and many of the tree branches, laden with fruits, leaves, and flowers, were sagging. Pairs of chirping birds and clusters of buzzing bees flew all around, and there were ponds full of swans, cranes, ducks, and chakravaka birds. Gorgeous women, who were protected by the gods, delighted in these pleasurable gardens.

King Bali's army was drawing nearer to the city.

The metropolis was encircled by motes full of Ganges water as well as by a high red wall that contained ramparts for fighting. Marble gates leading to the city were connected by various public roads. There were courtyards, wide roads, assembly houses, and not less than one-hundred-million airplanes. The crossroads were composed of pearl, and the sitting places were made of diamond and coral. Scented smoke of aguru incense drifted lazily from filigreed windows into the streets.

King Bali's host was getting closer.

The city was shaded with canopies adorned with pearls, and the palace domes bore flags that were inlaid with pearl and gold. All over, one could hear in concert the sounds of peacocks, pigeons, and bees, as well as *mrdanga* drums, conch shells, flutes, kettledrums, and stringed instruments. People were always dancing and the Gandharvas were often singing.

King Bali's army had now reached the city's outskirts.

The city women, shining like tongues of fire and attired in clean garments, appeared to be forever youthful and beautiful. They had firm breasts and were warm-bodied during the winter and cool-bodied in the summer. Often riding in airplanes, they sang pleasing, auspicious songs. And when flowers fell from their hair, gentle breezes carried the fragrance of them through the streets. The city was barred to anyone who was sinful, envious, cunning, greedy, lusty, falsely proud, or violent towards other beings.

After the space ships landed, Bali's soldiers hastened out of them. Then Bali blew his conch shell loudly and ominously, signifying a determined challenge for battle.

The women within the city precincts, hearing the fearsome sound, became alarmed.

Bali's soldiers began to attack the city furiously from all directions.

Indra, with several other gods, hastened to the roof of the fortification wall and looked down. He was amazed by the intensity of Bali's endeavor. "I've never seen him look so powerful," he said to one god.

"Neither have I," the god answered.

"He looks invincible," declared another.

"I think we should get some advice from our guru," said Indra.

"Yes!" they replied eagerly.

They thus hurried from the roof to Brihaspati's quarters. After offering the sage due respects, Indra described what he had just seen.

Brihaspati nodded silently.

"We defeated Bali sometime ago, yet—he looks stronger than ever now. Why?"

The sage closed his eyes momentarily. Then, after divining the cause, he said gravely, "The Brahmin descendants of the sage Bhrigu are pleased with him. Therefore, they have blessed him with immense power."

Indra felt anxious. "So—what can we do about that, my lord?"

"Nothing at this time."

"Nothing?"

"Nothing. You have to wait until Bali's situation is somehow reversed."

"And when will that be?"

"Later—when he insults the Brahmins."

"The ones who blessed him?"

"Yes. Until then, all of you should leave this planet."

"Leave it?" Indra was surprised.

"Unless you want to be defeated."

"But—where should we go?"

"Anywhere else. But be sure to disguise yourselves."

"Why?"

"If Bali's men see you, they'll attack."

"Thank you, my lord."

The gods accepted their guru's counsel. Assuming various unrecognizable forms, they left their heavenly planets and settled themselves on other planets. Although they were disappointed, they were not hopeless, for they knew that Bali's fortune was destined to change. But they wondered when and how this would happen.

King Bali then conquered the entire universe. The Brahmin descendants of Bhrigu were very pleased with him, so they engaged him in performing one hundred horse sacrifices—just as Indra had done long ago and which had entitled him to the heavenly throne. This type of sacrifice clearly established the sovereignty of a king over all other leaders. After Bali completed the sacrifices, he became formally entitled to Indra's throne, and he ruled from it accordingly. Thus, his fame in the three worlds—the lower, middle, and upper planets—increased significantly. Indeed, he shone like a full moon among the twinkling stars.

But little did Bali know that Indra's mother, Aditi, would become his greatest nemesis. Who could imagine that she would become the catalyst that would cause Bali to insult all the Brahmins who had empowered him? Although she was devoid of the physical or the fighting power of Bali, she had recourse to a far superior power—one whom she knew could never fail.

The sage Kashyapa had been away for many days in seclusion, meditating. After he arose from his trance, he returned to his ashram in Amaravati. When he entered the sitting room, his wife, Aditi, respectfully received and welcomed him. Sitting down, he noted that the ashram looked neither joyful nor merry, and that Aditi was quite sullen. "What's bothering you?" he asked.

Aditi found it difficult to answer him.

"Did you violate some ethical or religious principles?"

She shook her head.

"How are your sons faring?"

"Not well," she said sadly.

"Oh?"

"Bali and the demons, they've—"

"Yes?"

"Well, they've taken my sons' wealth and fame—even their homes."

"Where are they now?"

"Scattered all over the universe." Then she tearfully added, "My dear husband, you're a great sage. You have the power to grant blessings. Therefore, I would like you to bless my sons."

"With what?"

"With the return of everything that's been taken from them."

Kashyapa smiled and said, "Why are you so attached to those material illusions—sons, property, wealth, and fame?"

Aditi lowered her head and shook it morosely. She was not in the mood for high philosophy now. She simply felt the pangs of a bereaved mother and wanted practical relief.

Observing this, Kashyapa said, "If you perform devotional service to Lord Vishnu, He will surely fulfill your wish."

Aditi looked up and opened her eyes wide. "Please tell me exactly what I have to do."

He then explained to her the twelve-day Payo-vrata ritualistic ceremony. This consisted of observing an austere diet, chanting a specific mantra, uttering reverential prayers, and worshiping the Lord with certain items, as well as donating charity to the Lord's priests and devotees, offering oblations into a sacrificial fire, reciting scriptural passages, and feeding all caste members with holy food [that was first offered to and blessed by the Lord]. She would also have to observe complete celibacy, sleep on the floor, bathe three times daily, refrain from materialistic conversation, and avoid harboring envious thoughts.

"This is the best process," he concluded, "because it pleases the Supreme Lord."

"And if He's pleased, He'll satisfy my wish?" Aditi asked.

"Absolutely."

Aditi smiled hopefully, ready to begin.

Kashyapa's wife diligently followed her husband's instructions, concentrating her mind solely on the Supreme Lord, Vishnu. After she completed the twelve-day program, the Lord appeared before her in His four-armed form. Seeing Him, Aditi offered obeisances and was overwhelmed with transcendental bliss. Tears flowed from her eyes, and her body trembled. Then she expressed heartfelt prayers, emphasizing the Lord's unlimited mercy and divinity. Pleased by her discipline and devotion, God revealed how He intended to help her. But He strongly advised her to not disclose His plan to anyone, or it would not be successful.

After some time, Aditi became pregnant and gave birth to a boy. But this was no ordinary boy: He was Lord Vishnu Himself! At this time, souls everywhere felt immense happiness. Celestial beings played music, sang songs, danced, showered flowers on Aditi's residence, and glorified and praised the Lord. All over, the sounds of "Victory!" could be heard.

Then, something amazing happened. Standing before Aditi and Kashyapa, the child changed His four-armed form into that of a two-armed form, and He looked like a dwarfish *brahmachari* (celibate monk). Then the sages performed His birthday and sacred thread ceremonies and named Him Vamana. Each of the distinguished guests present—gods and sages—gave Him a gift, for wearing or carrying, that He needed for His monastic lifestyle.

One day Lord Vamana learned that King Bali was performing a horse sacrifice under the patronage of the Brahmins belonging to Bhrigu's dynasty. He therefore decided to show His mercy to the king by attending the event. It was being conducted on a field known as Bhrigukaccha, on the northern bank of the Narmada River. Arriving there, He immediately entered the outdoor sacrificial arena. When the Bhrigu priests saw Him, He looked so effulgent—like the rising sun—that He robbed all the assembly members of their splendor.

"Who is He?" asked one priest.

"Probably the sun-god," another priest answered.

"No, I think He's Sanat-kumara," a third priest said.

"He looks more like the fire-god to me," said a fourth priest.

Almost everyone there could not help gazing at Him. His blond hair was matted and twirled into a bun atop his head. He was wearing a deerskin, a straw belt, a sacred thread across His chest, *Rudraksha* beads around His neck, and was holding a staff, an umbrella, and a filled water pot. All the priests and their disciples first stood up from their seats and then respectfully welcomed Him by bowing down. Although they did not know who He actually was, they knew from His radiance that He was someone highly spiritual.

King Bali was joyful to see Him, so he offered Him a comfortable seat. He then washed His feet worshipfully and poured the holy water onto his own head. "O Brahmin," he said, "welcome to the sacrifice. Please accept my respects." Bali bowed down and then stood up. "Please let us know what we may do for you."

"Do?"

"Yes. By Your coming here, my ancestors, family, and dynasty have been blessed. And Your presence has made my sacrifice complete."

The Lord smiled affably.

"And all the pains I was destined to suffer from the sins I committed in the past—they've all been washed away by the water that just bathed my head. Please tell me how I may serve You. Take whatever You like—a cow, gold, furnished house, Brahmin wife, some tasty food and drink, thriving villages, horses, elephants..."

The Lord praised Bali for his ingratiating and accommodating manner. Although Bali had been born in a demon family, he nonetheless possessed many devotional qualities. This was because his grandfather, King Prahlada, was an exalted devotee of Lord Vishnu. Consequently, the Lord had blessed Prahlada's descendants to be devotionally inclined also.

Lord Vamana said, "I know that no one in your family has refused to give charity to the Brahmins or accept challenges by warriors. So you're an exemplary leader."

"O Brahmin, thank you," Bali said graciously. "But—how may I serve You.?"

The Lord considered Bali's offer.

"Is there something you would like?" the king asked.

"Yes, there is."

"Such as?"

"I would like some land."

"I'll be glad to oblige. Just tell me how much You want."

"As much as I can cover with My three steps."

"Three steps?" Bali thought He was joking.

"Yes, that will be enough."

"But—why such a small amount?"

"Because that's all I really need."

"Are You sure?"

"Yes. Definitely."

Bali smiled at Vamana affectionately. "My dear Brahmin, You're still a young boy—so I don't think You know what's in Your best interest."

"I don't?" the Lord asked with surprise.

Bali shook his head. "I can give You an entire planet—and all You're asking for is three steps' worth of land. I don't think that's very smart."

"Really?" the Lord grinned.

"Better take enough land so that You'll never have to ask for any more."

"No, three steps' worth is enough. If I take more, I'll just get greedy."

"I doubt that."

"Then My desires—they'll never end. And I'll have to keep reincarnating just to satisfy them."

Bali appreciated the boy's wisdom, but he still wanted Him to take more. However, Vamana firmly refused.

"All right," smiled Bali, "then take what You want."

Shukracharya, Bali's guru, had been listening to the conversation and studying Vamana. He called Bali aside and said to him, "Don't give the boy anything!"

"What?" Bali was surprised.

"That's right—nothing!"

"But He's a Brahmin and—"

"No," the preceptor interrupted, "He's not a Brahmin. He's Lord Vishnu!"

"He's *what?*"

"Yes! And He's come here to help your enemies—the gods."

Bali was stunned. "Are you sure?"

"Absolutely!" Shukracharya then explained to Bali what the Lord's plan was, and further said, "The demon dynasty is now in a dangerous position."

"I see. But—what can I do? I've made a promise to Him."

"Then break it."

"Break it? A promise to a Brahmin?" The proposition sounded crazy, for Bali believed that such betrayal could only bring him a profusion of bad karma.

"Yes!" emphasized Shukracharya. "The *Bahvrcha* scripture says that a promise can be considered truthful only when it is preceded by the holy sound 'Om.' Since you never said that word, in effect, you never really made a promise."

Bali found it difficult to accept such reasoning, for it did not appeal to his heart.

Noting the King's doubt, Shukracharya reassured him, "The scripture also says that one may lie if one's life is in danger."

But that also did not find favor with Bali, so he remained silent for awhile, deliberating carefully on the matter. Then he confidently said to his guru, "O Master, I don't think keeping my wealth is more important than keeping my promise."

"What?!" Shukracharya was surprised.

"Once I break my word, I become a cheater, and—"

"Are you challenging me?" interrupted Shukracharya.

"—and there is nothing worse than a cheater."

"You are, aren't you?"

"Even Mother Earth once said, 'I can bear any heavy thing—except a cheater.'"

"How dare you speak to me in this way!"

"O Master, I'm less afraid of hell, poverty, distress, demotion, or even death— than I am of cheating a Brahmin."

Shukracharya glared at Bali.

"Therefore, I will give this little Brahmin monk whatever He wants."

"You rascal!"

"I'm sorry, Master."

"You fool! How dare you pose yourself as a learned man before me?"

"I'm just trying to—"

"How dare you to speak so impudently—and disobey my order?"

"My lord, please try to—"

"For these offenses, you will soon lose your prosperity—without fail!" Shukracharya wheeled around and stomped towards his Brahmin associates.

Notwithstanding the curse, King Bali remained fixed in his determination. As was the custom, Bali's wife had a large golden water pot brought there for worshiping the Lord by washing His feet. Again, Bali bathed those lotuslike feet and poured the blessed water onto his own head as a benediction. In the sky, many celestials lauded the king's excellent qualities and showered down on him countless flowers. Then Bali said to the Lord, "You may now take Your three steps."

"Thank you," smiled Lord Vamana.

As everyone watched Him, the Lord did something extremely miraculous. He began increasing His size—until everything in the universe was within His body, including the earth, planets, sky, oceans, creatures, humans, gods, and saints, as well as the material elements, senses, mind, intelligence, false ego, and karma. King Bali thus saw everything in God's gigantic face and form, which now looked like Lord Vishnu. He had eight arms, and in each hand He held one of the following: a conch shell, sword, shield, flaming discus, arrow, bow, lotus flower, and club. His garment was yellow and He was decorated with a flower garland.

When Bali's demon followers saw this universal form, when they saw in the Lord's hand His whirling disc—which generates unbearable heat—and when they heard the tremendous sound of His twanging bow, they grieved deeply.

The Lord then covered the sky with His body, all the directions with His arms, and the entire surface of the earth with His *first* step. In fact, the tips of His toenails even pierced the covering of the material universe and penetrated the spiritual world. Through this hole, the Ganges water flowed down from the spiritual world to the material world. Then He covered all the heavenly planets with His *second* step. Thus, there was not a single spot remaining for Him to take His *third* step.

When Lord Brahma, in his lofty planet, saw that its light was insignificant compared to the illumination radiating from the Lord's toenails, he, along with some great sages and yogis, approached the Lord and offered Him prayers. He then washed the Lord's feet with the water in his pot, and the liquid became so pure that it was transformed into Ganges water. It then went flowing down from the sky and purified the three worlds (the upper, middle, and lower).

The Lord suddenly metamorphosed Himself back to His original diminutive Vamana form, and Lord Brahma, the chief gods, the sages, and the yogis hastened from Brahma's planet down to the planet on which Bali's sacrifice was being conducted. Lord Brahma and those companions then worshiped Vamana with water, fruits, roots, sprouts, flowers, grains, and lamps, and simultaneously offered Him prayers of glorification and veneration. They also sang, danced, and played musical instruments, repeatedly shouting, "Victory!"

Needless to say, Bali's demon followers, realizing that their leader had just lost all his prosperity, were angry. One of them said, "This Vamana is no Brahmin!"

"He's just a big cheater!" a second demon said.

"Masquerading as a Brahmin just to help the gods!" said the first.

"He's exploited our king's truthfulness," the second said.

"I say we kill this Vamana!"

The demons roared their approval. Grabbing their lances and tridents, they headed angrily towards Him.

"Stop!" ordered Bali. "Stop!"

But they ignored his command and sallied forth. As they neared Vamana, the Lord's guards suddenly appeared there and stepped in front of Him. Each possessed the strength of ten thousand elephants, and they readied their weapons for combat. "Don't come any closer!" one guard warned.

But the furious demons kept coming.

"Halt!" shouted another guard.

The demons ignored him.

The guards then repulsed and killed many of Bali's soldiers. Noting this, Bali bellowed to his men, "Stop fighting! Time is against us now! Stop!"

The demons looked at Bali curiously.

"We can't win now, so don't even try."

Feeling morose, the demons lowered their weapons and surrendered. They were later driven in ships by Lord Vishnu's guards to the lower regions of the universe.

Lord Vamana summoned His eagle carrier, Garuda. Understanding the Lord's desire, Garuda arrested Bali with the ropes of Varuna. Although the king lost his luster, he was, nonetheless, fixed in his determination to satisfy the Lord.

"O Bali," said Vamana, "you promised to give Me three steps' worth of land. But I have covered the whole universe with only two steps. Where should I take My third?"

Bali was at a loss for words.

"Since you have not kept your promise, the law is that you must live on one of the hellish planets."

"The hellish planets?"

"Yes."

Bali considered how he could fulfill his word. Then he realized he had one remaining option. "O Lord, I know where You can take Your third step."

"Oh? Where?" Vamana smiled.

"On my head."

"Your head?"

"Yes. I'm less concerned with losing all my possessions than I am of losing my honor. So please—step on my head."

"Are you sure?"

"Absolutely. To have Your lotuslike foot on my head will help destroy my false prestige...and show me who I really am." Bali smiled hopefully. "Thank You for Your mercy, O Lord."

At that moment Bali's grandfather, King Prahlada, one of the most glorious of the Lord's devotees, appeared there. He was tall, darkish, long-armed, lotus-eyed, and wearing yellow clothing.

Because Bali was bound by ropes, he could not properly respect Prahlada by bowing down, so he humbly lowered his head, tears flowing down his cheeks.

On seeing the Lord, Prahlada became ecstatic. He prostrated himself before Vamana and then rose to his feet, his palms prayerfully clasped. "My Lord," he said, "it was You who gave Bali the post of heavenly king. And it is You who have taken it away. This is Your mercy."

"Mercy?" the Lord asked.

"Yes. Bali's lordly position—as king of heaven—was deluding him. But You have disillusioned Him and made him realize how temporary and unfulfilling materialistic success is. Now he knows that the true goal of life is self-realization and not self-glorification...Such is Your mercy."

The Lord smiled affectionately at Prahlada.

Lord Brahma then said, "O Lord, King Bali has been punished enough, for You have taken away all his property. Please release him."

"Are you sure?"

"Yes. He doesn't deserve any more punishment. He offered You everything he had, including even his own body. So why keep him under arrest?"

"You are right. Although he has lost everything—including the blessings of his spiritual master—he has kept his promise and maintained his truthfulness."

"Without a doubt, my Lord."

"Moreover, he has shown great tolerance in adversity. Therefore, in the distant future, during the rule of Sarvani Manu, Bali will become the king of heaven."

Bali's tearful eyes opened wide in disbelief. *How was this happening?* he wondered.

"In the meanwhile," Vamana continued, "he will live on one of the lower planets—Sutala—which I ordered Vishvakarma, the heavenly architect, to create. And I have specially protected that place, so it is free of physical and mental sufferings."

Lord Brahma was gladdened to hear this.

The Lord then looked at Bali. "O King, you may now go there and live peacefully with your friends and relatives. No one will be able to conquer you there. Any demons who transgress your rule, I will kill with my disc. What's more, I will always be with you and protect you in all respects. Also, your materialistic ideas and anxieties that have come from your contact with the demons—they will all disappear. And you will always be able to see Me there...All good fortune to you."

With teary eyes, clasped palms, and a faltering voice, Bali ecstatically replied, "You have blessed me, a fallen demon, with more mercy than You have ever blessed any of the gods. Thank You, my Lord."

Bali was then released from the bondage of Varuna's ropes. Fully satisfied, he offered obeisances to Lord Vamana, Lord Brahma, and Lord Shiva.

The Lord then said to King Prahlada, "Go and join your grandson Bali in Sutala, and enjoy happiness with him and your other relatives."

"With pleasure, my Lord."

"Due to your divine bliss, You will see Me there in My four-armed form, and that will free you from any bondage to materialistic activities."

"Thank You again, O Lord." Prahlada and Bali, after offering the Lord their respects, then departed for the planet Sutala.

Vamana next looked at Shukracharya, who was seated nearby among the assembly of priests. "O Brahmin, do you still think King Bali committed an offense against you?"

"An offense?"

"Isn't that what you said to him?"

"Yes, I did, but—"

"Then?"

"My Lord, since he has obviously satisfied You, it would appear that—"

"Yes?"

"That *I* committed the offense—by cursing a faultless person." Shukracharya humbly bowed his head and folded his palms. "My Lord, please order me, since Your order will benefit not only me, but the whole world."

"All right. Then you should make amends for the offense you committed at Bali's sacrifice."

"Yes, I shall do so."

Thus Indra, the king of heaven, by the Lord's mercy, regained his rule over the lower, middle, and upper planets. Again supremely opulent, he became fearless and fulfilled. All the gods glorified Lord Vamana's extraordinary activities and praised the superlative effort of Indra's loving mother, Aditi. Had she not undergone the *Payo-vrata* process and invoked the unfailing grace of the Lord, her son would still be wanting and miserable.

We can thus understand how important it is to keep our promises— even when we may become apparently disadvantaged—in the course of striving to discover ourselves. Being greatly pleased, the Lord rewards us for such truthfulness with countless blessings—as King Bali so joyfully discovered.

If this story about Lord Vamana is recited at any ceremony—such as at a marriage, birthday, memorial, etc.—that occasion should be understood to be extremely auspicious. Whoever hears this story—or any story about Lord Vishnu—becomes free from all of one's future unfavorable karma (that would have resulted from one's past immoral activities); moreover, one may be elevated to the higher planets, or even to the spiritual world.

CHAPTER EIGHT

KING BHARATA'S FALL AND RISE

Although the king had renounced his throne to exclusively devote himself to self-discovery, he became slavishly attached to a pet, and this led to an unexpected misfortune. If we wish to discover the real self within, it is useful for us to exercise detachment (but not indifference) toward our loved ones; otherwise, we may encounter similar hindrances.

King Bharata had renounced his kingdom and family to live alone in the forest and pursue a life of God-realization. One day, after he had finished his morning ablutions, he seated himself on the bank of the Gandaki River and began chanting a holy mantra. At that moment, he saw a pregnant black doe ramble over to the water's edge and begin drinking. As she drank, a ferocious lion nearby began roaring thunderously. Frightened and disturbed, the doe fled the danger by hastily leaping across the river. However, as she jumped, she miscarried, and a fawn fell from her womb into the coursing stream. Exceedingly distressed, the doe doddered into a nearby cave, collapsed, and died.

As Bharata watched the helpless, motherless fawn floating down the river, he became overwhelmed with compassion. So he hastened to the stream, waded into the water, caught hold of the fawn, and rescued it. Then he carried it to his thatched hut, laid it down, dried it with a cloth, and began petting it affectionately. Little did Bharata know that his merciful concern for the fawn would prove to be his great undoing.

When Bharata had been a king, he had ruled the entire world. Married to Panchajani, he gave her five sons. Especially learned and experienced, he ruled all the citizens affectionately and kept them properly engaged in their occupational duties. To worship and please the Lord, the king performed many ritualistic sacrifices, following all the regulations strictly. This enabled him to become free from all materialistic contamination, such as lust and anger. His devotional service to Lord Vishnu increased day after day.

King Bharata becomes enamored of a deer

After a very long period of rulership, Bharata lost all interest in and attachment to his family and kingdom. He therefore divided his wealth and property among his grown-up sons and retired from family life. Departing from his opulent paternal palace, he journeyed to Pulaha-ashrama, which exists near the holy city of Hardwar. The sacred Gandaki River, presided over by the famous female saint Tulasi Devi, flowed past Pulaha-ashram. In its waters, there were innumerable Shalagrama stones, each one a worshipable incarnation of the Supreme Lord, Vishnu.

Bharata lived alone here. With a full head of black, curly hair and a deerskin wrapped about his loins, he appeared quite handsome. Collecting a variety of flowers, twigs, roots, fruits, and Tulasi leaves, he offered them regularly and lovingly to God. His every moment was a moment of worship, and he felt complete satisfaction within his heart. Day by day, his heart grew purer till at last he became free from all desires for materialistic enjoyment. This enabled him to one-pointedly devote himself to the loving service of the Lord. Consequently, he became exceedingly blissful, his body hairs standing up straight and tears flowing from his eyes.

Instead of caring for the rescued fawn till it could move about easily on its own, and then releasing it to the surrounding deer community, Bharata chose to adopt it as a pet. Feeling strong affection for the fawn, he daily fed it grass and carefully protected it from predatory animals. He would also scratch its itches, pet its soft hair, and endeavor to make it feel very comfortable. Sometimes, when the fawn would look up at him helplessly, he would lovingly kiss it. Gradually, Bharata became increasingly attached to raising it—so much so that he began to forget the rules and regulations for advancing spiritually and even to forget to worship the Supreme Lord.

He rationalized his behavior by thinking, *This poor fawn has taken shelter of me. It doesn't know anyone but me. I've become its father, mother, brother, and relatives. It has complete faith in me. So it's my duty to raise, protect, caress, and please it. How can I neglect it? To do so would be improper.*

Because of his affectionate bond with the fawn, Bharata would sleep with it, stroll with it, bathe with it, and even eat with it. And when he desired to enter the forest to collect provisions—wood, leaves, fruits, roots, etc.—he feared that dogs, jackals, tigers, or other predators might kill it. Thus, he always kept the fawn in tow when he proceeded through the woodlands. Sometimes Bharata would even carry the fawn on his shoulders as a doting father might carry his child. In fact, he loved the fawn so much that he would at times place it on his lap or sleep with it on his chest. And when affectionately stroking it, he would feel enormous pleasure.

Bharata was so attached to the fawn that when he was worshiping the Lord or engaging in some ritualistic ceremony, he would suddenly stop his practice and wonder how the animal was faring. If he had any doubt about its well being, he would discontinue his practice and begin searching for the fawn to make certain it was situated securely. And when he would discover that all was well, he would feel joyful in mind and heart. Thus, he would bless the fawn, "May you be happy in every respect."

But sometimes, after he would search for his pet, Bharata would not find it. He would thus become very perturbed. Anxiety would overwhelm him and, due to separation from the fawn, he would grieve intensely. Moreover, he would begin babbling like a frightened madman: "How terrible! My pet is now helpless—due to my cruelty. The deer put his faith in me, yet I've betrayed him. Will he ever come back and place his faith in me again? Or—has he been eaten by some hungry wolf, dog, boar, or tiger? What an unlucky day for me! The sun is now setting and my pet has not yet returned."

Then Bharata would fondly reminisce about it. "When I'd pretend to meditate, he would circle around me, wanting to play. Then he would fearfully touch me with the points of his soft horns. Or when I'd place all the sacrificial ingredients on the *kusha* grass, my pet would touch it with his teeth and pollute it. Then, when I'd chastise him by pushing him away, he would become so apprehensive that he would sit down, stay still, and stop playing."

Unable to tolerate the separation from his pet, Bharata would go outside and begin searching for it. When he would spot his pet's footprints, he would praise them out of love and say, "How fortunate Mother Earth is—to have my deer's footprints on her. And how small, beautiful, soft, and holy they are. In fact, these footprints have blessed this land, making it a suitable place for spiritual practices." And when he would look at the dark spots of the rising moon, he would wonder whether it had given his pet shelter there—to protect it from the dangerous attacks of a lion. "How I'm suffering!" Bharata would say.

"My heart is burning like a forest fire! But at least the moon is shining soothingly on me, just as a friend sprinkles water on another friend who has a high fever."

Thus Bharata had become mad about the deer. While it had been correct for him to initially express compassion and affection for it, it was wrong for him to allow those feelings to expand so enormously. They had made him feel that he was indispensable to the deer's welfare—which he was not; only God was. But Bharata had gradually forgotten this. Thus, he had re-awakened his former worldly need to feel important, necessary, and loved—a true bane to spiritual growth—and to taste the illusory pleasure of these feelings.

After some time, Bharata was on the verge of death. Lying on his mat, he saw his pet sitting by his side and looking at him sadly. Unable to withdraw his eyes from the deer—and filled with deep affection and attachment for it—he finally fell unconscious and died. Because his mind and heart were so absorbed in his pet, after his soul left his body, it was transferred to the womb of a doe and born as a deer in the Kalanjara Mountains. However, due to the rigorous devotional service to God he had performed in his previous lifetime, he was not born as a typical deer. The Lord graced him with perfect understanding of why he had been born in this species and with complete remembrance of the incidents leading up to this lower birth.

Nevertheless, because a human body is generally necessary to achieve God realization, Bharata could virtually make no spiritual advancement now. Therefore, he tolerated his animal form and tried to make the best use of it so that in his next lifetime he would, hopefully, attain a human birth. Thus, he constantly repented for his past foolishness and thereby became completely detached from materialistic interests. In fact, he would not even associate with other, pleasure-loving deer. After awhile, he left his deer family and returned to Pulaha-ashram. There, standing in the wooded background, he listened intently to various saintly preceptors discoursing on spiritual subjects to their students.

After some time, the deer died. Because his mind was focused on the Lord's transcendental teachings, his soul took its next birth in a pure Brahmin family. His father had excellent qualities—he was always content, tolerant, gentle, learned, charitable, and self-controlled. His first wife had given him nine equally qualified sons, and his second wife gave him twins—a boy and a girl. The boy was the reincarnation of King Bharata. Known as Jada Bharata in this lifetime, he could remember the important incidents of his past lifetimes.

Though born in a Brahmin family, Jada Bharata was quite fearful of his relatives and acquaintances. This was because, being more interested in ritualistic and sacrificial performances, they were not devotees of God. He therefore remained cautious, for he wanted to avoid having another spiritual downfall. To discourage people from talking to him, he presented himself as a madman—very dull, partially blind, and slightly deaf. This enabled him to always remember the Lord's lotuslike feet and mentally recite His superhuman glories, which help save one from materialistic enslavement. Thus, he always remained immersed in blissful God consciousness.

Jada Bharata's father, filled with profuse love for his son, tried to educate him in the Vedic teachings, especially in cleanliness. In his heart, he desired that Jada Bharata become a learned scholar. However, his son, acting like a hopeless moron, rejected his father's instruction. For example, although he was taught to wash his hands after defecating, Jada Bharata would always wash them *before*. Thus, no matter how hard his doting father tried to educate him, he could not succeed. After awhile, he just stopped trying.

Sometime later, Jada Bharata's father and mother died. Although his nine brothers were learned in those Vedic scriptures that encourage materialistic activity, they were not at all educated in devotional service to God. Therefore, they were incapable of comprehending the spiritually elevated position of their apparently moronic brother. Often they called him crazy, dull, deaf, and dumb. And they mistreated and exploited him, usually engaging him in arduous farming activities. They paid for his heavy labor by throwing him scraps of uneatable food—broken rice, oil cakes, rice chaff, and wormy and burned grains. But Jada Bharata accepted them all as though they were quite delectable. What's more, he never held any grudges against his inconsiderate brothers.

Extremely muscular, Jada Bharata's body was as strong as a bull's. He was indifferent to winter or summer, wind or rain. Never covering his body, he wore only a dirty loincloth and a sacred Brahmin thread. He would never smear oil on his body or take a bath, and he would indifferently sleep on the hard ground. His filthy body concealed his spiritual illumination, just as dirt can hide the brilliance of a precious jewel. When he wandered about, materialistic people mocked, insulted, and neglected him. However, because he was always absorbed in the joy of divine consciousness, these slights could not disturb him.

One day, the leader of a gang of robbers, desiring to have a son, sought the blessings of Goddess Kali. He therefore decided to sacrifice to her a primitive man—one with limited intelligence and learning. After he spied such a person, he captured him and bound his hands and feet. However, at night, by intense effort, the primitive loosened his restraints and escaped from the camp. When the leader noted this, he ordered his gang to search for and re-capture him. But hard as they tried—looking here, there, everywhere—they could not find him.

However, as the robbers were walking across a paddy field, they saw Jada Bharata sitting there alone. He was guarding the area against the attacks of wild deer and pigs. The robbers studied him carefully, considering whether he might be a good substitute for the escapee. Since Jada Bharata looked dull and dirty—like a primitive—one of them said, "He looks good to me. What do you think?"

"Yeah, I think he's perfect."

"Then let's take him."

They quietly sneaked up on Jada Bharata, seized and bound him with ropes, and quickly dragged him to their leader at the Kali temple.

Although Jada Bharata was strong and smart and could easily have defended himself and fled, he chose not to. This was because he had completely surrendered his life to the will of God and depended fully on His mercy. In other words, whatever the Lord desired to do—protect him or kill him—Jada Bharata would gladly accept, since he believed God knew what was best for him. Thus, he was neither worried about what might happen to him nor resentful towards those who had captured him. In fact, he remained indifferent to them, meditating happily within himself on God's beautiful form.

Actually, there was no injunction in the Vedic scriptures denoting that to obtain Goddess Kali's blessings a primitive must be sacrificed to her. Rather, the thieves had concocted this horrific ritual based on their own barbaric mentality. To kill a Brahmin, like Jada Bharata, was considered by spiritual authorities to be the worst of sins. And even though Jada Bharata wore an identifying Brahmin thread across his torso, they foolishly ignored it. In their degraded minds, their prisoner was little more than an animal, one whose blood they believed the goddess would ecstatically relish. Thus, they now prepared him for the sacrifice.

They bathed him and decorated him with sacred markings, sandal-wood pulp, and flower garlands. Then they anointed him with fragrant oils, adorned him with ornaments befitting an animal, and dressed him with new clothes. After feeding him lavishly, they brought him before the altar on which a statue of the goddess had been installed. Next, they respectfully offered the deity incense, ghee lamps, garlands, parched grain, newly grown twigs, sprouts, fruits, and flowers. Then they reverently sang songs and prayers to her while they spiritedly played drums and bugles. After this, they made Jada Bharata sit down before the statue.

One of the thieves, acting as the chief priest, grasped a sharp sword and consecrated it by uttering a sacred prayer to Kali. Then he raised the sword high in the air and shouted, *"Jaya Kali Ma! Jaya Kali Ma!"* and was just about to decapitate Jada Bharata—when quite suddenly and resoundingly the statue burst apart!

The rogues could scarcely believe what they saw.

Out of the statue emerged the actual Goddess Kali! Her body was burning with an intense and intolerable brilliance, and some of her hands were clutching sharp deadly weapons. Flashing her fiery eyes and bearing her sharp teeth, she was hideously frightening.

The thieves were aghast.

Jada Bharata was surprised.

Suddenly, Kali's naked female devotees—all powerful witches—materialized and began cackling wildly.

The robbers became even more horrified.

Kali violently leaped from the altar, grabbed the sword from the chief priest, and hastily beheaded him and all the other thugs. Then she and her helpers drank with gusto the hot blood spurting from the sliced necks. This quickly intoxicated the witches, so they sang loudly and danced frenziedly, as though prepared to destroy the whole world. Then they playfully began tossing the robbers' heads back and forth, as if they were sporting with balls. After awhile, Goddess Kali and her followers, fully satisfied, disappeared from the macabre scene.

But why had the goddess appeared there at all? Simply because the Supreme Lord repeatedly declares in numerous scriptures that He protects His devotees and destroys the demons who try to harm them. Since Jada Bharata, a pure devotee, had humbly taken shelter at the feet of Lord Vishnu, God felt obliged to uphold His word. Thus, He ordered Goddess Kali, one of whose functions is to destroy evil in the world, to do the needful. And of course, she did so with full enthusiasm.

Sometime later, Jada Bharata began wandering all over India. One day he was sitting on the bank of the Ikshumati River, meditating on God. King Rahugana, the ruler of the Sindhu and Sauvira states, was headed in his direction with a small entourage. On his way to Kapilashram, Rahugana was sitting on a palanquin that was being carried by four men—two at the front and two at the rear—each bearing a pole on his shoulder. However, one of the carriers became indisposed, so another qualified man was needed to replace him. Searching for one on the riverbank, the carriers noticed Jada Bharata. One of them said, "He looks strong enough to me. What do you think?"

"Sure," replied his coworker. "Let's use him."

The first bearer approached Jada Bharata, explained the situation, and commanded, "Come with us."

Since Jada Bharata understood that he had no choice, he rose to his feet and proceeded with them to the palanquin. Each man then lifted one of the palanquin poles, placed it on his own shoulder, and began walking. However, Jada Bharata, in the rear, was walking considerably slower than the others. This was because he was deliberately trying to avoid stepping on the many ants along the path. Feeling love for all creatures—from the largest down to the smallest—he refused to harm any of them unnecessarily. However, his hesitant steps were causing the palanquin to jerk, jarring the king uneasily on his seat.

Disturbed, the king angrily shouted to the carriers, "What's the matter with you? Why is the palanquin jerking like this?"

One of the carriers fearfully answered, "My lord, it's the new man."

"What are you talking about?"

"He can't keep up with us, so the palanquin is jerking."

"Then stop it for a moment!"

The carriers stopped.

Then the king looked to the rear and carefully studied Jada Bharata. Noticing how strong and healthy he looked, the king concluded that he was just a lazy, disrespectful lout. He therefore tried to rouse some energy and sense into him by addressing him sarcastically. "You must be worn out because, after all, you've been carrying my palanquin all alone—without any help. Right? And you've been shouldering it for such a long distance. Haven't you? And what's more, you're such an old man—so weak and skinny. Aren't you?"

But Jada Bharata, unaffected by the king's barbs, said nothing.

Hoping that the newcomer felt ashamed enough to walk faster now, the king ordered the carriers, "Start moving!" Then he looked tellingly at Jada Bharata and bellowed, "And I mean move!"

The carriers began walking. But again Jada Bharata slowed his steps to avoid stepping on the ants. This again jarred the king, and he almost fell backwards. Considering Jada Bharata to be insolent and thoughtless, the king was livid. "You clumsy rascal! How dare you!"

The palanquin stopped.

"Are you dead despite being alive?" the king yelled. "Don't you realize that I'm your master—and that you're not carrying out my order!?"

Bharata said nothing.

"I will now punish you for this disobedience—just as the lord of death punishes the wicked. Maybe then you'll come to your senses and act properly!"

Jada Bharata, smiling knowingly and pityingly at the king, boldly answered, "Although you've spoken to me sarcastically, your words are actually true."

This reply surprised King Rahugana.

"You've indicated that I haven't really been working. And that's correct, because only my *body* has been working. But I, the soul—I've just been watching."

"What?!" The king was further surprised.

"You've also indicated that I'm not strong or healthy. And that's also true, because only my body is. Not I, the soul."

The king now gazed curiously at Jada Bharata. Was he trying to be philosophically cute or clever?

"You said that you're my master and that I'm your servant. This may be true today. But in your next lifetime, I may be the master and you may be the servant—depending on our karma. But you're thinking and acting as if your position today is permanent. Aren't you?"

King Rahugana looked baffled.

"Aren't you?"

The king could not deny it.

"That's like living in a dream and thinking it's real. In other words, you're in illusion. And you'll remain in illusion—with all its miseries—unless you realize who you truly are."

The king suddenly understood that the carrier was not some shift-less, irresponsible fool. He could see that Jada Bharata was a self-realized soul—far superior to himself—who had been concealing his exalted spiritual position. He therefore ordered that the palanquin be lowered to the ground. He then emerged from it and humbly lay face-down on the path, his head near the holy man's feet and his palms clasped. "O sage, I'm sorry for my offenses. And I beg your forgiveness."

Considering the king's submission to be humble and sincere, Jada Bharata kindly said, "O King, I forgive you."

King Rahugana then rose to his knees and confessed, "I'm attached to my family life and my worldly activities. And I'm blind to knowl-edge about my higher self. Would you please teach me about this? I would consider it a great blessing."

"Yes, I'll be glad to. What would you like to know?"

King Rahugana then submissively asked Jada Bharata numerous questions about the soul, God, material nature, mind, karma, and reincarnation. And the sage answered all of them to the king's full satis-faction.

Jada Bharata then advised the king to renounce his royal position. "Give up attraction to sense objects and take hold of the sword of spiri-tual knowledge. Sharpen this sword by the flint of devotional service to God. Then you'll be able to cut away your ignorance—with all its illusions—and become truly free and happy."

King Rahugana thanked Jada Bharata profusely for enlightening him about his real position—as an eternal soul who had a permanent relationship with the Supreme Soul. Feeling free from the stress of all his materialistic problems, the king again offered his respectful obeisances to the sage. Graciously accepting them, Jada Bharata bid the monarch farewell and left his company.

The sage continued wandering all over the earth. Insulating himself against all the allurements of materialistic living—so that he would never again become deviated—he achieved an extremely high level of devotional love for Lord Vishnu as well as the transcendental bliss that naturally accompanies it. Jada Bharata was thus no longer attached to anyone or anything in the material world. Totally tied to God now, he served Him steadfastly with his whole heart and mind.

Pingala tries to entice customers

CHAPTER NINE

PINGALA THE PROSTITUTE

One night Pingala realized how empty and futile her life was unless she sincerely devoted it to serving God. Unless we understand and act on this principle, we may have difficulty discovering the real self within.

In the city of Videha, the moon showered Pingala with beams of soft light as she stood in the doorway of her mud flat, waiting for lustful customers. She was youthful and attractive, and very eager to earn money. Wearing a tight black cholee and a sleek reddish skirt, she fully exposed her midriff. She stood with her hands on her full hips and her ample breasts raised as high as possible, looking extremely sensual. Her hair was black and flowing—deliberately parted on the left side to announce her occupation—and her body radiated the scent of jasmine.

Pingala gazed at the dark road before her where a stream of men sauntered in both directions. However, after a few hours elapsed, not a single man had sought her services. This made Pingala extremely anxious. Then she saw an eager man coming towards her. *He looks like he wants me*, she thought, switching on her bedroom smile.

The man glanced at her for a moment but then walked away.

He just doesn't know what he's missing, she thought.

Three dogs in the road began barking and fighting, and after awhile, they disappeared in the woods.

Pingala saw another man coming towards her. *He looks pretty rich*, she thought, *so I'm sure he can pay.*

But he just walked by her without even giving her a glance.

Maybe he wasn't so rich after all, she rationalized. *Looks can be deceiving.*

A few minutes later, another man headed towards her. *Oh, here comes one of my old customers*, she thought. *Now I'll finally make some money.*

The man nodded, smiled, and waved to her, but he just kept walking.
Oh well, maybe next time, she consolingly thought.

Several peacocks in the nearby forest began crying loudly, making Pingala very edgy. Then she saw a handsome man coming towards her. *Oh, he'll be a real pleasure*, she thought.

But he just shook his head and walked away. After awhile, Pingala became so anxious that she nervously began walking in and out of her house. *I've got to get some business tonight, otherwise—* she dreaded the thought.

The hours slipped by, and soon it was midnight. Still, no man had stopped. Pingala was tired and weary from hoping and expecting. *Why was this happening?* she wondered.

Although she stayed out for about another hour, the road remained deserted. Deeply disappointed, she decided to retire for the night. Then, in the distance, she noticed a lone man coming. As he drew closer, she desperately prayed, "Oh please, let me make you happy. Please."

But he just walked by, as if she weren't even there.

Pingala now felt frustrated and angry. It all seemed so hopeless— because she had no control over it. This made her very gloomy—so much so that her face looked like a dried leaf. Even her cheap makeup couldn't hide her abject dismay.

And then suddenly she realized that there was absolutely nothing she could do about it. God was completely in control and was giving her what He wanted to. And since He was infinitely more powerful than she, all she could do was tolerate it. Realizing how helpless she was, Pingala decided to stop worrying. She entered her house, shut the door, and became indifferent to it all. *Do what you want with me, Lord. I have nothing more to say.*

Whether the Lord made her wealthy or poor, or gave her pleasure or pain—she couldn't care less now. She understood that whatever she might gain would one day be lost. For at death, God would take everything away from her. Therefore, what was the point of grieving? Pingala thus accepted her lot with philosophical indifference.

Then something amazing happened. A new feeling washed over her that she had never before experienced. It was a feeling of peaceful happiness—totally different from the sensual satisfaction she usually felt. And it arose from her conscious dependence on and need for God. With this, various realizations streamed through her mind. "How illusioned I am," she said to herself. "I stupidly desire sex from ordinary, useless men—because I can't control my mind."

She walked over to the mirror hanging on her wall and gazed at her face. "You fool! Why have you given up serving God? He's in your heart and ready to give you real love and happiness. But what have you done? You've neglected Him! You've been serving worthless men who've brought you only fear, worry, illusion, and sorrow. How can they ever satisfy your real desire?"

She turned away from the mirror and started pacing the room. Looking at the soft bed she had shared with numerous lovers, she winced and asked herself, "What do I really desire?" Then she firmly answered, "To be happy! But not just for a few seconds or minutes or hours—but always! And who can make me happy always? Only the Supreme Lord. For He's all bliss and He lives in my heart. So if I serve and please Him, He can make me blissful too—and always."

As she understood how pathetic her life was, tears began to glide down her cheeks. They were not tears of self-pity but tears of regret and remorse. "How uselessly I've tortured my soul! I've sold my body to greedy, pitiful men. And I've engaged in the most abominable work—prostitution! Yes, I hoped to get rich and have sex pleasure—thinking that would make me happy. How foolish I've been!"

She looked out the window and saw a silvery cloud gliding past the moon. "The Supreme Lord can give me everything I need. But I've neglected Him—and thought I didn't need Him. How dumb! For He's the one who's been giving me food, clothing, shelter, health, and strength. And He can take them away from me whenever He wants."

Pingala walked away from the window and sat down on her bed. "And yet—in spite of my neglecting Him, He's allowed me to have all the things I need in order to live. I deserve to be heavily punished for being so sinful. But—He has spared me. How merciful, kind, and loving He is! Is there anyone more worthy of my love than He? Is there anyone else I should serve but Him?" Thus Pingala renounced her life of prostitution forever.

"Right now, I'm feeling very happy," she continued, "so I must have pleased the Lord. I have full faith in His mercy. Therefore, I'll maintain myself with whatever He sends me. And I'll enjoy life with Him only—because He's the only source of real love and happiness. And He's the only one who can free me from misery and hopelessness."

She rose, extinguished the light of the two table lamps, and then lay down on her bed. The room was dark save for a ray of moonlight that caressed her face. Closing her eyes, a faint smile played about her lips and new hope entered her heart. Like a secure, satisfied child in its mother's arms, she fell asleep completely peaceful and happy. She was sure that the Lord would take care of her—even more so than He already had.

CHAPTER TEN

GOD'S NAME RESCUES AJAMILA

If Ajamila had not, in his youth, cultivated and practiced devotion to God, he never would have discovered who he really was later on. Similarly, if we desire to discover who we are, it is very useful to cultivate and practice devotion to God.

The eighty-eight-year-old Ajamila was dying—and fast! Though his material eyes were closed, he could see through his astral eyes the subtle world of ethereal beings. And what he saw was absolutely terrifying. Standing before him were three horrible-looking men, their forms darkish and muscular. They had fierce twisted faces, deformed bodily features, and upraised hair on their bodies. They threw their ropes over Ajamila's ethereal neck and began to tighten them.

Ajamila was horrified. He knew they were servants of the Lord of Death. And that they had come to drag him to their master, who would surely sentence him to a long life in hell. But why had they come now? He wasn't ready to go. He was so much in love with his little, son Narayana that the thought of separation from him was intolerable.

And yet—it was happening! *Where is my Narayana?* he wondered.

Ajamila's lips quivered, tears trickled out of his eyes, and grief possessed him totally. "Narayana!" he screamed. "Narayana!" As the servants yanked on the ropes and uttered wrathful sounds, Ajamila felt himself being slowly dragged out of his physical body. He felt alone, helpless, afraid, heartbroken. "Narayana!" he cried. "Narayana!"

But what had Ajamila done to warrant this? And why did he believe that he was headed for hell? Had he committed some colossal crime or offense?

When Ajamila was a young man, he had lived an ideal, saintly life. Born as a Brahmin and residing in the city of Kanyakubja, he had excel-

Ajamila is on the verge of dying

lent character, good conduct, and fine qualities. He studied the Vedic scriptures, faithfully executed their injunctions, and chanted their mantras. Mild and gentle, he controlled his mind and senses. He was pure, truthful, upright, and benevolent to all living beings. Always respectful to his spiritual preceptor, to the fire god, to guests, and to the elderly members of his household, he never spoke nonsense or envied anyone. Nor had he ever had an illicit sexual relationship with any woman. His only contact with the opposite sex had been with his young wife.

One day his father said to him, "Please go to the forest and collect some fruit and flowers. Also, bring back some *samit* and *kusha* grasses."

"Yes, Father." Ajamila bowed his head, folded his palms, and departed, wearing only a dhoti and sandals.

In the woods, Ajamila collected all the needed provisions and then started for home. As he proceeded, he heard the distant singing and laughter of a young man and woman. This provoked his curiosity, so he stopped and listened for a few moments. *Who are they? And what are they doing?* he wondered. *Should I go and see? Or should I just ignore them and return home?*

Intuitively, he knew he should go home, and yet—he couldn't. His mind was now riveted on the singing and laughter. So he dropped his provisions and walked curiously, slowly, toward the sound. As he did, he could not help noticing the birds flying about the trees and the beautiful flowers wafting their intoxicating fragrance everywhere.

Then, hiding behind a tree, he saw the couple—although they could not see him. He could see, from her dress and hair, that the woman was a prostitute; and that the man was no better than a sex-driven brute. The couple stopped singing and laughing and began embracing and kissing.

Ajamila's eyes opened wide and his breathing quickened. He saw that both of them were drunk, their eyes reeling and their bodies swaying. Then, as they sighed and gasped, the prostitute's dress loosened and the man held her tightly. Ajamila wanted to leave, wanted to stop watching, but couldn't. He was now mesmerized. Although he remembered the scriptural warning—that he should not observe such things—he found it impossible to depart. Thus, his dormant lustful desires became intensely aroused.

After Ajamila returned home with the provisions, he could not forget the prostitute. Enamored of her wild, careless behavior, he

continuously thought of her—while eating, working, bathing, evacu-
ating, worshiping, praying, reading, and even sleeping. Soon his
thoughts of her burgeoned into a full-blown desire—a desire that totally
consumed and overwhelmed him. Now he could not live without her, as
a drug addict cannot live without his high. Her lusty glances and her
provocative poses had now become everything to him! Unless he could
enjoy those perverse charms daily—as his own personal possessions—
it would be impossible for him to go on living.

Ajamila therefore hired her as a servant in his house—and then
enjoyed sex with her regularly. He soon renounced the company of his
pretty, young wife, who hailed from a very respectable Brahmin family.
Because the prostitute knew Ajamila was slavishly attached to her, she
demanded numerous gifts from him: new expensive saris, *cholees,*
shawls, rings, bangles, earrings, makeup, perfumes, oils, and shoes.
And of course, just to keep her pleased, he would satisfy her each and
every whim. This continued for many years.

When Ajamila's parents grew old, they needed care and attention.
Ajamila was their only son, so he was expected to assist them. But
because of his strong attachment to the prostitute, he seriously
neglected them, leaving them in extreme difficulty. When they finally
died, Ajamila inherited their life savings. But what did he do with
them? Did he use them in the performance of daily Brahminical activities—such as deity worship, fire sacrifices, bathing ceremonies, and
purificational rites? Not at all. Due to the prostitute's wicked influence,
he neglected to perform these holy rituals—so that he could spend more
time with her serving his ever-increasing sensual wants.

After some time, Ajamila squandered all his inheritance on the
prostitute. During that period, she bore him a number of children. And
to support them and her, he earned money in whatever way he could—
legally or illegally. He gave trouble to others by arresting them, by
cheating them in gambling, or by plundering them. He was no longer
concerned about ethics or morality. Thus, he spent his long lifetime
living extravagantly and transgressing all the regulations of the holy
scriptures.

Although nine of Ajamila's ten children were grown up, his son
Narayana was yet a toddler. As the old man lay dying on his bed, he was
about to leave the child, from whom he could not bear to be away for
even a moment. Therefore, as the unsightly-looking servants of the

Lord of Death, called Yamadutas, began dragging Ajamila's soul from the core of his heart, Ajamila screamed loudly, fearfully, desperately, "Narayana! Narayana! Narayana!"

Then, something extraordinary occurred. Four dazzling divine beings suddenly appeared there and shouted to the Yamadutas, "Stop! Stop!"

The Yamadutas, surprised and disturbed, glared at the intruders. "Who are you?" one of them angrily asked.

"We are the servants of Lord Vishnu," one replied.

"Lord Vishnu?"

"Yes. We are known as the Vishnudutas."

"But why are you interfering?" another Yamaduta suspiciously queried.

"Because our master ordered us to."

"Ordered? But this world is under our master's control!"

"True, but your master is under our master's control," the Vishnuduta said pointedly.

The Yamadutas gazed curiously at the radiant interlopers. Resembling Lord Vishnu—fresh, handsome, and youthful—their complexions were bluish and their eyes were like lotus petals. Dressed in yellow silken garments and adorned with lovely lotus garlands, they wore glowing helmets and sparkling earrings. Each servant had four long arms, and each held a bow over one shoulder and a quiver over the other. Each Vishnuduta also held a club in one of his hands, a conch shell in his second hand, a disc in his third, and a lotus flower in his fourth. They were obviously much more powerful than the Yamadutas, who fearfully recognized this.

"But this man Ajamila—" protested one of the Yamadutas, "he committed many sins! And he never underwent any atonement for them."

"Are you sure?" the Vishnuduta said doubtfully.

"Of course. Therefore, we have to bring him to our master for sentencing."

"Sentencing?" The Vishnuduta smiled mildly.

"Yes. He has to be punished and corrected."

"That's not true! He's already atoned for all his sins."

"He's what?!" The Yamadutas were bewildered.

"Yes. As he was dying, he called out one of God's names—Narayana."

"So?"

"God's name is so powerful that it canceled all the sinful reactions, or punishment, that he was supposed to get."

"What do you mean 'canceled'?"

"I mean that he doesn't have to be punished for all those sins."

"Just by calling out God's name—he atoned?" The Yamadutas were incredulous.

"Yes—because he did so in an offenseless manner."

"Offenseless?" They were puzzled.

"When Ajamila cried out God's name," explained the Vishnuduta, "he did so in a helpless manner—without any ulterior motive, such as to again commit sins after being excused for them. And he didn't blaspheme the Supreme Lord or the Lord's devotees or the Lord's scriptures. Those are just a few examples of offenses."

"This is hard to believe," said one of the Yamadutas.

"Well, just ask your master about it. God's name is so powerful that even if one recites it but actually means something else, one will still be freed from having to suffer for one's sins."

"Even if he means something else?"

"Yes. When Ajamila called out God's name, he meant his son Narayana, not Lord Narayana. But even then, the Lord's name freed him —not only from the punishment due him from the sins he committed in *this* lifetime, but also from those he committed in his *past* lifetimes."

"Are you serious?"

"Absolutely. Even if he would have recited God's name as a joke or in a song or without any care about it—the name still would have freed him—just the way a medicine acts to cure a disease regardless of whether or not a patient knows anything about the medicine."

The Yamadutas stood there stupefied and dismayed.

"But best of all, by reciting God's name, he cleansed his heart, reduced his desire to commit new sins, and awakened an interest in developing love for God. That goes far beyond atonement, which doesn't really stop one from committing new sins. Only when one's heart becomes purified does one want to stop committing them."

Dreading the power and authority of the Vishnudutas, the Yamadutas stopped protesting. They then departed for the court of Yamaraja, the Lord of Death. There, they explained to him all that had happened, and he confirmed that what the Vishnudutas had told them was perfectly true. He also said that in the future they should disregard any sinner who recites any of God's names while dying—as Ajamila had.

The Vishnudutas then released Ajamila from the nooses around his neck. Realizing they had saved him from death, Ajamila was now free from fear. He bowed his head at the Vishnuduta's feet and felt greatly obliged to them. For they had not only saved him from death, but also from hell. Feeling greatly purified by their holy presence, Ajamila felt deeply regretful and contrite over having committed so many sins in the past. He thus rebuked himself repeatedly. Then, just as he was about to say something to the Vishnudutas, they mysteriously vanished from his presence.

Ajamila suddenly became fully conscious of his physical body, his bed, and his room. "Was that a dream I just saw or—or was it real? Some dreadful men came with ropes to arrest me and drag me away." Ajamila looked about wondrously. "Where have they gone? And where have the Vishnudutas gone?" Then he understood why he was so fortunate. "It was all due to my earlier spiritual practices—when I was a young man. If I hadn't performed devotional service to the Lord then, I never would have gotten the chance to call out God's name when I was dying. It was by His grace that I had decided to name my son 'Narayana.'

"I'm just a shameless cheater who abandoned my Brahminical culture. Yes, I'm sin personified. Next to the chanting of God's name, I'm nothing! And yet—I now see that I have a wonderful opportunity. But to use it, I've got to control my senses, my mind, and my intelligence. And I've got to always practice devotional service to God. That way, I won't again fall into the darkness of materialistic living. I'll become free from my illusions and absorb myself in transcendental consciousness."

Just from the brief contact he'd had with the Vishnudutas, Ajamila was able to resolutely detach himself from all his materialistic desires. Freed from all sensual attractions, he renounced his home life and started for the holy city of Hardwar. There, he took refuge at a Vishnu temple and practiced daily the process of bhakti yoga. Fully engaged in devotional service, he always meditated on the beautiful name and form of Lord Vishnu.

After some time, as Ajamila sat chanting God's holy name on the bank of the Ganges River, he again saw the four Vishnudutas.

Immediately, he offered them his humble obeisances. Then, quite suddenly, he became free of his material body—permanently—and manifested his original spiritual body. The Vishnudutas beckoned him to their golden airplane, and he cheerfully boarded it. The plane then hastily flew through space and, in only a moment's time, reached Vaikuntha, the eternal, spiritual world.

Ajamila was saved forever.

Whoever hears or describes this story with faith and devotion is no longer doomed to hellish life—regardless of having a material body and regardless of how sinful one may have been. Indeed, the Yamadutas do not draw near to such a person. After finally departing from one's body, one returns to the eternal world, where one is respectfully greeted and worshiped by the holy, effulgent residents there.

CHAPTER ELEVEN

DHRUVA'S INCREDIBLE VICTORY

Although he was only five years old, Dhruva, by his intense determination, discovered himself and realized God. If we desire to discover ourselves, it is helpful to have great determination— as Dhruva had—otherwise we may be impeded by many obstacles.

Prince Dhruva was only five years old when he decided to leave home. Extremely defiant and determined, he walked on a path that would soon lead him into a dangerous forest. Although he knew there were wild lions, tigers, elephants, boars, hyenas, and snakes there— which could easily kill and eat him—he wasn't worried in the least. This was because he had taken shelter of the Supreme Lord and fully trusted that God would protect him. More than that, he fully believed that the Lord would help him achieve his incredible goal: to obtain the most powerful position in the universe! Only then would he prove to his haughty stepmother, who had viciously insulted him, that she was wrong; only then would he expunge the vengeance that was festering in his wounded heart; only then would little Dhruva ever be happy.

But what had made this five-year-old child so miserable?

Dhruva's father, King Uttanapada, had two queens—Suniti and Suruchi. Dhruva was Suniti's son, and Uttama, about the same age, was Suruchi's. Favored by the king, Suruchi felt herself far superior to her co-wife. One day, the king was in one of his chambers sitting on his throne while Suruchi, Uttama, Dhruva, and several palace residents were present. The king placed Uttama on one of his knees and began patting his head. Seeing this, Dhruva also wanted his father's affection. So he tried to climb onto the king's other knee, but his father did not welcome him. This was because he wanted to especially please Suruchi.

Dhruva is insulted by Queen Suruchi

As Dhruva tried to clamber onto his father's knee, Suruchi looked at him with utter contempt. Did the boy think he was equal to *her* son—and could receive equal attention from the king? "Dhruva," she said, "you don't deserve to sit on the king's lap or throne."

"I don't?" he asked, looking up at her scornful glance.

"Of course not. If you did, you would have been born from me."

"But I'm also the king's son."

"Yes, you are, but you can never become the king."

"Why?"

"Because *my* son will become the next king!"

"But *I'd* like to become the king."

"Really?" she snickered. "Well, that's impossible now. The only way you could is by performing severe austerities and satisfying the Supreme Lord."

"The Lord?"

"Yes. Then, if He favored you, you would have to be born again—but from *me.*"

"From you?"

"Yes."

Dhruva felt humiliated and looked up at his father for support.

But the king, to please his wife, remained silent—although he knew she had verbally and emotionally abused her stepson.

Dhruva began breathing very heavily—like a snake just struck by a stick—and became incensed. Seeing that the king was ignoring him and still patting Uttama, Dhruva ran out of the chamber and hastened to his mother's apartment. When he entered it and went to her, his lips were trembling and his eyes were tearing. Very concerned, Suniti immediately lifted Dhruva onto her lap and hugged him tightly, smelling his head affectionately. As she soothed him, a few of the residents who had witnessed Suruchi's abuse entered and related all the unpalatable details to her.

Suniti became overwhelmed with grief and began to sob. Trying to think of a practical remedy to alleviate her son's, as well as her own, grief, she failed. However, she felt she had a duty as a mother to try to calm and instruct Dhruva. Therefore, she said in a trembling voice, "My dear son, please don't wish anything bad to others. Whoever purposely causes pain to anyone, ultimately has to suffer that same pain."

But Dhruva's wrath towards Suruchi continued to grow—like a forest fire.

Suniti's quavering voice continued. "What your stepmother said was true. Your father doesn't consider me his wife or—or even his maidservant. He's ashamed to accept me." She gently stroked the back of Dhruva's head. "So you've been born from an unfortunate woman. But if you want to sit on the same throne as your stepbrother, don't be envious of him. Instead, immediately begin worshipping the Lord's lotuslike feet. That's what your great grandfather Brahma did."

"He did?"

"Yes. And he became the creator of this world and the most powerful person in this universe—all by God's mercy."

"Really?"

"Yes. So just think of the Lord in your heart, take shelter of Him, and always engage in His service. He alone can take away your misery."

Dhruva wiped the tears from his eyes, hopped off his mother's lap, and said, "Thank you, Mother." He then walked out of her room, firmly determined to try to obtain God's mercy. In fact, he decided to leave home immediately, enter the forest where the saints dwelled, and ask them to show him how to practice austerities. He would do whatever was necessary to become the most powerful person in the universe— yes, even more powerful than his great grandfather! And if he could achieve this stupendous feat, he would gain the satisfaction of seeing his stepmother Suruchi eat her abusive words. Which is all he lived for now.

Wearing only a loincloth, Dhruva walked resolutely along the dusty, tree-lined road towards the ominous forest. Along the way, the great saint Narada, whom the Lord had informed of Dhruva's firm desire, suddenly, if not mysteriously, appeared before the boy. Patting Dhruva's head warmly, he said, "Hello, little prince."

"Hello," answered Dhruva, bowing his head respectfully.

"You look rather angry."

"I am."

"At what?"

"My stepmother."

"Oh? What did she do to you?"

"She insulted me." Dhruva described what had happened.

"Well, you're only a child, so why even think about that?"

"I can't help it."

"Of course you can. A boy like you should just play and have fun—and forget about what she said."

But Dhruva shook his head firmly and looked at the ground.

Seeing that the boy was obstinate, the sage philosophically said, "Then try to realize that she insulted you because you probably insulted her in one of your past lifetimes. You're just getting it back."

"Back?"

"Yes. And if you insult her again, then she'll insult you again. And it will never end. So the best thing to do is to stay content—as if she had never said anything to you."

"I wish I could."

"But you can—if you try. That will put an end to the karmic reaction, and you'll become a wise person."

Dhruva looked up at Narada sternly. "No! I—I have to prove her wrong. I have to."

"And how will you do that?"

"I'll practice austerities—and gain great power."

"Dhruva, please go home. When you're grown up, you can practice austerities."

"No. I want to do them now!"

Narada stared at the child, amazed by his military spirit and dogged determination.

"Would you help me?" Dhruva asked. "Please?"

Having tested the boy's sincerity and resolve, Narada realized that Dhruva could not be dissuaded by any means. He thus crouched down and looked affectionately into the boy's eyes. "All right, I'll help you."

"Thank you," Dhruva smiled. "What should I do first?"

Narada explained that Dhruva would have to become completely absorbed in devotional service to the Supreme Lord. "I want you to go to the bank of the Yamuna River in Madhuvana Forest. It's a very sacred place and perfect for attaining your goal." Then Narada explained the specific duties and practices Dhruva would have to perform daily. They were so severe and arduous that any ordinary man—let alone a five-year-old child—would never even dare to attempt them. But Dhruva, with Suruchi's insult still blazing in his heart, was undaunted. No price was too high for him to pay.

When Narada was about to depart, Dhruva folded his palms prayerfully, circled the sage three times out of respect, bowed down to his feet with deep reverence, and then headed for the forest.

But how long would Dhruva's determination last? A few days? A few months? Or would he actually complete the painful program? This remained to be seen.

After the child entered Madhuvana Forest, Narada considered it prudent to visit Dhruva's father and see how he was faring. He traveled through space and arrived at the palace in just a few seconds. When the sage entered the monarch's chamber, the king was grieving profusely. Trying to control himself, Uttanapada offered the sage a comfortable seat as well as his humble obeisance.

"My dear king," said Narada, "your face appears to be drying up. Is something bothering you?"

"Yes, O sage."

"Such as?"

"It's about my son—Dhruva."

"Dhruva?"

"Yes. Just earlier today, he tried to climb up on my knee and—" Uttanapada's voice choked up.

"Yes?"

"Well, he just wanted to express his love to me, but—I ignored him. I didn't even pat his head as a loving father should." The king's eyes became glassy. "I'm so hardhearted!"

"That's because you're too attached to one of your wives."

"Yes, I'm addicted to her. So I practically banished my other wife, Suniti, and her son, Dhruva. I'm so unmerciful!"

"It's good that you've realized this."

"Yes, but much too late. My poor son ran away from the palace—all alone—to live in the forest and devote himself to God."

"O King, please don't worry about what's hap—"

"Don't worry?!" the king interrupted. "How can I *not* worry? He's only five years old! And unprotected! And maybe hungry. Or—he may have been attacked and eaten by vicious wolves."

"Listen to me, Uttanapada."

"How cruel I am! How utterly cruel!" The king began to weep remorsefully.

"I was just with your son."

The king's eyes opened wide. "You were? How—how is he? Is he well?"

"Yes, he's fine. In fact, he's well protected by the Supreme Lord."

"Well, that's good. Good. But I've got to bring him home now."

"No, don't even try. He's fixed on achieving a certain goal—and no one can deter him—not even I." Narada then explained Dhruva's present aim and resolve. After this, the sage vanished just as mysteriously as he had appeared.

Uttanapada remained aggrieved, so much so that he practically abandoned all his royal duties. For all he could think about was his apparently helpless five-year-old son living alone in the dangerous forest. Despite the sage's assurances—would the boy really survive? The monarch could not stop worrying.

At Madhuvana Forest, Prince Dhruva began the program of austerities that Narada had outlined for him. He would bathe three times a day in the sacred, auspicious Yamuna River. To control his life air, mind, and senses, he would practice three different breathing exercises. Then he would meditate on the handsome face and figure of four-armed Lord Vishnu. Dhruva focused his attention on the Lord's beautiful eyes, nose, lips, jeweled helmet, necklaces, bracelets, and ankle bells. He also concentrated on the Lord's merciful glance, loving smile, and peaceful disposition, as well as on His transcendental activities.

The boy would utter the powerful mantra *Om namo bhagavate vasudevaya* at three different periods of the day. After he constructed, out of mud and water, a small statue or Deity of Lord Vishnu, Dhruva would offer Him flowers, fruits, vegetables, grasses, and Tulasi leaves. Then he would worship the Lord with love and devotion. Whatever fruits or vegetables were available, he would eat, remaining subdued, peaceful, and satisfied. He also remained aloof from any and all kinds of sense gratification.

Little did Dhruva realize that the program Narada had given him was designed to produce a different result from the one for which the prince aspired. If Dhruva seriously continued his practices, he would become surprised and amazed by the ultimate outcome. Yes, Narada had tricked him!

During the first month of his austerity program, Dhruva ate only fruits and berries every third day. In the second month, he ate only dry grass and leaves once every six days. During the third month, he drank only water every ninth day. And in the fourth month, having become a master of breath control, he inhaled air once every twelve days. By the fifth month, the child had controlled his breathing so adeptly that his mind became very steady—so steady that he was able to stand on one leg only and perfectly meditate on the Supreme Lord's form.

Because Dhruva was incredibly steady and faithful in his practices, something very extraordinary and mystical began to occur: first, the whole world began to tremble; then, as he stood on one leg, his big toe pushed down half the earth; and finally, everyone in the universe began to breathe with great difficulty. It was not that Dhruva desired that these anomalies should occur. Rather, they happened quite spontaneously due to his intense determination and severe austerities.

When the gods in the heavenly planets began to suffocate, they became unable to perform their administrative duties. They therefore went to Lord Vishnu's domain and sought His shelter. One of them helplessly said, "Dear Lord, everywhere everyone is suffocating. We've never experienced anything like this. Please—save us from this danger!"

The Lord then explained to them what was happening and what He planned to do about it. The gods, reassured, returned to their respective planets.

Lord Vishnu then boarded His eagle carrier, Garuda, and directed him to the Madhuvana Forest, where King Uttanapada's son was residing. When He reached the spot and approached the boy, Dhruva was deeply absorbed in meditation on Lord Vishnu. But then suddenly his meditation broke and he could no longer see God within his heart. This perturbed him, so he opened his eyes. And there, standing before him, was the same glorious being he had been meditating on. Overwhelmed with ecstasy, Dhruva offered the Lord his humble respects and obeisances.

His palms clasped prayerfully, the prince desired to offer the Lord beautiful prayers in suitable language. But being only a small boy, with limited speaking skill, he felt quite incapable. However, the Lord could appreciate His devotee's heartfelt desire, therefore He touched His conch shell to Dhruva's forehead and empowered him to speak eloquently.

"O my Lord," he began, "I desired a powerful position, so I underwent harsh types of penance and discipline. You are difficult for even the great gods, saintly persons, and kings to attain. But now I've found You. I was looking for a piece of glass but instead found a most valuable gem. Thus, I'm so satisfied that I don't even wish to ask You for any blessing."

Uttanapada's son then glorified the Lord, emphasizing that the bliss derived from meditating on God's lotuslike feet and from hearing about His greatness from pure devotees was far superior to that of merging into the Lord's infinite light or of ascending to the heavenly planets. Then he asked God to bless him to be able to keep company with His great devotees who are constantly engaged in His transcendental loving service.

"O Lord," Dhruva continued, "I've discovered that engaging in devotional service is far better than becoming a king or ruling a kingdom. You are very merciful to ignorant devotees like me. You always nourish and protect me. Thank you very much." Dhruva now gratefully realized that his guru, Narada, under Divine guidance, had earlier provided him with instructions that would result in love for God and transcendental ecstasy—instead of supreme dominion and power over the universe, as he had originally desired.

The Lord then told Dhruva what he wanted him to do for the rest of his life, and what would happen to him after he finally left this world. Being a devotee fully surrendered to God, Dhruva agreed to fulfill His wish. The Lord then bid farewell to Dhruva, who longingly watched Him on His eagle carrier soar into the sky towards His eternal residence.

Since Dhruva had now stopped his harsh austerities and rigid practices, the worldwide temblors ceased, the earth stopped sinking, and people everywhere could once again breathe normally. Then Dhruva remembered—his stepmother, Suruchi, and the vengeance he had harbored against her. Feeling greatly ashamed of himself, he declared, "What a fool I was—praying for things that are temporary and thinking of my stepmother and stepbrother as my enemies!"

In obedience to the Lord's wish, Dhruva started walking towards his father's palace.

When King Uttanapada heard from a messenger that the prince was headed home, he could scarcely believe it. Considering himself a most wretched father, he wondered how it was possible for him to gain such good fortune. Nevertheless, feeling greatly elated, he rewarded the messenger with a very valuable necklace. Extremely eager to see his son, the king asked the Brahmins, his family members, officers, ministers, and immediate friends to join him in welcoming Dhruva home.

The king mounted a chariot bedecked with golden filigree and drawn by fine horses, and his two queens, Suniti and Suruchi, along with her son Uttama, sat on a palanquin. Then, like a huge ocean wave, the joyful procession moved forward along the road.

As soon as the king saw Dhruva ambling towards him, he jumped off his chariot and happily hastened to greet him. Although only six months had elapsed since his son had left, it had seemed like eons. Breathing heavily and with great affection, the monarch hugged his son tightly with both arms. He felt as if he had regained his life. Smelling the boy's head again and again, he bathed Dhruva with torrents of tears.

Dhruva bowed down before his father, who honored him by asking various questions. He next bowed his head at the feet of his two mothers. When the proud Suruchi saw that Dhruva had fallen at her feet, she immediately lifted him up and hugged him tightly. With tears streaming down her cheeks, she blessed him: "My dear boy, may you live long!" Then Dhruva and Uttama, filled with affection, embraced each other fondly, the hairs on their bodies standing up. And when his mother, Suniti, hugged him, her tears and breast milk soaked his whole body. The palace residents praised and congratulated her, emphasizing her great fortune.

The exuberant king then seated Dhruva and Uttama on the back of an elephant and ordered the procession to return to the capital. Shortly after, everyone enthusiastically entered it and noticed that the city was lavishly decorated with fruits, flowers, trees, leaves, and branches. The domes of the palaces glittered, as did the turrets of the gods' space ships that hovered over the city. The many palaces, gates, and surrounding walls were adorned for this occasion with golden ornaments. The streets and crossings were thoroughly cleansed and sprinkled with sandalwood water; and rice, barley, fruits, flowers, and other favorable offerings were scattered all about the city.

As Dhruva passed by on the road, all the household ladies showered blessings on him along with such auspicious items as mustard seeds, barley, curd, water, new grass, fruits, and flowers. They also sang lovely songs of glorification as he, with the king, entered the extremely opulent palace, which contained marble walls, bejeweled engravings, lush gardens, lotus-filled lakes, and colorful birds. When the monarch heard about Dhruva's superlative activities and saw how influential and remarkable he was, he felt extremely satisfied.

After Dhruva became fully grown and mature, the king carefully examined his son's character. Seeing many sterling qualities in him, Uttanapada believed that Dhruva was now fully qualified to become the next sovereign. However, to be certain, he asked his ministers and the citizens for their opinions. Being very fond of Dhruva, they all concurred that he was the most suitable person to lead them. Uttanapada then happily installed him on the throne, detached himself from all worldly affairs, and retired to the forest to perform spiritual activities.

But why had Dhruva, who no longer had any desire to rule or control, accepted this kingly position? Simply because when he had met the Lord personally at Madhuvana Forest, God had ordered him to rule the kingdom for thirty-six thousand years. He had also told him to perform many sacrifices, give abundant charity, and be an exemplary leader so that all of his subjects would try to emulate him. And He had blessed him to always remain youthful, providing him with the energy and drive necessary to create a prosperous and happy kingdom. Submissively accepting the Lord's order, Dhruva assumed his royal responsibilities with alacrity.

King Dhruva married Brahmi, and she bore him two sons. He also wed Ila, and she delivered to him one son. After some time, his brother Uttama, still unmarried, proceeded to the Himalaya Mountains on a hunting expedition. However, he was killed by a mighty Yaksha (a supernatural being). His mother, Suruchi, maddened by hearing about his death, went searching for him in the forest, but she was devoured by a fire.

When Dhruva heard about his brother's death, he became sorry and angry. Determined to punish the Yaksha who had caused it, Dhruva climbed onto his chariot and had his charioteer drive it north to the city of Alakapuri. There, in the valley, he saw a city full of Yakshas, all of whom were devotees of Lord Shiva. To announce his challenging presence, Dhruva blew his conch shell and it resounded loudly throughout the sky in all directions.

On hearing the sound, the Yaksha wives became anxious, as it portended a battle for their husbands. The warriors found the blast intolerable and prepared for combat. On the battlefield, Dhruva, in his chariot, charged them. Firing three arrows at a time, he killed many in their ranks. Although Dhruva was their enemy, the Yakshas could not help admiring his dexterous fighting. Nonetheless, the Yakshas then threw twice as many arrows at him—six from each of their 130,000 troops. They also showered him with many other weapons, such as swords, tridents, lances, spears, etc. Dhruva looked like a mountain being helplessly pelted by a thunderstorm. The Yakshas then thought they had defeated Dhruva.

But Dhruva somehow recovered and shot an incessant barrage of arrows at them. His bow twanged and his arrows hissed, filling his enemies with mortal fear. Then, splitting apart their various weapons, Dhruva decapitated some of the warriors and cut off the limbs of many others. Noting Dhruva's amazing military prowess, the remaining Yakshas fled from the battlefield, hoping to save their lives. When all the soldiers were gone, Dhruva considered entering the city proper. He discussed this with his charioteer, mentioning that the Yakshas had many mystic powers. Thus he might not be able to predetermine their next move.

Then suddenly, they heard a tremendous oceanic sound and, from all directions, a monstrous dust storm began blowing over them. In a moment, the sky was filled with clouds and lightning, and rain began to abound. But this was no ordinary rain, for it consisted of blood, mucus, pus, stool, urine, marrow, and even body trunks! Then Dhruva and his charioteer saw a huge mountain in the sky, and from all quarters hailstones dropped, along with lances, clubs, swords, iron bludgeons, and massive rocks. There were also large angry snakes vomiting fire, along with furious elephants, lions, and tigers bent on devouring him. Then, a furious ocean with foaming waves and roaring sounds rushed before Dhruva. It appeared that he was now overpowered by the Yakshas' mystic illusions.

Even so, there were sages who, by their mystic powers, were watching the fierce battle from the sky. To encourage Dhruva, one of them flew down and said to him, "May the Supreme Lord destroy your formidable enemies. God's name is as powerful as God Himself. Just by chanting and hearing it, many persons can be protected from death easily. Thus a devotee is saved!"

Hearing these encouraging words, Dhruva touched water for purification. Then he took up an arrow made by Narayana Rishi himself and fixed it firmly to his bow. Immediately, the Yakshas' horrendous illusions vanished, just as light makes darkness disappear. Then, from that one arrow, numerous arrows flew out—all with golden shafts and swanlike feathers. Sounding like peacocks' crowing, they pierced many of his enemies. However, those who were not hit raced towards Dhruva with upraised weapons. But Dhruva fatally cut his enemies to pieces, scattering their arms, legs, heads, and bellies.

When the great sage Svayambhuva Manu, the original lawgiver and father of mankind, saw his grandson Dhruva killing so many Yakshas who were not actually offenders, he felt great sympathy for them. Therefore he, along with other sages, appeared before Dhruva and said, "My dear son, please stop. It's wrong to be unnecessarily angry—and it leads to hellish life. You're going much too far by killing these faultless Yakshas."

"What do you mean?"

"I mean that it's not approved by spiritual authorities and is unsuitable for our family members. We're supposed to know what is and what isn't religious law."

"But one of them unnecessarily killed my brother."

"True. But does that mean you have the right to kill others who are innocent?"

"No, but it enraged me, and—"

"I'm surprised at you," interrupted Manu, "because you're supposed to set an example for others to follow. Why have you done this?"

Dhruva found himself speechless.

"The Lord becomes pleased when his devotee shows tolerance, mercy, friendship, and equality to others. Then He frees him from materialistic miseries and fills him with spiritual bliss."

Dhruva nodded respectfully.

"Actually, the Yaksha who killed your brother is not the real killer, for the Supreme Lord alone gives everyone his karmic reactions. Therefore, please surrender to God, who is the ultimate controller. Give up this false sense of 'I' and 'My' that you're exhibiting, as if you were your physical body. And act from the position of self-realization."

"I'll try, Grandfather."

"And remember: anger is the worst enemy on the path of self-realization, for it reinforces the false idea that you're a material body instead of an eternal soul."

Dhruva understood clearly.

"By killing so many Yakshas, you've disturbed their leader, Kuvera, Lord Shiva's brother and the treasurer of the gods. Thus, you've disrespected them. I therefore suggest that you pacify Kuvera with soft words and prayers, so that his anger doesn't harm our family."

Accepting his grandfather's wise instructions, Dhruva thankfully offered him his humble obeisances. Manu, along with the other sages, then departed for their residences.

King Dhruva's anger subsided and he ceased killing the Yakshas. Then Kuvera, who had heard what Dhruva had done, suddenly appeared before him. Other celestials also arrived and began worshiping Kuvera. Dhruva folded his palms and stood humbly before the god, who said, "I'm glad to see that you've given up your hostility. So I'm pleased with you. May the Lord constantly bless you with good fortune. Since you're always engaged in devotional service, you're worthy of receiving a blessing. Therefore, please ask me for one."

Dhruva begged, "May I always have faith in the Supreme Lord and remembrance of Him. Only then can a person easily cross over the ocean of ignorance."

"Granted," replied Kuvera, smiling with satisfaction.

Kuvera then returned to his own abode. And Dhruva, with his chariot driver, journeyed back to his capital city, where he performed many great ceremonial sacrifices to please God. As Dhruva carried out his devotional service, he could see that everything exists in God and that God exists in all beings. He was always kind to the poor and innocent, and he continuously protected religious principles.

King Dhruva ruled over his kingdom for thirty-six thousand years, just as the Lord had ordered. Since that period of time was known as Satya-yuga, the golden age or the dawn of civilization, it was normal for people then to live up to one- hundred-thousand years. Dhruva soon realized that his body, wives, children, friends, army, wealth, palaces, and pleasure grounds were all creations of the illusory energy, which made them appear permanent and satisfying. However, he found no interest in them anymore. Therefore, he bestowed his kingdom on his son and retired to Badarikashram Forest in the Himalaya Mountains. There, he resumed some of the spiritual practices and austerities he had seriously undertaken when he was five years old.

Meditating on Lord Vishnu, Dhruva entered into a deep trance. Experiencing transcendental bliss, his eyes streamed tears, his heart melted, his hairs stood on end, and his body trembled. Totally forgetting his bodily existence, he was immediately freed from the thralldom of the material world. And when he opened his eyes, he saw a gorgeous shining spaceship descending from the sky. In the ship, he also saw two handsome servants of the Lord, who closely resembled God—each with four arms, blackish complexion, lotuslike eyes, attractive garments, and sparkling adornments.

Out of respect for them, Dhruva immediately stood up. Then he offered them his obeisances with his palms clasped, reciting and glorifying the Lord's holy names. Those beings were intimate companions of God and their names were Nanda and Sunanda. When Dhruva stood up, his palms folded and his head bowed, one of Lord Vishnu's servants said to him, "Dear King, all good fortune to you. Please listen carefully. We have been specifically ordered by the Lord to fly you to the pole star, where He eternally dwells."

The other servant added, "You have achieved this by your devotion and austerity. Even the great sages and gods haven't attained this position; nor have your forefathers. The pole star is the highest in the galaxy, and the inhabitants of all other planets worship it. So come— and live there eternally."

Dhruva then took his sacred bath, dressed himself with proper ornaments, and performed his usual religious duties. He next offered his respectful obeisances to the glorious sages living there and gladly received their infallible blessings. Then he worshiped the spaceship and bowed to Lord Vishnu's servants.

Suddenly, his body became as shining and glowing as molten gold, and he proceeded to board the ship. But then something very strange happened: death personified unexpectedly approached him and bowed his head. Having no interest at all in death, Dhruva stepped on his head and climbed aboard the plane, which was as large as a house.

Kettledrums resounded in the sky, the chief celestials began to sing, and other gods rained flowers on Dhruva. Just as the ship was about to lift off, Dhruva remembered his mother, Suniti. *How can I go to the eternal world and leave my poor mother behind?* he mused. *For when I was only five years old, she was the first person to help me take shelter of God.*

Nanda and Sunanda could perceive his concern, so they showed Dhruva that Suniti was flying to the same destination in a different airship. This satisfied Dhruva completely.

As the space ship ascended and passed through the galaxy, Dhruva saw all the planets of the solar system, as well as the gods showering blossoms on him. Although Dhruva no longer wished to have the most powerful position in the world, the Lord, out of affection for him, decided to fulfill his former wish and make him the ruler of the pole star. It is the highest position in this universe, and all the heavenly bodies continuously and respectfully revolve around it. Even when all the stars and planets dissolve at the end of Lord Brahma's one day (4,320,000,000 years), the pole star remains fixed and unaffected.

Thus Dhruva, by the grace of the Supreme Lord, attained both his material and spiritual goals. And to this day, throughout the Vedic literature, the pole star is referred to as Dhruva-loka, or the Star of Dhruva.

By listening to or reciting this story, we can fulfill our worldly and spiritual desires, as well as counteract all the punishments due to us from our past immoral actions. If we try with faith and devotion to understand Dhruva's pure character, we will become a pure devotee of God and perform unalloyed devotional service. Moreover, we will acquire sublime qualities like Dhruva's, as well as attain immortality.

CHAPTER TWELVE

LORD VISHNU TRICKS VRIKA

*Showing a conspicuous lack of appreciation after he received
a powerful blessing, Vrika met with great misfortune. To discover
our true selves, it is useful to feel and express appreciation to the
Lord for all His blessings—else He may withdraw some of them
to teach us how valuable they are.*

Vrika grabbed his hatchet and cut off a piece of flesh from his thigh. Indifferent towards his profuse bleeding, he then flung the flesh into the sacrificial fire he was sitting near. "Lord Shiva!" he shouted. "Please appear from the fire! I need to see you—and ask you for something!"

But Lord Shiva did not appear.

So Vrika continued to chop off pieces of his own flesh and feed them into the flames—in the hope that Lord Shiva would at some point be satisfied and manifest himself.

But he didn't.

"Why don't you come?" demanded Vrika. "You're supposed to be easily pleased. Isn't my flesh enough to satisfy you?"

Apparently, it wasn't.

But what had driven this crazy person to this horrifying extreme?

Vrika wanted a special blessing and only a god of exceptional power could grant it. Several days earlier, he had wondered which of the three presiding deities he should worship in order to obtain it—Lord Brahma, Lord Vishnu, or Lord Shiva? Then he met the great sage Narada and asked him for his advice. "Which of those three are most quickly satisfied?"

Understanding Vrika's sinister intention, Narada answered, "Lord Shiva. He quickly satisfied Ravana and Bana with great wealth—simply because they prayed to him."

So Vrika journeyed to Kedarnatha, in north India near Kashmir,

Vrika tries to kill Lord Shiva

where many devotees of Lord Shiva go. With snow-capped mountains in the background, Vrika ignited a sacrificial fire in Lord Shiva's name. He thought that Shiva would be especially pleased if he offered him his own flesh in the fire, for it is through fire that the gods eat the devotional offerings. Thus, day after day, for six days, Vrika sliced off many pieces of his own flesh and offered them into the flames. But in spite of these severe attempts, Lord Shiva did not appear.

"Why don't you come?!" Vrika angrily demanded. "I need to see you—and ask you for something! Please!"

On the seventh day, Vrika became so frustrated and enraged that he decided to try a more drastic means. First, he took a bath in a nearby lake. Then, while his body and hair were still wet, he grabbed his hatchet. Raising it above his head and leaning over the fire, he was just about to chop off his head as a final offering. But at that moment, Shiva suddenly rose from the fire and cried, "Stop! Stop! I'm here."

Vrika's eyes opened wide. It was he—Lord Shiva—stepping out of the fire.

Lord Shiva grabbed both of Vrika's arms to prevent him from killing himself. Just by touching him, Shiva miraculously healed all the gaping wounds on Vrika's limbs and body. But why had Shiva bothered to appear to such a madman? Simply out of compassion—to save Vrika from committing suicide. Even an ordinary person—let alone a god— would do that. "My dear Vrika," he said appeasingly, "you don't have to cut off your head to please me. I'm satisfied by an offering of just a little water. Now ask me what you want."

"You'll give it to me?"

"Yes."

"Promise?"

"Of course."

Vrika then grinned devilishly. "All right. Then bless me that when I touch someone on his head with my hand, his head will crack open and he'll drop dead."

Although reluctant to grant this boon, Lord Shiva knew he had no choice, for he had made a promise and would not violate it. None- theless, at heart, he was very sorry to give Vrika a blessing that could endanger human society, since it was like offering milk to a poisonous snake. Thus, he hesitatingly said, "Your wish...is granted."

"Thank you," said Vrika. Then he gazed at Lord Shiva for a few moments, wondering whether or not Shiva had really blessed him.

Well, the only way to find out was to use it on someone. But who? Who? Vrika then thought lustfully about Lord Shiva's beautiful wife, Gauri. *Yes, with Shiva gone,* he thought, *I could then take her for my own pleasure. Great idea!*

Smiling demonically and reaching out, Vrika hastened towards Lord Shiva. Seeing that his life was now in danger, Shiva backed away. But the demon eagerly pursued him. So Shiva, using his mystic powers, shot up into the sky. But Vrika, just as mystical, also flew up. Lord Shiva then flew through the sky to other planets, but Vrika stayed right behind him. Lord Shiva even went beyond the higher planets, but Vrika pursued him there, too. Along the way, Lord Shiva appealed to some of the predominating gods to help him—such as Lord Brahma, Lord Indra, and Lord Chandra—but all of them, incapable of baffling the boon Shiva had given Vrika, remained silent.

Lord Shiva finally reached the radiant realm of Shvetadvipa, or Vaikuntha, where Lord Vishnu resides along with His peaceful, loving devotees. Being omniscient, Lord Vishnu fully understood that Lord Shiva, His glorious devotee, was in great danger. He therefore conceived of a plan to save him. Assuming the body of a celibate student—with the proper belt, deerskin, staff, and prayer beads—Lord Vishnu intervened and approached Vrika, giving Lord Shiva a chance to hide himself.

Lord Vishnu offered Vrika his respects and obeisances just to attract his sympathy and attention. Then, to create a sense of familiarity, He said, "Aren't you Shakuni's son?"

"That's right."

"You look pretty tired."

"Yeah, I am." He was breathing rapidly.

"Then why don't you rest here for awhile?" The Lord indicated a grassy mound.

"Thanks."

"It's not good to overtax the body."

"No."

"With the body, we can satisfy our desires. Right?"

"Right." Vrika then sat down on the knoll.

When the Lord saw that Vrika had recovered from his fatigue, He asked him, "Can you tell me why you've come here?"

"Why?"

"Yes. Perhaps I can help you."

Totally disarmed, Vrika freely explained. But the Lord replied with surprise, "Lord Shiva gave you that blessing? Really?"

"That's what he said."

"Well, I can hardly believe it. As far as I know, Lord Shiva went crazy."

"Crazy?"

"You didn't hear about it?"

"No." Vrika was now bewildered.

"Well, when he had a quarrel with his father-in-law, Daksha, he was cursed to become a ghost."

"Lord Shiva?"

"Yes. Now he's a leader of ghosts and goblins."

Vrika looked very surprised.

"So—I'd never place any faith in Shiva's words."

"You think maybe he cheated me?"

"Maybe. The only way to find out is to make a test."

"What kind?"

"Well, just take your hand and—place it on your head."

"My head?"

"Yes. And if nothing happens, then you can kill the bluffer."

"Hmm. That's a great idea."

"That way he'll never cheat anyone again."

"Right...Right."

Illusioned by Lord Vishnu's wily words, Vrika placed his hand on his head. Instantly, his head cracked open, as if hit by a lightning bolt, and he fell down dead.

The gods rained flowers on Lord Vishnu and gladly prayed to Him: "Victory! Obeisances! Excellent!"

When Lord Shiva came out of hiding and approached Lord Vishnu, the latter said, "This demon was killed by his own sinful reactions."

"Yes."

"Whoever offends saintly persons—especially persons like you—can never hope for good fortune!"

Lord Shiva bowed his head gratefully, realizing that Lord Vishnu had saved his life.

Anyone who recites or listens to this account will be freed from all foes and from the repetition of birth and death.

Bhrigu tests Lord Vishnu

Chapter Thirteen

Bhrigu Discovers Who God Is

When the sage Bhrigu seriously offended Lord Vishnu, the latter reacted with extraordinary humility. Unless we develop such humility, we can scarcely hope to remain undisturbed by another's offenses. Such disturbances can seriously prevent us from discovering our true identity.

"**I** say that Lord Brahma is the Supreme Lord!" said one sage. "Absolutely not! Lord Vishnu is!" argued another.

"You're both wrong!" a different sage insisted. "It's Lord Shiva!"

This wrangling continued among the assembly of sages for some time.

They had all come to the holy Saraswati River to perform a great sacrifice called Satra. But they could not agree on who, among the three predominating deities, was supreme. Determined to find out, one of the sages said, "We have to discover which of the three possesses the quality of goodness in full."

All the sages agreed. After further discussion, it was decided that the sage Bhrigu would test each of the deities. He therefore made an excellent plan and decided to implement it immediately.

By his mystical powers, he instantly reached Brahmaloka, where his esteemed father—the four-headed, four-armed Lord Brahma—ruled. Coming before him, Bhrigu deliberately failed to show him the customary respect he was entitled to. Since Lord Brahma was not only his father but also the creator of this world, Bhrigu was expected to greet him by humbly bowing down and offering prayers of glorification and appreciation. But Bhrigu just stood there in a casual manner, as if Brahma were no more important to him than a pebble on the street.

Lord Brahma could not believe his eyes—that Bhrigu was acting so offensively. "What's wrong with you?" he asked.

"Wrong?" Bhrigu shrugged his shoulders innocently. "Nothing."

"Nothing?! Is that how you greet your father?"

"Sure, why not?"

"You impudent wretch! Why are you acting this way?"

"What way?"

"Disrespectfully!"

"Disrespectfully? You think so?"

As Brahma glared at him furiously, Bhrigu could see that his father was about to curse him. However, because Bhrigu was his son, Brahma made a strenuous effort to control his anger. And after awhile, although his anger subsided, it did not disappear. Bhrigu then had to conclude that since his father was still subject to anger, he was not full in the quality of goodness. Thus, he could not be the Supreme Lord!

Bhrigu then went to Mount Kailash, where his brother Lord Shiva resided. Arriving there, he noted the high, snow-covered mountains, gushing streams, colorful foliage, and warbling birds. Bhrigu walked towards Lord Shiva, who, under a tree, was sitting cross-legged on a tiger skin with his wife, Parvati, and conversing with her. She was wearing a plain, brown sari and he, a simple orange loincloth. Lord Shiva's darkish body had been smeared with ashes, so it had a pale, whitish glow. Most of his brown matted hair hung loosely over his shoulders while the rest of it was twirled above his head, Ganges water spouting from the top of the twirl. The pole of his trident was stuck firmly in the ground.

When Lord Shiva saw Bhrigu coming towards him, he was very happy to see his brother. He therefore stood up and, as Bhrigu approached him, opened his arms to give him a warm, fraternal embrace. However, Bhrigu jumped back, his eyes filled with profound disgust and contempt.

Lord Shiva was surprised. Never before had Bhrigu acted like this. "What's the matter?" he asked.

"What's the matter? Look at you!" he declared condescendingly.

"What about me?"

"You're filthy!"

"I'm what?"

"Filthy! You're covered from head to toe with cremation ashes."

Lord Shiva glowered at Bhrigu. He could scarcely believe what he was hearing.

"So don't contaminate me!"

"What?!" Lord Shiva's eyes were red with fury.

"You heard me!" answered Bhrigu.

Clutching his trident tightly, Lord Shiva raised it and was just about to stab Bhrigu—when Parvati dove in front of her husband's feet and screamed, "No! Don't! Don't!"

Lord Shiva glared at her. Why was she interfering?

"He's your brother!" she shouted. "Your brother!"

"Yes, and he's treating me like an enemy!"

"Just ignore it! Please! It will be a great sin to kill him!"

"Who cares? It'll teach him a lesson."

"Don't! Please!"

"But—"

"Why care if he doesn't know your greatness? Better to pity him than to kill him."

"Pity—?

"Yes. All he sees is your ashes—and nothing else. He doesn't see your purity. So pity him."

"Pity him."

"Yes."

Thus, Parvati, by her urgent entreaty, dissuaded Lord Shiva from killing his brother.

Bhrigu now realized that the quality of ignorance was still somewhat prominent in Lord Shiva. He therefore concluded that since Shiva was not fully in the quality of goodness, he could not be the Supreme Lord.

Bhrigu then traveled to the realm of Shvetadvipa, or Vaikuntha, Lord Vishnu's realm, determined to test Him.

He entered a magnificent jeweled palace and, without even announcing himself, walked right into Lord Vishnu's bedroom. There, Bhrigu saw the Lord lying on a bed of flowers with His wife Lakshmi present. Approaching Him, Bhrigu lifted his foot and kicked Lord Vishnu firmly on the chest, as if this were perfectly good behavior.

Although Bhrigu had committed a heinous offense, Lord Vishnu felt no anger towards him. Rather, He saw Bhrigu as a Brahmin—a priest and teacher of society, worthy of the highest respect. Thus, in accordance with etiquette, He immediately forgave him and forgot the infraction. Then, along with His wife, He rose from the bed and offered Bhrigu His respectful obeisance. Standing up, He gave Bhrigu a cushion to sit on and said, "My dear Brahmin, how fortunate I am to have you here! I'm sorry that when you entered, I couldn't receive you properly. Please pardon Me for this offense."

Bhrigu was astonished by Lord Vishnu's reaction.

"You're so pure and glorious," Vishnu continued, "that the water that washes your feet can even purify pilgrimage places. Therefore, please further purify this planet of Mine."

"You want *me* to purify this planet?" Bhrigu asked in amazement.

"Yes! And there's something else. I know that your feet are quite soft, and that My chest is very hard. So you must have hurt your foot when you kicked Me. Therefore, I'd like to massage it to relieve your pain." He then had Bhrigu sit down on the cushion and proceeded to knead his foot. As He did, He said, "My chest has now become sanctified by the touch of your foot. Thus, I'm sure Lakshmi will be happy to live there forever."

Nevertheless, Bhrigu was not so foolish as to believe that he was purer or even *as* pure as Lord Vishnu. Thus, he was struck with wonder by the Lord's humility, affection, and sympathy. Feeling intense gratitude, Bhrigu's voice choked up and he was unable to answer the Lord. He therefore bowed his head, and tears streamed uncontrollably from his eyes.

Bhrigu realized that the first offense he had committed—to his father, Brahma—was with his mind. In other words, he had thought of not offering him respect and had manifested this thought by neither speaking nor acting. His second offense—to his brother Lord Shiva—was with his speech. He had insulted and criticized him for having unclean habits. This offense was certainly worse than the first one. But his third offense—which was even worse than the previous two—was with his body. He had kicked the Lord's chest, and in the presence of His wife Lakshmi! Yet, because Lord Vishnu was so merciful and loving, He had not only considered the kick inoffensive, but considered *Himself* the offender for not having risen to greet Bhrigu respectfully and for having bruised the sage's foot with His hard chest! And above that, He had felt that His chest had become even more sacred than it had been prior to the kick!

(Nevertheless, it has been said that Lakshmi, the goddess of fortune, had not regarded the kicking of her husband's chest with the same indifference. In fact, she had become rather angry over it. Consequently, in remembrance of that incident, she has often withheld her blessings from the Brahmins and left them quite poor.)

When Bhrigu returned to the sages on the bank of the Saraswati River and described the experiences he'd had, they came inescapably to the conclusion that of the three predominating deities, Lord Vishnu was the greatest. His greatness had been shown by His ability to tolerate an extremely disturbing situation. But Lord Brahma and Lord Shiva had lost their serenity upon even a slight provocation. Hence, how could they maintain the tranquillity of their devotees? The sages thus agreed that Lord Vishnu obviously possessed the quality of goodness in full; and that if one wanted true peace and freedom from all fear, one would have to take shelter of Him.

Thereafter, those sages rendered devotional service to the Lord, became fully self-realized, and achieved the transcendental qualities necessary to enter the eternal world.

Narada sees the Lord in his heart

CHAPTER FOURTEEN

NARADA SEES GOD EVERYWHERE

By constantly remembering the Lord, Narada discovered himself as well as God. Similarly, if we wish to discover the real self within, we need to try to constantly remember Him.

The angry snake lay coiled in the grass, waiting to spring at the oncoming feet.

The feet belonged to Narada's mother, who couldn't see the agitated viper. Not only was it too dark, but her mind was centered on getting to the cowshed. There, she would milk a cow and then bring the milk back to the house.

The snake saw the feet coming closer...closer... Then, just as one of the feet was about to trample it, the serpent lunged and sank its deadly fangs into the foot, venom squirting rapidly into its victim's bloodstream.

Narada's mother screamed and gazed down fearfully. Seeing the snake attached to her foot, she grabbed it by the neck, pulled it off, and flung it as far away as she could. As she hastily continued towards the barn, she suddenly felt a weakness, a limpness, come over her. She halted, rubbing the side of her head where it had begun to throb. Then, no longer able to stand, she helplessly collapsed to the ground. Her breath came in tense, painful gasps. She tried to cry for help, but her weakened voice failed her. Feeling alone, distressed, and helpless, she knew she would soon be dead!

When her five-year-old son, Narada, learned that she had passed away, he could not help thinking about her. She had been a maidservant at a Brahmin's house while trying to raise him. He recalled the last rainy season—when it had just begun. Several itinerant devotees of

Lord Vishnu had asked for and received shelter at the house. The master had assigned Narada's mother to cater to their needs during the four months they would be there. Gladly serving them, she delegated some of her duties to her son. Narada would, for example, deliver their food to them and clean their quarters.

As a result of serving the holy men—and receiving their blessings—Narada suddenly became very spiritually inclined. He was self-controlled and uninterested in childish sports. Never ill behaved, he spoke only that which was necessary. One day, while he was taking away the renunciants' leftover foods—*prasadam*, or eatables that had been offered to and blessed by God—he asked if he could eat them. Understanding his purpose, they gladly consented, and Narada consumed and relished all their remnants.

Just from this holy contact, all the karmic punishments that Narada would normally have received from the sins he had committed in his past lives were instantly eradicated. Thus, his heart became purified and he became strongly attracted to transcendental living. He therefore eagerly listened to the sages describing the attractive activities of Lord Krishna. And with each telling, he became increasingly enrapt—so much so that his taste for knowing about Krishna's divine exploits escalated daily. This resulted in his realizing that he was not his material body or mind but was an eternal, spiritual soul.

As Narada continued serving the sages, he developed strong faith in them. They, in turn, instructed him in confidential, spiritual knowledge. He learned where souls originally come from, why they are in this world, what causes them to suffer, and how they may become free from all misery. He also discovered that he had an eternal relationship with God; and even though it had become dormant, he could actually revive it by the process of bhakti yoga or devotional service to Him. He further learned that he could eventually enter the divine world—where God dwells and acts—and personally meet and serve Him there. To Narada, there was no higher goal than this.

At the end of the rainy and autumn seasons, the holy men bid Narada goodbye and wandered off to other places.

Now that Narada's mother was dead, what would he do? Who would attend to him? Considering this, he felt quite helpless. Though he was sad from being separated from his mother, he knew that she had merely gone to another realm—and that the Lord would take good care of her.

He also understood that her leaving him while he was so young was God's special mercy, for now he would have to depend solely on the Lord to guide and help him. Since he had full faith in God, he left the Brahmin's house and walked onto the road. Completely alone and determined to be an itinerant devotee—just like the sages who had initiated him—he now headed north.

Narada passed through many thriving cities, towns, villages, valleys, vegetable and animal farms, flower and nursery gardens, and natural forests. He saw hills and mountains full of gold, silver, and copper, as well as land tracts with water reservoirs filled with attractive lotus flowers fit for the residents of the heavenly planets. He ventured through numerous forests, bamboo reeds, sharp grasses, weeds and caves, which were difficult for him to forge through alone. And he saw dark and dangerous forests that were the playgrounds of snakes, owls, and jackals.

After awhile, he not only felt physical and mental exhaustion, but also intense hunger and thirst. However, he soon came upon a lake, and after bathing in it and drinking its water, he felt relieved and refreshed. Continuing on, Narada discovered an uninhabited forest, where he sat down under the shade of a banyan tree and began to meditate. Then, as the sages had taught him, he focused his attention on the Supersoul in his heart. Gazing resolutely at the Lord's lotuslike feet, his heart became filled with transcendental love, and tears flowed from his eyes.

Narada instantly saw Lord Krishna in his heart, and this filled him with indescribable happiness. Each and every part of his body became thrilled and enlivened with ecstasy. In fact, Narada became so blissful that he could no longer see the Lord. And yet—he wanted to continue seeing Him, for the vision gave him total satisfaction. Perturbed by the loss, Narada concentrated firmly on his heart and endeavored again and again to see that divine form. But hard as he tried, he could not succeed. This greatly frustrated and distressed him.

Noting the child's grief, the Lord within suddenly but gravely said to him, "Narada, I'm sorry to say that you will not see Me for the rest of your life."

"What?!' Narada was taken aback.

"I'm sorry."

"But—why?"

"Because you're still incomplete in devotional service."

"Incomplete?"

"Yes. However, the more service you perform, the purer your heart will become."

"But—how come You let me see You today?"

"Just to increase your desire for Me."

"Increase?"

"Yes. The more you remember Me and hanker after Me, the more you'll be freed from your worldly desires."

"And when I'm free from them, will I be able to see you then?"

"Yes, always—and everywhere."

Narada became hopeful.

"By My mercy, you will never forget Me."

When the Lord stopped speaking, Narada felt relieved and grateful. He therefore offered Him his obeisances.

From that time on, Narada remembered and chanted the Lord's name and glories regularly, for he knew how immensely beneficial those practices were. Thus, he continued traveling all over the world, fully satisfied, humble, and content. At the end of his life, he was free from all materialistic desires and karma. The Lord then awarded him a transcendental body—which is eternally knowledgeable and blissful, and which enables one to see the Supreme Lord always.

Many years later, when Lord Brahma's day ended [after 4,320,000,000 years] the world was destroyed. At that time, Narada, along with Brahma, entered into the Supreme Lord's body and remained there in divine consciousness. At the end of Lord Brahma's night [4,320,000,000 years], when Brahma awoke, he once more created the world. Then Narada appeared from Brahma's body in the same transcendental form he had when he had previously entered God's body. Since then, by the grace of Lord Vishnu, Narada travels everywhere without restriction, both in the material and spiritual worlds, performing devotional service for Him.

Wherever Narada travels, he always sings God's glories and plays devotional music on his vina. This stringed instrument is charged with transcendental sound and was given to him by Lord Krishna Himself. As soon as Narada sings about the Lord's holy activities and plays a devotional melody, Lord Krishna, as if summoned, instantly appears in Narada's heart.

Narada's message to everyone is: "You can cross over the rough ocean of materialistic desires, anxieties, and miseries with the boat of constant conversation about the transcendental activities of the Supreme Lord. This gives you pure love of God and complete delight and fulfillment. Possessing these, you need nothing else."

Thus, Narada not only achieved his spiritual goal—of being able to see God always—but by his expert teaching and perfect example, he continues to instruct many other souls on how to do the same.

Lord Krishna orders Arjuna to kill Ashvatthama

CHAPTER FIFTEEN

ASHVATTHAMA PUNISHED

Ashvatthama ruined his life by being bitterly vengeful. To discover ourselves, we should not only become free from vengeance, but should also learn to be forgiving.

When Ashvatthama, under the cover of darkness, secretly entered the Pandava military camp, he had one thing in mind: murder! And not just ordinary murder— mass murder!

But can I accomplish it? he wondered.

He moved stealthily forward, looking for his first victim's tent— Dhrishtadyumna's. As he searched, he vengefully remembered how Dhrishtadyumna had unfairly and cruelly killed his father, Drona, in the war between the Kurus and the Pandavas, which had just about ended. He recalled how his father, a general of the Kuru army, was invincible and relentless on the battlefield. Skillful and powerful, Drona had killed thousands of the Pandava soldiers on that fatal day. In fact, it had appeared that he would destroy the entire enemy army—until Lord Krishna, a well-wisher and relative of the Pandavas, suggested a tactic to defeat Drona.

Implementing it, Bhima, one of the five Pandava brothers, killed an elephant named Ashvatthama. Then, so that Drona could clearly hear him, Bhima roared, "I've killed Ashvatthama!" Drona, of course, thought that Bhima was referring to Drona's *son* Ashvatthama and not to the elephant. This greatly disturbed Drona, incapacitating him from further fighting. Yet he wanted to be sure that what Bhima had said was true. Therefore, he inquired from Yudhishthira, a Pandava known for his truthfulness. Trying to execute Krishna's tactic while at the same time endeavoring to uphold morality, Yudhishthira replied, "Yes, it's true, Ashvatthama has been killed—" Then, in a scarcely audible voice, he added, "Ashvatthama the elephant."

However, because of the surrounding din of warfare, Drona did not hear the last three words. Thus, he concluded that his only son was dead. Greatly attached to him, Drona became so distressed that he lost his will to live. Thus, he discarded his weapons, sat down in a yoga posture on the floor of his chariot, and entered into a spiritual trance. It was then that Dhrishtadyumna, a general of the Pandava army, climbed aboard the chariot, drew his sword, and lopped off the elderly warrior's head.

If Ashvatthama could understand that Lord Krishna had wanted the Pandavas, and not the Kurus, to win the war—because the Pandavas were the most exemplary and enlightened rulers of the world—he might not have harbored such vengeance towards them or Dhrishtadyumna. But he failed to understand the will and position of Krishna. Like so many misguided and deluded persons at that time, he viewed the Lord as an ordinary, fallible being.

However, the Pandavas, being eternal companions of Krishna's, not only knew He was God, but perceived themselves as His surrendered devotees. Had this not been so, their high level of virtue and morality would have totally prevented them from carrying out Krishna's infallible stratagem. But they fully understood that Krishna's will was superior to and transcended all considerations of mundane morality. Thus, they accepted His advice.

Ashvatthama found and quietly entered Dhrishtadyumna's tent. Seeing him sleeping on an excellent silk-sheeted bed, he irately noted the flower garlands strewn about him. *Your hero days are over!* he thought. Seized with rage, Ashvatthama lifted his foot and kicked Dhrishtadyumna hard. Waking up and seeing Drona's son, Dhrishtadyumna began to rise from his bed. But before he could do so, Ashvatthama grabbed him by the hair, dragged him off the bed, and slammed him onto the ground. Then he kicked him in the throat and chest, causing Dhrishtadyumna to squirm and squeal, like a helpless animal. Next, with his heels, Ashvatthama repeatedly struck his enemy's vital parts—till he was unmistakably dead.

Ashvatthama then proceeded to other tents, viciously killing warrior after warrior. Next, he entered a tent in which five young men—who were the sons of the Pandavas, delivered by their wife Draupadi—lay sleeping. Suffused with vengeful glee, Ashvatthama gripped his sword tightly and beheaded one son after another. But that was not the end of his onslaught, for by night's end, he had killed thousands of Pandava warriors—and most, while they were sleeping. Drenched in blood and filled with joy, he felt he had properly avenged his father's death—even if by improper means. *Who cares about the means?* he thought. *Hadn't the Pandavas used improper means to slay my glorious father?*

Carrying the five heads of Draupadi's sons, he sped on his chariot to the place where Duryodhana, the commander-in-chief of the Kuru army, lay dying. He then presented the heads to him as a prize, hoping to uplift him. But after learning of the heinous means Ashvatthama had used to kill them, even the demonic Duryodhana disapproved. In fact, he was not at all pleased.

At the Pandava camp, when Draupadi heard about the slaughter of her five sons, she felt great sorrow and cried heavily. One of her husbands, Arjuna, tried his best to pacify her. Incensed, he said, "Rest assured, I will cut off Ashvatthama's head with my arrow! And after I present it to you, I'll wipe away your tears. Then you can stand on Ashvatthama's head while you take your bath."

Draupadi was somewhat mollified.

After dressing in armor and gathering his devastating weapons, Arjuna mounted his chariot. He asked Lord Krishna, his friend and charioteer, to find and follow Ashvatthama. Krishna drove the chariot with amazing speed and, after only a short while, spied him on his chariot.

Ashvatthama saw that Arjuna, whom he knew to be much more powerful than himself, was chasing him. Therefore, he whipped his horses forcefully, trying to make them accelerate. But the horses were tired, and thus unable to fully cooperate. Ashvatthama looked back. Arjuna was getting closer...closer...closer. He realized that if he continued on his present course, he would soon be captured and killed. To avoid the danger, he stopped his horse and jumped off his chariot. Then he touched water for purification, snatched a blade of grass from the earth, and recited a mantra. The blade was instantly converted into one of the most powerful weapons in the world—the Brahmastra! Having learned this art from his illustrious father, he then commanded the weapon, "Destroy the Pandavas!"

As the blade shot into the air, it exploded into an ever-expanding effulgence. The power unleashed from this mantra was thousands of times more devastating than the nuclear weapons invented fifty centuries later. The sky thundered, thousands of meteors fell, the earth trembled, and fear gripped all living beings. Thinking his own life to be in danger, Arjuna had Krishna stop his chariot and said, "You're the Supreme Lord, You're most powerful, and You know everything. So please explain to me why that dangerous light is spreading all around?"

"Because Ashvatthama has thrown a Brahmastra."

"A Brahmastra?" Arjuna was surprised and stunned.

"Yes. He's afraid you'll kill him. So he's trying to kill you first."

"That weapon can destroy the whole world if he doesn't withdraw it."

"That's right. And he doesn't know *how* to withdraw it," said Krishna.

"He doesn't?" Arjuna was amazed.

Krishna shook his head. "His father hadn't taught him that yet."

"Then what should I do?"

Krishna told him, and they alighted from the chariot.

Arjuna then touched water for purification, reverently walked around Krishna three times, and fixed a shaft to his bow string. After uttering the mantra for materializing the Brahmastra, he ordered it, "Go and combine with Ashvatthama's weapon." Instantly, the weapon blazed up and shot into the sky, merging with Ashvatthama's Brahmastra. The whole sky looked like a circle of fire, and the light spread through outer space to all the other planets. The radiance was so bright and hot that everyone in the universe was scorched by it. Some people even thought that the world was coming to an end.

Seeing how disturbed people were, Arjuna retracted both Brahmastras, their light and heat immediately vanishing. Next, he angrily arrested Ashvatthama, tied him with ropes, as if he were an animal, and led him to his chariot.

Krishna fumed, "Although he's the son of a Brahmin, don't show him any mercy. He's killed innocent young men while they were asleep. He's worse than an animal!"

"I agree."

Krishna then reminded Arjuna that it was unethical for a warrior to kill a boy, a woman, a foolish creature, or a surrendered soul; or to kill an enemy who was careless, intoxicated, insane, asleep, afraid, or chariotless.

Arjuna nodded.

"A person who is cruel and wretched," continued Krishna, "who lives at the cost of others' lives, should be killed. Otherwise, in his next lifetime, the karmic reaction will destroy him. Besides, I heard you promise Draupadi that you would deliver his head to her."

"Yes," Arjuna said hesitantly.

"This man murdered your family members. He's also dissatisfied his commanding officer. And he's degraded himself unlimitedly. Therefore, kill him immediately!"

Although Arjuna knew that Ashvatthama was a heinous murderer, he was reluctant to kill him at this moment. "I'd like to first hear what Draupadi has to say."

Arjuna and Krishna helped Ashvatthama onto their chariot. Then they themselves mounted it and Krishna drove it back to the military camp, where they met Arjuna's brothers, as well as Draupadi. Arjuna then presented Ashvatthama to Draupadi, who was still lamenting over her murdered sons. When she saw him—tied up and silent—she showed him the respect due to a Brahmin, even though he no longer deserved it. Because she was a virtuous and sympathetic woman, she found herself unable to deviate from the noble way in which she had been trained.

"Release him," she said.

"What?!" Arjuna said, surprised.

"He's a Brahmin, our spiritual master."

"But he's a murderer!"

"Still, it was by his father's mercy that you learned how to shoot arrows and master weapons.

"His father would never do what he did!".

"Perhaps not. But the son represents the father, so his father is, in a sense, still alive. If you kill him, it will be like killing his father."

Arjuna looked at Krishna uncertainly, then back at his wife.

"And you'll make his family members grieve—especially his mother. Just as *I* can't stop crying over *my* sons' death, why should she also have to grieve?"

Arjuna admired her sympathy and compassion.

"If the warriors offend and enrage the Brahmins," Draupadi continued, "then the fire of that rage burns up the entire royal family—and makes everyone grief-stricken."

"I agree with her," said Yudhishthira. "Her points are in accordance with religious principles. They're glorious, merciful, and fair."

Arjuna's younger brothers, Nakula and Sahadeva, as well as others there, all agreed. But his brother Bhima disagreed and urged, "No, he should be killed! He killed our sleeping sons for no good reason!"

Krishna, smiling slightly, turned to Arjuna and authoritatively said, "The scripture says that a Brahmin's friend should not be killed. But if he's an assailant, he must be killed. So—you have to act to satisfy your wife, and also to satisfy Bhima and Me."

Arjuna instantly comprehended the Lord's equivocal orders and decided on a compromise. Drawing his sword, he first cut off Ashvatthama's hair, which, in a sense, cut off his dignity and respectability. Then Arjuna cut off the mystical jewel implanted between Ashvatthama's eyebrows. It had the power to bestow on the wearer freedom from fear of weapons, disease, hunger, robbers, gods, or demons. Thus Ashvatthama, bereft of his strength, wealth, weapons, reputation, and luster, stood there in abject humiliation. For a preeminent warrior—as Ashvatthama had been—this punishment was even worse than death.

Then Lord Krishna decided to add something to it. "You are a coward and a sinful wretch!" He boomed. "You killed defenseless young men while they were sleeping. Now you must pay the price for this sin. Therefore, for the next three thousand years you will wander over the earth—through many countries—without a friend and without anyone to talk to. Your body will be filled with all kinds of diseases— and you will stink from pus and blood. No one will want to go near you. And you will live in menacing forests and dismal swamps... Now go!"

Ashvatthama shuffled off and shamefully headed for the forest.

Draupadi then asked her husband Yudhishthira, who was now king of the world, to wear Ashvatthama's jewel and regard it as a gift from his deceased guru, Drona. Placing the celestial gem on his forehead, Yudhishthira looked powerful and beautiful, like a mountain in the moonlight.

After that, the Pandavas and Draupadi, overwhelmed with grief, performed the necessary funeral rites for their sons.

Several days later, Ashvatthama trudged through the dreary forest, filled with humiliation and rancor. He felt he had failed to fully avenge his father's undeserved death. Although he had found some satisfaction in killing the Pandavas' sons and many of the Pandava warriors, he would never be fully satisfied unless or until he killed the five Pandavas themselves and Arjuna's yet-to-be-born grandchild. "Therefore," he affirmed, "I will kill them all now!"

The degraded warrior touched water for purification, grabbed an iron arrow from his quiver, charged it with the Brahmastra mantra, and commanded it, "Go and kill the five Pandavas and the baby in Uttara's womb!" Then he hurled the deadly dart into the sky and, as it soared upwards, it blazed with terrifying splendor. Watching it, Ashvatthama smiled proudly. *Finally*, he thought, *the Pandavas will be dead—and my debt to my father will be fully paid.* Although Ashvatthama knew that his future would be terribly miserable, he now felt he would at least have some consolation, some pleasure knowing that the Pandava dynasty was irrevocably doomed.

Some moments later in Hastinapura, Lord Krishna, about to leave for his kingdom, was sitting on his chariot and bidding farewell to the Pandavas and their relatives.

Suddenly, the pregnant Uttara anxiously pushed her way through the immense crowd and breathlessly reached Krishna. "My Lord!" she blurted out hysterically, "Help me! Please!

"What's wrong?" Krishna asked.

"Look!" She pointed to the sky.

Everyone looked up and was amazed to see the blazing iron arrow headed towards them.

"Don't let it kill my baby, Lord! Please!"

Instantly, the five Pandavas grabbed their bows and arrows.

"I don't care if it burns me," cried Uttara, "but please—save my baby!"

Krishna knew that there was not enough time for the Pandavas to counteract the fiery arrow. Therefore, as it neared the Pandavas, Krishna hurled his Sudarshana disc at it and diverted it from its course. However, the arrow then sped into Uttara's womb and instantly burned her fetus to death.

Uttara screamed in agony, clutching her abdomen.

But the soul of her fetus remained there helplessly.

Although Krishna was watching Uttara sympathetically, He also existed in another form, in her heart, as the Supersoul. Thus, from her heart, He entered her womb and neutralized the Brahmastra's devastating heat.

Outside, Krishna assured her, "Don't worry. Your baby is alive."

"It can't be—I felt it die," Uttara said tearfully.

"No, it's all right. Believe me."

But she couldn't—even though she wanted to.

Inside her womb, Krishna miraculously created another fetal form which exactly resembled the one that had just been burned to death and which now bore the same soul.

Uttara soothed her abdomen with her two hands and began to feel mild kicking movements. It was her baby—alive! Tears of gratitude streamed down her cheeks, for she knew that Lord Krishna had miraculously saved it.

Within Uttara's womb, the baby clearly observed the four-armed Supersoul—a sight it would never forget. It would always remember the Lord's thumb-high form, blackish body, yellow garments, golden helmet and earrings, and reddish eyes. It would also recall the Lord whirling His club about His head, dispelling the last traces of the Brahmastra's radiation, and then Himself disappearing.

But why had Krishna saved the child from death?

The Lord knew that the infant would one day become a saintly warrior—named Parikshit—and would therefore be most qualified to succeed King Yudhishthira on the throne. Parikshit would protect the virtuous, orderly, and enlightened government that Yudhishthira would soon establish. This, of course, would insure the development and perpetuation of worldwide happiness, which was one of the reasons the Lord had appeared in this world. Having a king like Parikshit rule the kingdom would provide the people with an ideal leader who could inspire and encourage them to live up to the highest level of spirituality. Thus, it was absolutely necessary for the Lord to save the child.

But what about Ashvatthama?

In his ignorance, he thought he could destroy the Pandavas. He did not know that they were great devotees of the Lord, that Krishna was omnipotent, and that under His protection, the Pandavas could never be vanquished. Therefore, by attempting to destroy the Pandavas, Ashvatthama only worsened his own already pathetic situation by acquiring even more bad karma. This is generally the plight of persons who complacently violate God's laws. However, those who dutifully observe them and devote themselves to His pleasure—as did the Pandavas—ultimately live in peace, joy, and happiness.

CHAPTER SIXTEEN

KING YUDHISHTHIRA SEES EVIL OMENS

When Arjuna returned from Dwarka, because of his strong attachment to Lord Krishna, he felt intense pangs of separation. Similarly, to discover ourselves, it is helpful for us to try to develop attachment to Krishna, for this can cause us not only pangs of separation, but also abundant feelings of bliss.

In Hastinapura, King Yudhishthira saw evil omens everywhere—omens that eerily signified future misery. For example, the seasons were now occurring at the wrong time. People were extremely greedy, dishonest, and angry. They were earning their livelihood by improper means. Affairs and exchanges, even among friends, were duplicitous. And there were always misunderstandings and quarrels between family members, well-wishers, and married couples.

Standing near the palace with his brother Bhima, Yudhishthira morosely said, "Evil signs are everywhere—including in my own body."

"In your body?"

"Yes. My left side and my thighs, arms, and eyes are trembling. And due to fear, my heart is palpitating."

Bhima nodded sympathetically.

"When the sun rises, the female jackal cries and vomits fire. Dogs bark at me fearlessly. Useful animals like cows pass me on my left side, and lower animals like asses circle me. And when my horses see me, they begin crying."

A pigeon suddenly swooped down in front of them.

"This dove is like a messenger of death!"

"Yes," said Bhima.

Some owls and crows nearby began to shriek.

"They make my heart tremble," said Yudhishthira, "for they sound like they want to empty the universe."

King Yudhishthira notices evil omens

Smoke began circling the sky, making the earth and mountains appear as if they were pulsating. And although there were no clouds in the sky, thunder and lightning were perceivable. The wind began gusting violently, dust blew everywhere, and darkness pervaded the area. And when clouds suddenly appeared, they released a downpour of blood.

"These are ill omens, Bhima."

"They certainly are!"

"The rivers, reservoirs, and the mind are all upset. Butter no longer ignites fire. This is extraordinary. What do you think is going to happen?"

"I don't know."

"I noticed that the calves refuse to suck the cows' udders, and the cows fail to give milk. In fact, the cows just stand about crying. And the bulls—they take no pleasure in the pasturing grounds."

"Yes, I noticed."

"And did you see the temple Deities?"

"What about them?"

"They seem to be sobbing, sorrowing, and perspiring, and they look as if they're about to leave."

"Leave?"

"Yes. And all the cities, villages, towns, gardens, mines, and hermitages have lost their beauty and happiness... I wonder what disasters are about occur."

"Hmph!"

"I think that all these disturbances mean that the world is about to lose its good fortune."

Just then, a horse-driven chariot clattered through the nearby gate. It was driven by Arjuna—the younger brother of Yudhishthira and Bhima. He had been sent by Yudhishthira seven months ago to the city of Dwarka to find out what Lord Krishna's future agenda would be. Seeing his brothers, Arjuna brought the car to a halt and dismounted.

When Arjuna bowed at the king's feet, Yudhishthira noticed that he was extremely depressed. His head hung down, and tears flowed from his lotuslike eyes. "Arjuna, please tell me whether our friends and relatives are well and happy." He then mentioned many of them by name. Next, he asked the most important of all his questions: "How is Lord Krishna?"

Arjuna rose to his feet but was unable to speak.

"Arjuna," said Yudhishthira, "is your health all right? You seem to have lost your bodily glow. Has someone spoken to you in an unfriendly way—or threatened you? Or—were you unable to give charity to someone who asked for it? Or could you not keep your promise to someone?"

Arjuna wanted to speak, but his sorrow was too overwhelming.

"Were you unable to protect Brahmins, children, women, and the sick—when they asked you for shelter?...Or have you associated with a low-class woman?...Or have you been defeated along the way by someone who is your inferior or equal?"

Arjuna wiped the tears from his face. He tried to answer, but each time he uttered a word or two, his dry voice halted.

"Or have you committed some terrible offense?" After several more seconds, Yudhishthira said, "Arjuna, please let us know what's paining you."

Breathing heavily, Arjuna composed his thoughts and began to speak haltingly. "O King, Lord Krishna...has left...this world!"

Yudhishthira and Bhima felt extreme anguish, as if their very life had just been stolen from them. The meaning of the evil omens Yudhishthira had been seeing was now clear to him. Lord Krishna had established order and virtue all over the world. But now that He had left, Kali-yuga, or the age of darkness, would commence and the force of evil would begin spreading everywhere.

His voice quavering, Arjuna said, "My most intimate friend has left me alone. Thus my great power, which even amazed the gods, has also gone. It was by Krishna's grace that I was able to defeat all the lusty princes who had come to King Drupada's palace to compete for Draupadi's hand. It was because of Him that I was victorious over the king of the gods in the Khandava Forest. It was by Krishna's grace alone that Bhima killed the powerful demon Jarasandha and that the sage Durvasa was prevented from cursing us when we were dwelling in the forest. Yes, it was the Lord who allowed me to astonish Lord Shiva and his wife and receive from Shiva the gift of his mighty weapon."

Arjuna paused for a few seconds, gulping and holding back his tears. "When I stayed for some time on the heavenly planets, I protected the gods by killing their powerful enemy Nivatakavacha. And on the battlefield of Kurukshetra, the Kauravas were like an insurmountable ocean; but by Krishna's grace, I was able to cross over it and triumph. Yes, it was He who really killed our enemies, although He made me appear to be the hero. None of the great enemy generals could touch a hair on my head."

Again Arjuna wiped the tears away from his cheeks. Then a nostalgic smile lit up his anxious face. "O King! I loved the way He joked and talked with me, and the way He smiled. I remember the affectionate way He would call me—'O son of Pritha,' 'O friend,' 'O son of the Kuru dynasty.' This overwhelms me now. We used to live together—and sleep, sit, and loiter together. And I would sometimes joke sarcastically with Him, but He would tolerate it and excuse me, as a true friend excuses a friend or a father excuses his son. O Emperor, I now feel separated from my friend and best well-wisher, so my heart feels as if it's empty."

Arjuna then showed surprise and amazement. "And listen to this: after Krishna left this world, I tried to guard His queens from any rogues. But I was defeated by a number of infidel cowherd men—men who in the past I could conquer or kill without the slightest effort. I have the same Gandiva bow, the same arrows, the same chariot drawn by the same horses, and I use them in the same way I once did. But in Lord Krishna's absence, all of them, in a moment, have become useless."

Yudhishthira and Bhima could scarcely believe this, since Arjuna once had the power to fight one thousand warriors simultaneously— and win. With few exceptions, he had truly been the greatest fighter in the world.

"All our friends and relatives in Dwarka," continued Arjuna, "were cursed by Brahmins. Consequently, they became drunk on rice wine and fought each other with sticks, never even recognizing one another. Now…they're all gone—except four or five of them. This is also the Lord's will. At this moment, I feel strongly attracted to those instructions Krishna taught me on the battlefield of Kurukshetra. For I know they can relieve my burning heart—anytime, anywhere."

Thus, Arjuna began to meditate on some of those profound Vedic teachings, which later came to be known as the *Bhagavad-gita*, or the *Song of God:*

Never was there a time when I did not exist, nor you, nor any of these kings; nor in the future shall any of them cease to be.

That which pervades the entire body you should know to be indestructible. No one is able to destroy the imperishable soul.

Although I am unborn and My transcendental body never

deteriorates, and although I am the Lord of all living beings, I still appear in every millennium in My original transcendental form.

Always think of Me, become My devotee, worship Me and offer your homage unto Me. Thus you will come to Me without fail. I promise you this because you are my very dear friend.

Abandon all varieties of religion and just surrender unto Me. I shall deliver you from all sinful reactions. Do not fear.

One can understand Me as I am, as the Supreme Lord, only by devotional service. And when one is in full consciousness of Me by such devotion, he can enter into the kingdom of God.

After remembering these and other teachings, Arjuna's mind became pacified and free from all materialistic desires. His continuous recollection of Lord Krishna's lotuslike feet quickly increased his devotion. His doubts disappeared, he was delivered from the qualities of ignorance, passion, and goodness, and he entered a state of transcendence, or Krishna consciousness. He could no longer be entangled in birth, death, and rebirth—the process of reincarnation—for he was free from all the attachments that compel one to be repeatedly reborn. Shortly afterwards, he and his brothers entered the eternal world to continue their loving service and relationship with Lord Krishna.

Whoever hears this story with faith surely obtains the devotional service of the Lord—which is the highest perfection of life—and ultimately returns to the divine world.

CHAPTER SEVENTEEN

KALI'S EVIL CHALLENGED

Kali generated immoral and unethical conduct in human society. However, unless we live morally and ethically— according to God's laws—we will always be in anxiety and thus unable to discover our real selves.

On the bank of the Saraswati River, a terrible tragedy occurred: With his sword raised, the black demon, whose name was Kali and who was disguised as a king, stood menacingly beside the fearful bull. Then he raised his sword higher and swiftly brought it down, lopping off one of the bull's hind legs.

The bull screamed painfully, but Kali just laughed.

He then cut off the bull's other hind leg and also one of its forelegs. As the bull wobbled helplessly on one leg, Kali began walking away. "I'll be back in a while," he promised, "to get rid of your last leg!"

Kali then went into the city to spread his evil influence wherever he could. His only business was to establish the Iron Age of quarrel, wherein people would hate and harm each other and ultimately destroy one another. During the reign of King Yudhishthira, who had firmly established righteousness all over the world, Kali had found it impossible to insinuate his evil presence. Likewise, when Yudhishthira's successor, King Parikshit, had assumed the throne, it had been equally difficult. However, Kali had recently found some weaknesses in Parikshit's administration, and thus he began to take full advantage of the situation.

In Hastinapura, in his palace chamber, Emperor Parikshit was sitting on his throne and considering an important state matter when one of his trusted spies entered.

After offering the king his respects, the spy said, "My lord, I have some bad news."

King Parikshit threatens to kill Kali

"Oh?"

"The demon Kali is influencing many of your subjects."

"In what way?"

"Well, they've begun to eat meat, gamble, and—"

"What?!" the king interrupted. He was surprised, for those practices had been prohibited in his realm.

"Yes, and also to intoxicate themselves and engage in illicit sex."

"That's terrible! They'll all become corrupt and the state will degenerate!"

"I agree," said the spy.

"When people kill animals unnecessarily and eat their meat, people become merciless towards one another. When they gamble, they begin cheating and lying to each other. When they intoxicate themselves, they become undisciplined and neglect their duties and families."

The spy nodded dolefully.

"And when they engage in illicit sex, they not only become careless and unclean, but they acquire unwanted children and various diseases."

"So what do you plan to do?"

"What do you think?" asked Parikshit rhetorically.

The king then notified his army to prepare for battle. Parikshit mounted his gold-embossed chariot, which bore a flag marked with the picture of a lion and was tethered to black horses. He then signaled for the chariots, cavalry, elephants, and infantry to proceed out of the capital. Having been trained in warfare by his grandfather and granduncles—the preeminent Pandavas—the king was invincible in battle. Thus, he sallied forth to correct the threatening immoral situation in his empire.

While the king was traveling east towards the Saraswati River, the one-legged bull happened to meet a cow there. Actually, the god Dharma (Virtue) had assumed the form of the bull and the goddess Bhumi (Mother Earth) had assumed the body of the cow. Dharma's three missing legs represented discipline, mercy, and cleanliness, and the one on which he was now hobbling represented truthfulness. All four legs constituted the pillars on which an enlightened society rested and flourished.

Dharma noticed that the beauty of Bhumi's body was gone, her face had become dark, and she was crying. Concerned, he said, "Madam, you don't look very healthy. Are you suffering from some internal disease, or are you thinking about some relative in a far-off place? Are you grieving over the loss of my three legs? Or are you afraid that the unlawful meat-eaters will soon exploit you?"

Bhumi was so overwhelmed by sorrow that she could not speak.

But Dharma continued questioning her. "Are you upset because no one is performing sacrifices and the gods aren't getting their share of the offerings? Or is it because the living beings are suffering due to famine and drought? Are you feeling sympathy for the miserable women and children who've been abandoned by their husbands and fathers?"

Dharma paused to allow Bhumi to answer, but she was still too overcome.

"Are you sad," he continued, "because Brahmins have become addicted to immoral activities? Or because they have taken refuge in leaders who disrespect morality and religion? Or because Kali has influenced the administrators to create chaos in state affairs? Or because people have stopped following the rules and regulations for eating, sleeping, drinking, and mating—and now perform them wherever they want to?"

Bhumi seemed like she was almost ready to speak.

But Dharma further asked, "Are you sad because Lord Krishna left this world, and you now feel bereft of His company? What is the root cause? What has made you so weak? It appears that time might have forcibly taken away all your fortune."

Now somewhat composed, Bhumi tearfully replied, "Once you had four legs and, by the Lord's mercy, you increased happiness all over the world." She then glorified Lord Krishna by naming forty of His transcendental qualities, such as compassion, cleanliness, contentment, equanimity, leadership, and magnanimity.

Dharma listened intently.

"I had been overburdened by the military divisions of the atheistic kings. But Krishna had them all killed and thus relieved me. Similarly, you too were in a troubled condition and could hardly stand, but Lord Krishna also relieved you. Then He finished His divine pastimes on Earth and returned to the eternal world. But recently, the evil Kali has begun spreading his influence again. That's what makes me grieve."

Bhumi paused for a few moments, recalling her greatest joy. "When the Lord was here, I was decorated by the marks left by His lotuslike feet—the flag, thunderbolt, goad, and lotus flower. Just when I was feeling so fortunate, the Lord left me. Now I'm feeling the pangs of separation from Him. When He walked over my surface, I would be covered by the dust of those merciful feet. Consequently, my hairs in the form of grass would stand up in ecstasy."

At that moment, Kali returned. He gazed malevolently at both Dharma and Bhumi.

Dharma became terrified as he remembered how Kali had, in the past, destroyed his three legs.

Kali began maliciously kicking Dharma's and Bhumi's legs.

In the distance, Emperor Parikshit, with his army, was riding on his chariot and heading towards them. Seeing Kali kicking the animals, he became upset and urged his charioteer to drive faster.

Kali raised his club and smashed it firmly against Dharma's one remaining leg. The bull became so frightened that he trembled and urinated.

Outraged, King Parikshit declared, "That rogue!"

Then Kali began clubbing Bhumi's legs, weakening her and making her cry.

Reaching the shore, Parikshit angrily shouted, "Stop what you're doing!"

Kali turned and saw the king gazing hotly at him.

Parikshit jumped off his chariot, hastened to Kali, and defiantly asked, "Who are you?"

"Me? I'm—I'm Kali," he said fearfully.

"Kali? Why are you trying to kill these helpless beings?"

"Why?"

"Yes. Don't you know that's illegal in my kingdom?"

"Yes, but—"

"But that doesn't matter to you, does it?"

Actually, it didn't.

"Have you forgotten that the cow is like a mother to us—providing us with life-giving milk and other products? And that the bull is like a father—helping us to produce life-giving grains?"

Kali couldn't care less.

"Look at you—dressed like a king but acting like a wretch! Do you think because Lord Krishna and Arjuna aren't around any longer, you can get away with this crime?"

Now Kali became anxious. Was the king going to punish him?

"You deserve to be killed for this!"

"Killed?"

"Yes!" The king turned to the bull and the cow. "You don't have to worry about him anymore."

Kali began to tremble.

When the king noticed that Dharma was standing on only one leg, he asked him, "Who cut off your three legs—and made you so miserable?"

Dharma hesitated to answer.

"You can tell me," urged the king.

Nodding pensively, Dharma said, "Well, it's hard to say."

"Why?"

"Because different philosophers give different reasons."

"Such as?"

"Some say one's own self is responsible. Others say superhuman powers are. Some say it's due to our past activities. And still others say nature is the culprit. So—why don't you decide."

King Parikshit was impressed. "By your answer I can tell that you're more than just a bull—you're Dharma, the personality of virtue."

The bull nodded.

"Originally, you had four legs, and they represented discipline, cleanliness, mercy and truthfulness. It appears that by Kali's influence, pride, lust, and intoxication have destroyed three of those legs. And gambling is now trying to destroy your last leg, truthfulness."

"Yes."

"Therefore, it's my duty to kill Kali!" Parikshit removed his sword from its sheath and raised it high.

Eyeing the sharp blade, Kali became terrified.

"And I will!" asserted Parikshit.

To save himself, Kali quickly removed his royal robes and crown and affirmed, "I surrender!" Then he bowed his head and folded his palms entreatingly.

Because it was not ethical for a warrior to kill a surrendered enemy, the king halted and smiled compassionately at him. He was smiling because Kali had revealed himself to be not a king but a low-class man—a coward who refused to accept Parikshit's challenge. "I will spare your life," said the king. "But you can't stay in my kingdom."

"Why not?"

"Because you influence people to become greedy, untruthful, thieving, treacherous, quarrelsome, and vain."

"But I—"

"No! You may not reside where my subjects live for the pleasure of God."

"All right. But then where can I live—without having to worry about you killing me?"

The king carefully considered the question. He knew that a surrendered soul must be given some shelter. Therefore, he replied, "You may live wherever gambling, intoxication, prostitution, and animal killing are going on."

"That will be fine, but—could you please give me one more place to stay?"

"Why?"

"Well, just in case I can't find any of the other places."

The king deliberated for a few moments. "All right. You can stay wherever there is gold."

"Gold?"

"Yes.

"Why gold?"

"Because lying, intoxication, lust, envy, and hostility usually exist there."

"Oh. All right."

"Now go—immediately!"

Kali, happy to have his life, ran away as fast as he could.

After this, King Parikshit restored Dharma's lost legs, and Bhumi became gladdened and productive. The king accomplished this by conquering all parts of the Earth and exacting tributes from various leaders. Reestablishing his rule and authority, he punished and replaced the miscreant princes who had allowed or encouraged their subjects to violate moral principles. Meat-eating, intoxication, gambling, and illicit sex were unqualifiedly prohibited throughout his domain. He also confiscated improperly used gold and engaged it correctly in religious sacrifices, ceremonies, and charity. Thus he helped all his subjects become receptive to spiritual enlightenment.

In whatever cities, towns, and villages the king visited, he continually listened to the accounts of the glorious deeds of his great ancestors—all devotees of the Lord—and of the remarkable exploits of Lord Krishna. Pleased by the singers and narrators of such glories, Parikshit awarded them valuable necklaces and clothing. When the king heard that the Supreme Lord, Krishna, who is universally obeyed, rendered various services to his Pandava relatives—as a chariot driver, messenger, friend, etc.—just as a humble servant would, Parikshit felt intense devotion to the Lord.

Although the king had allowed Kali to stay only in places where sin existed, he, in effect, had tricked him. After the king traveled over the earth and re-established moral principles everywhere, Kali could not find any place where gambling, intoxication, illicit sex, or meat-eating occurred. Thus, he had no place to stay and wreak mischief or havoc. Consequently, Kali had to wait a long time before he could again begin asserting his baleful influence.

CHAPTER EIGHTEEN

GAJENDRA FIGHTS THE CROCODILE

As soon as the elephant began to pray to the Lord for relief from its terrifying ordeal, something very beneficial happened. Similarly, if we wish to discover ourselves, it is useful to cultivate the habit of praying to God often.

Two bulging eyes eerily peeked out of the lake's transparent water. They were the crocodile's, as he waited angrily for Gajendra. Yes, today he would prove that the monstrous elephant wasn't invincible after all. Although other creatures—such as lions, rhinoceroses, snakes, and deer—usually fled on seeing the elephant, the crocodile was now ready to confront him and show him who really was the king of this territory!

But where was Gajendra? the crocodile wondered. *Why hadn't he yet arrived? This was his usual time for bathing and drinking.*

As the crocodile waited menacingly for the elephant, he glanced at the beautiful scenery around him.

The clear lake, adorned with golden lotuses, was a part of the god Varuna's garden. A sporting and frolicking ground for celestials, the lake was filled with swans, cranes, fishes, and tortoises. On the bank, there were beautiful trees that always bore colorful flowers, delicious fruits, and intoxicating fragrances. Multihued birds, flying here and there, merrily chirped enchanting melodies.

But where was Gajendra? What was keeping him?

Beyond the garden was the immense Trikuta Mountain—decorated with creepers and shrubs, studded with sparkling jewels and minerals, and splashed with refreshing waterfalls. Surrounding the three-peaked mountain was the famous ocean of milk, which had once been churned by the gods and demons and from which ambrosia had been produced.

In the distance, the crocodile heard stomping. *Was it Gajendra?* he

Gajendra begs for God's help

wondered. Then the thuds grew louder. And the ground began to tremble. He was almost sure it was the elephant king.

Or could it have been some other big elephant?

As the tread grew deafening and the ground quaked, the crocodile was certain—it had to be Gajendra. No other elephant had such a thunderous gait.

Followed by male, female, and young elephants, Gajendra emerged from a grove of blossoming trees and headed straight towards the lake. He was perspiring heavily, liquor dripped from his lips, and he appeared to be intoxicated and fatigued.

As the elephant reached the bank, the angry crocodile submerged and hid himself underwater.

Gajendra left his herd and plunged sportively into the lake.

Stealthily, the crocodile began paddling towards him.

Gajendra bathed himself completely, dispelling his fatigue.

The crocodile swam closer to Gajendra's front legs.

The elephant drank the cold, clear, nectarean water—mixed with lotus-flower and water lily pollen—until he was fully satisfied.

The crocodile was now only a few feet from Gajendra's front legs.

Unsuspectingly, Gajendra urged his wives and children to enter the lake and imbibe its waters. As they did, he sucked water into his trunk, raised it high, and cheerfully showered them all. Some of them played in the water and trumpeted with pleasure.

The crocodile quickly rose to the surface and furiously opened its mouth wide.

Gajendra raised one of his legs to walk forward.

But the crocodile clamped his sharp teeth into the elephant's ankle.

Gajendra screamed.

The crocodile bit deeper.

Gajendra screamed louder. He tried vigorously to free himself. He moved his leg back and forth and up and down.

But the crocodile held on tenaciously.

Gajendra tried to drag the crocodile here and there.

But the reptile's teeth remained tightly fastened.

Gajendra jerked his body this way and that way—kicking, splashing, twisting, and falling.

But the crocodile refused to let go.

Seeing Gajendra in that grave condition, his wives began to weep. All they could do was watch, wait, and hope that he would somehow free himself. But they were sorely disappointed. For days passed without any change...then months...then years...then centuries...then a millennium.

It seemed like the battle would last forever. But Gajendra's strength and enthusiasm finally began to wane. And why not? He had been out of his natural element—the forest—for such a long time. And he had not even eaten a morsel since his ordeal had begun. On the other hand, the crocodile was in his natural habitat, so during momentary pauses in the fight, he had been able eat things. This increased his power and fervor. He was sure now that he would triumph.

Gajendra realized he was in serious danger and became greatly afraid of dying. So he stopped fighting and thought, *None of my elephant friends or relatives have been able to rescue me. I think this situation was arranged by Providence. Therefore, what choice do I have now but to take shelter of God? He's the shelter of great saints and sages. Maybe He'll also help me. No one is more powerful or merciful than He. Therefore, I surrender to Him and beg for His mercy.*

Gajendra then meditatively fixed his attention on his heart. Suddenly, and greatly to his surprise, a Sanskrit mantra bubbled into his consciousness. In his entire life, he had never uttered such a mantra— had never even heard it from anyone—yet now, in his mood of utter helplessness and desperation, he mentally recited it: "*Om namo bhagavate tasmai* [I offer my respectful obeisances to the Supreme Lord Vishnu]."

How was this happening—a dumb elephant uttering a holy Vedic mantra?

In his previous lifetime, Gajendra was the famous King Indradyumna. He had been the monarch of Pandya, which was in the South Indian province of Dravida. When the king had retired from family life, he journeyed to the Malaya Hills and built a modest cottage there in which he practiced spiritual austerities. He let his hair grow long and matted, wore a loin cloth and tree bark for clothes, and worshiped and meditated regularly on Lord Vishnu. One day, while observing a vow of silence, he was worshiping God and experiencing ecstasy.

At that moment, on a surprise visit, the great sage Agastya arrived, surrounded by his disciples. The holy man entered the ashram and, seeing the king seated, smiled and greeted him.

But the king remained silent and indifferent, apparently too engrossed in his blissful worship to be concerned about the sage.

Agastya was surprised, for such conduct was a serious violation of Vedic etiquette. Perhaps if the sage had been far beneath King Indradyumna in spiritual status, there might have been some justification for neglecting him, at least temporarily. But Agastya was one of the greatest sages in the universe, so the king should have immediately stood up, folded his palms prayerfully, and then offered the sage obeisances. Next, he should have provided him with an appropriate seat, offered him drinking water, washed his holy feet, and provided him with foodstuffs. And last, he should have worshiped him with respectful and appreciative prayers.

But the king had done none of these. Therefore, Agastya affirmed, "Indradyumna is not at all gentle. He's degraded and uneducated, and he's insulted a Brahmin. I therefore curse him to enter the plane of darkness—and become a dull, dumb elephant!"

The sage quickly left the ashram with his disciples.

Having spiritual understanding, Indradyumna welcomed the curse as the Lord's wish—to correct and purify him. After the king left his physical body, he transmigrated to an elephant form in the Trikuta Mountains. Thus, by the Lord's mercy, Gajendra was now remembering what he had once known and practiced—how to worship and pray to God.

But what about the crocodile? Who had he been during his past lifetime?

There was once a king named Huhu who ruled on the Gandharva planet, where heavenly musicians called Gandharvas reside. One day he, along with several stunning damsels, went to Varuna's lake in the Trikuta Mountain. As the great sage Devala was taking his bath there, they decided to frolic in the water. Hearing them giggling and playing, the holy man became displeased by their lack of consideration and manners. But when King Huhu frivolously pulled Devala's leg—as a joke—the sage was highly incensed and cursed him to become a crocodile. However, because the king was truly repentant, the sage gave him a benediction that would materialize sometime in the future.

Gajendra's ankle was still between the crocodile's teeth. Because he had performed devotional service in the past, the elephant remembered how to worship and supplicate the Lord. With flagging strength and zeal, he prayed desperately, *My dear Lord, You are the ultimate cause of all causes and results, and are the witness of everyone and everything. You are the giver of unalloyed happiness and the master of the transcendental world. You are all pervading and the basis of all incarnations. You alone can give liberation and shelter to Your children. You personally appear in the minds of spiritually advanced souls. I therefore bow down to you again and again.*

Since You are all-powerful, I beg You to free me from this danger. If You do, I no longer want to be an elephant. It makes no sense. My body and mind are filled with ignorance. I want to be liberated from them. Please protect me and release me from this crocodile. You are my only shelter now. I therefore bow down to You again and again.

Gajendra was so exhausted and weak that he was about to collapse. The water was now around his chest...then his neck...his chin... He glanced up at the sky to take one last look at it.

And then he saw something far away. It was hard to discern what it was, but it was moving rapidly in his direction. It looked like an eagle—with someone riding on it. And on either side of the bird were several flying beings who looked like gods and sages. A moment later, he recognized the four-armed being on the eagle—it was Lord Vishnu, whom he had formerly worshiped daily!

In the water, Gajendra saw a lotus flower near his neck. He wanted to present it as a love offering to the Lord, but he felt so feeble and pained. Nonetheless, he would try. He limply grabbed it with the end of his trunk and agonizingly held it as high as he could. Then he thought, *O Lord Vishnu, master of the universe, I offer my respectful obeisances to You!*

Garuda, the Lord's eagle carrier, zoomed down quickly, landing right in front of the elephant. Then the Lord affectionately accepted the flower. Dismounting, he grabbed Gajendra's trunk and began pulling him and the attached crocodile towards the shore. There, the Lord hurled His whirling disk at the crocodile's mouth, cutting it into two pieces.

I'm free! Gajendra thought joyfully. *Free!*

The chief gods and advanced sages there praised Lord Vishnu and showered flowers on Him and Gajendra. In the heavenly planets, the residents celebrated by beating kettledrums, dancing, and singing.

Lord Vishnu immediately transformed the crocodile back into King Huhu. This was the blessing the sage Devala had given him after the

Gandharva had repented for his disturbing offenses. Deeply appreciating God's mercy, the king prostrated himself at the Lord's feet and offered him lofty prayers of glorification and gratitude. He then rose to his feet, respectfully circled the Lord, and again bowed down to Him. The Lord freed the king from all the pain he would normally experience in the future from his past sins. Thus, King Huhu returned to his Gandharva planet as a spiritually liberated man.

Lord Vishnu then glanced kindly at Gajendra. The elephant was instantly transformed into a servant of Lord Vishnu and resembled Him facially and bodily, as do many of the servants in Vaikuntha, the eternal world. He had four arms, carried a disc, club, lotus flower, and conch shell, and wore the same apparel and adornments as the Lord. Feeling intense appreciation and affection, Gajendra was speechless. He knew he could never repay the Lord for this merciful benediction. Thus, all he wanted to do now was serve Him forever.

The Lord said, "Persons can be freed from all future pain stemming from past sins by rising from bed at the end of night and meditating on My form, residence, adornments, companions, activities, holy rivers, incarnations, and saints. And if they recite the prayers you offered Me, they can reside in My eternal world at the end of their lives."

Lord Vishnu then blew His conch shell and urged Gajendra to mount Garuda, which he did. After the Lord also mounted, Garuda flew into the shining sky and headed for the Lord's residence, where Gajendra would serve Him eternally.

Whoever hears this narration becomes qualified to be promoted to the planets where spiritually advanced souls dwell. Such persons become known as devotees of God, they are unaffected by the evils of Kali-yuga [the present age of quarrel and ignorance], and they never experience nightmares. Therefore, those who desire their own welfare should recite this narration.

King Chitraketu is shocked by the news

CHAPTER NINETEEN

KING CHITRAKETU'S AWAKENING

The king became miserable because he had become too possessive. Unless we become detached from our possessions—and understand that God is the true owner of everything—we will not only become unhappy but also unable to discover our true selves.

King Chitraketu was not just miserable but extremely miserable! And yet, from all appearances, it seemed that he had nothing to be miserable about. The earth was productive and his subjects were satisfied. He was handsome, magnanimous, and youthful. Born in a noble family, he had been fully educated and was exceedingly wealthy. And his numerous wives—they all had gorgeous faces, attractive eyes, and beautiful bodies.

Then why was he so miserable?

Because something important was missing from his life.

And there was nothing he could do about it.

He had tried to improve the situation by acquiring new wives—but to no avail. They had been unable to help him. Filled with anxiety and despair, he now felt that his throne was worthless. For unless he could solve his problem, both his subjects and his ancestors would be greatly displeased with him. Day after day, he brooded about what he could or should do to remedy the situation. But as always, he felt it was futile. Thus, his depression and despair deepened daily.

Then one day the eminent sage Angira, who travels all over the universe, paid the king a friendly visit at his palace. Chitraketu wondered whether the sage could help him overcome his problem. Rising from the throne, he offered Angira worship, drinking water, and eatables, and then seated him comfortably. The king respectfully sat on the floor beside the holy man's feet. He would wait for the right moment to broach the distressing subject.

"You are very humble and hospitable," the sage smiled.

The king bowed his head, deprecating his own importance.

"I hope that your body and mind, as well as your royal associates and paraphernalia, are well."

The king looked up curiously.

"I mean your guru, ministers, kingdom, fort, and treasury, as well as your warriors and friends."

"Oh yes, they're all well, my lord."

"Is everyone and everything under your control?"

"To my knowledge, they are."

"And what about yourself?"

"Myself?"

"Yes. Your mind—it seems disturbed."

The king nodded modestly.

"Was this caused by you or by others?"

"My lord," the king began helplessly, "you're a great yogi. So—I'm sure you know better than I."

"Still—why don't you tell me what's bothering you?"

The king nodded, paused for a few seconds, and began. "I have no interest in my empire, my wealth, or my possessions, because—" Chitraketu hesitated, finding it difficult to speak.

"Yes?"

"Because I have no son."

"No son?"

"All my wives are barren!"

"All of them?"

"Yes. Who will inherit my throne? And when I die, who will perform my funeral ceremony? And each year after that, who will perform my shraddha ceremony—so that I and all my ancestors continue advancing spiritually?" The king shook his head hopelessly, then looked up at the sage pleadingly. "Can you help me—to get a son?"

Angira smiled compassionately. He asked the king to bring various sacrificial ingredients, as well as his most favored queen. Then the sage performed a sacrifice by offering oblations of sweet rice to the god Tvashta. Next, he offered the sacrificial remnants to Queen Kritadyuti, who eagerly ate them. Looking at Chitraketu, he said, "My dear king, she will bear you a son."

The king and the queen gazed at each other happily. Then Chitraketu said to the sage, "O my lord, thank you! Thank you so much! You have no idea what this—"

"Just a moment," interrupted Angira.

"Yes?"

"Please keep one thing in mind: your son will bring you joy—but he will also cause you sorrow."

And without saying another word, the holy man abruptly left.

The queen curiously asked her husband, "What did the sage mean by—'joy and sorrow?'"

"Probably that we'll be joyful when our son is born."

"And what about our sorrow?"

The king considered this. "Probably because he'll be our only son, he'll become proud of his great wealth and empire. And he'll probably be very disobedient to me."

"Oh…"

"But what difference does it make? A disobedient son is certainly better than no son at all." Swept up in the elation of the moment, Chitraketu had no idea of what he was saying. If he had, he might have had second thoughts about having a son.

Shortly after the king and queen had sexual intercourse, Kritadyuti conceived, and in due time, she gave birth to a son. When all the residents of the state of Shurasena, the king's capital, heard the great news, they became extremely jubilant. "Long live the prince!" echoed in every house and street.

After bathing and adorning himself, the king engaged learned Brahmins to bestow blessings on the child and perform his birth ceremony. Chitraketu donated gold, silver, garments, ornaments, villages, horses, elephants, and many cows to those Brahmins. And to assure his son's reputation, wealth, and longevity, he contributed everything desirable to everyone else in the kingdom. Every day the king's and queen's affection for their son increased greatly. But when the monarch's other wives saw his son, they became very disturbed, for they too wanted to have one.

Gradually, Chitraketu lost affection for and interest in his barren queens. Because the king neglected and slighted them, they pitied themselves and envied Kritadyuti. Their chronic affirmation was, "How unfortunate we are!" Consequently, day after day, their jealousy of Kritadyuti intensified. They all wondered, *How can we regain the king's affection? Was it even possible?*

One day Queen Kritadyuti entered the palace playroom where her son was lying in a crib. "Sleep well, my son," she said, passing by him. Several feet away, she turned back and smiled at the boy. "I love you!" she said, her heart bursting with maternal joy. She left the room and busied herself with other household duties for several hours. Then, in the sitting room, she ordered the nurse, "Would you please bring my son here?"

"Certainly, O Queen."

Smiling, the nurse proceeded to the playroom and then to the child's crib. Looking down, she amiably said, "Oh, what a big sleeper you are. Well, you're going to grow up to be a big, strong king. And everyone will say, 'What a great king you are—just like your father!'" She leaned over the crib. "Isn't that so? Of course it is!"

A few moments later, the queen heard the nurse sobbing convulsively and crying out loudly, "Now I'm doomed! Finished!" Kritadyuti wondered what had happened to make the nurse so hysterical. Curiously, she wandered into the playroom and saw the nurse writhing on her back and striking her chest repeatedly. Hastening to her, she asked, "What's wrong?"

But the nurse was unable to speak.

"Tell me what's wrong!" she asked, kneeling beside her.

"Your—your—"

"My what?"

"Your son—"

"What about him?"

"He's—he's—"

"He's what?"

But the nurse's sobs became so convulsive that she could not speak.

Kritadyuti stood up and hurried over to her boy's crib. Looking down at him, she saw nothing strange or unusual. He was fast asleep—finishing his daytime nap. So why was the nurse sobbing? Suddenly, Kritadyuti noticed something curious. His eyes, her son's eyes—they were slightly open and looking upwards. *He probably just woke up*, she thought. *Of course.* "Did you have a nice sleep?" she asked him. "Hm?"

The boy didn't seem to hear her.

She reached down and clutched his arms: they were icy. A horrid suspicion loomed in her mind. *Ridiculous!* she argued. But to make certain she was correct, she placed her palm above her son's nostrils.

Hoping she would feel his breath, she discovered—he wasn't breathing! This filled her with anxiety, so she placed her hand over his heart. There was no heartbeat! Now she knew why the nurse was grieving so profusely. "He's dead! My son's dead!" she screamed. And she collapsed on the floor, unconscious, her hair and the flowers adorning it scattering. When she regained consciousness, she wept and wailed uncontrollably.

Hearing the loud crying, all the palace residents, including the king's other queens, entered the playroom. When they learned what had happened, they became equally aggrieved and sobbed heavily. After the king was informed, he became almost blind from grief. Surrounded by his ministers, officers, and learned priests, he blundered into the playroom and approached his son's body. Gazing at it, the king fell to the floor unconscious, his hair and clothes disarrayed. Upon regaining consciousness, he stood up, wept heavily, and was speechless.

When Chitraketu could finally talk, he looked at his wife. "How did this happen?"

She shook her head, indicating she did not know.

The king looked at all the sad faces assembled there. "Do any of you know?"

Everyone shook his or her head.

"How could this happen?" he asked. "He was only a child. He was happy, healthy. There was nothing wrong with him. A child like that doesn't just suddenly die."

They all nodded sympathetically.

"There must be some reason." He looked up towards the heavens. "Why, God? Why?" Then his head dropped as he began sobbing again.

Several minutes later, as the king and queen were bemoaning their fate, along with everyone else in the kingdom, the sages Angira and Narada suddenly appeared in the playroom. Seeing them there, everyone respectfully knelt and bowed down to the floor. Raising his head but still kneeling, King Chitraketu pleaded, "Help me, O sages. Please help me."

"Yes, that's why we have come," said Angira. "This is my brother Narada."

The king and queen bowed their heads to him. Then, looking up, and in a quavering voice, the king asked, "Why—why has my son died?"

"Did you think he was going to be here forever?" Angira inquired.

"No, but—" Chitraketu felt helpless.

"Nothing in this world is permanent—even though we act as if it were."

"Yes, that's true, but—"

"And you—like everyone else—have forgotten that. Therefore, you're now surprised and aggrieved."

"But—he was only a child."

"True, but children also die. Don't they?"

"Yes, they do, but—why should my child die?"

"For the same reason that any child dies."

"His karma?"

"Yes. He was destined to leave this world early."

The king nodded glumly.

"And you were destined to suffer as a result of that."

"From some sinful action I performed in my past?"

"Of course. You once caused someone grief."

"And—I never atoned for it?"

"Correct. So today you experienced the same grief you caused."

The king nodded, still feeling very morose.

"But there is an even deeper cause for your grief."

"And what's that?"

"You don't know who you are."

"I don't understand."

"You think you're your material body."

"My material body?"

"Yes. And because it brings you pleasure, you've become attached to it."

The king nodded, realizing it was true.

"You see your son as an extension of your material body, don't you?"

"I—I guess I do."

"And since he brought you lots of pleasure, you've become attached to his body also."

Chitraketu agreed.

"Therefore, you're miserable because you feel as if a part of you— a part that brought you much joy—has died. Isn't that so?"

"Yes, I feel as if I'm half dead!"

"That's because you have failed to identify yourself with your eternal soul."

"My soul?"

"Yes. Once you identify yourself with your eternal soul, you'll realize that your son is not his material body but is also an eternal soul."

"But—"

"So if he's eternal, you have nothing to lament about—since he really hasn't died. Isn't that so?"

"Then where is he? Why isn't he here—in his body?"

"Because his karma made him leave this body and has sent him on to another body—where he'll work out another set of karmic reactions."

"I—I just find it difficult to accept his loss. I wish I could, but I can't." The king again began to weep.

Narada placed his hand sympathetically on the king's shoulder. "Perhaps I can help you."

"I don't think so," said the king.

"Come with me," said Narada. He walked to the child's body, which was on its back on a blanket. Then he sat down on a cushion facing the little boy. "Everyone come closer."

Everybody there gathered around the sage and wondered what he was about to do. Was he going to recite some prayers for the well-being of the child's soul? Or was he about to perform some religious rite for the tranquillity of all the aggrieved? It all seemed so mysterious.

Narada closed his eyes for a few moments and meditated on the deceased child. Then he began to speak to it. "Oh, living being, please return to your body."

The king and queen looked at Narada with astonishment. Everyone else looked at each other curiously and then back at the sage. Was this some type of prank? Was the sage mocking their bereavement? Or was he about to—? The proposition was preposterous! And yet...

"My best wishes to you," Narada said to the child.

The child's eyelids began to blink.

"Just see your father, mother, relatives, and friends—they're overwhelmed with grief because you've left them prematurely. You still have a long life ahead of you. So why not enjoy it with your friends and relatives? And become the next king."

The child slowly sat up.

The king and queen, as well as everyone else, were mystified.

The child looked at the king and queen, then back at Narada. "I've been reborn many times in many species. And I've had many mothers and fathers. Therefore, how can I accept these two persons as my only parents?"

The king and queen were incredulous. They wanted to hug their child, show him their love, yet they found themselves unable to. For the child sounded very much like a disinterested philosopher.

"Although people come together," the child continued, "and form many different relationships, all these relationships are temporary and therefore illusory. The only real thing is the soul—because it's eternal and imperishable. Its quality is the same as the Supreme Lord's. And it can't be affected by friends, enemies, well-wishers, or mischief-mongers; for it's only a witness, an observer of the different qualities of people."

Chitraketu and Kritadyuti were stunned, for they had never before heard their child speak this way. What had happened to that adorable little boy they had loved and hugged so frequently? Was this the same boy? They could scarcely believe it.

"And finally," the child resumed, "the soul is part and parcel of the Supreme Soul and never dies. Thus, none of you have anything to grieve about. I'm not dead and I never will die. So stop crying." The child then closed his eyes, lay back on the blanket, and again apparently died.

Chitraketu and Kritadyuti, grasping the meaning of their son's words, stopped lamenting. They realized that the only real relationships that exist are those with the Supreme Lord and with the devotees of the Lord. This is because such relationships are permanent, based on serving and glorifying God rather than on serving and glorifying one's body and mind. They further understood that they had regarded their child as their own possession meant for their own pleasure instead of as the Lord's possession meant for His pleasure. They now accepted that God was ever free to do what He wanted with His own possession—whether giving it to or taking it from them. Thus reconciled to their fate, they cut the shackles of their false affection and attachment for their son.

Then suddenly, several of the king's other queens burst into loud sobs.

"What's the matter?" asked Chitraketu.

"We—we—"

"What?" asked the king.

"Poi—pois—" they sobbed.

"What are you saying?"

"We poisoned—we poisoned your son."

"What?!" He and everyone else there were shocked.

The king waited until their sobbing subsided and asked, "But—why?"

"Because—we were jealous. When Kritadyuti gave birth, you gave her all your attention."

"We felt neglected...abandoned."

Chitraketu wanted to chastise and punish them for their heinous act. They had no right to kill his only son. It was wrong—totally wrong. Yet, after considering the wise words with which the sages had blessed him, he refrained from taking any action against his wives. He realized that by ignoring them and loving only Kritadyuti, he had aroused jealousy and violence in them. Therefore, he reasoned, the responsibility was partly his. Nonetheless, because his wives had committed a terrible crime and would have to suffer for it in the future, the king asked the Brahmins what the women should to do to prevent such suffering. The priests advised that his wives bathe in the holy Yamuna River and atone for their sin.

The sage Angira encouraged the king to consider who he really was—body, mind, or soul; to consider where he came from and where he will go after departing from his body; and to consider why he fell under the influence of grief. "In this way, try to understand your true position. By so doing, you will be able to renounce your useless attachment. You will also be able to renounce the illusion that this temporary world is eternal. Thus, you will gain serenity."

The sage Narada said, "O King, I will now give you a most sacred mantra. If you chant it according to my instructions, you will see the Lord directly in seven nights." After Narada instructed him, he and Angira departed for Lord Brahma's planet.

Chitraketu fasted and drank only water, as well as chanted the mantra continuously, for one week. Besides attaining control of the planet of the Vidyadharas (as a side benefit), Chitraketu became enlightened, experiencing face-to-face contact with Lord Vishnu. The king was instantly cleansed of all materialistic desires and illusions and was thereby established in his original God-conscious position.

Chitraketu became silent and solemn. He was filled with pure love for the Lord; thus, tears glided down his cheeks and his hair stood on end. The king humbly bowed down, then rose to his feet. He wanted to offer choice prayers, but his overwhelming ecstasy choked his words. Nonetheless, after awhile, he regained his speech and expressed beautiful prayers of glorification and gratitude. Deeply impressed, the Lord further enlightened Chitraketu by disclosing more transcendental knowledge to him. Then, as the king looked on, the Lord disappeared.

Whoever listens to this account of King Chitraketu from a pure devotee of God becomes freed from the miseries of materialistic existence. And whoever rises early in the morning and recites this story—controlling his mind and words, and remembering the Supreme Lord—will easily return to the spiritual world.

CHAPTER TWENTY

LORD INDRA FIGHTS VRITRA

After King Chitraketu mocked an incarnation of God, he was cursed to become a demon. We would do best to never mock exalted beings, but instead, praise and honor them. This will help us gain their favor and blessings, which can certainly help us to discover our true identity.

"O enemy of Indra, kill your foe immediately!" said the god Tvashta, offering oblations in the sacrificial fire.

As the fire blazed, a terrifying monster emerged from it. He was gigantic, blackish, and radiant, and looked as though he were ready to destroy the whole world. His beard, mustache, and body hair were rust-colored, and his eyes were as searing as the noonday sun. Holding his fiery trident, he looked invincible. As he danced and bellowed, he created frightening earthquakes. And when he yawned, he appeared to be trying to swallow the whole sky with his deep, cave-like mouth. His tongue was long and his teeth were sharp, and he looked as though he were licking up the stars and gobbling down the universe.

His name? Vritra.

Whoever saw the mighty demon anxiously fled from him.

But why had he been invoked to kill Indra, the leader of the gods? What had Indra done to deserve this? Had he committed some offense or sin to arouse such hostility?

It had all started some time ago, many years after Lord Vishnu had blessed King Chitraketu with His personal presence. One day the king had been traveling through space in the glistening airplane the Lord had given him. He then chanced to fly to a place where Lord Shiva was sitting in an assembly of illustrious saints and sages. As Chitraketu flew close, he noticed that Lord Shiva, while engaged in a discussion, was embracing his wife, Parvati, who was sitting comfortably on his lap.

Vritra is created to kill Indra

The king laughed loudly and spoke within Parvati's hearing range.

"Of all people, how can Lord *Shiva* do that? He's a great spiritual teacher—an instructor in religion. He's performed severe austerities and penance. He's the chairman of that meeting. And yet—he's acting like a shameless, low-class person. Even *ordinary* men embrace and enjoy their wives in *solitude*. This is truly amazing!"

Lord Shiva smiled and stayed quiet, as did the assembly members.

But Parvati, resenting the criticism of her husband, who was far more advanced spiritually than Chitraketu, became extremely angry. She thought, *He thinks he can control his senses better than Lord Shiva—and can now judge him! Hmph!* Then she sarcastically blurted out to the others, "Has this upstart just been installed as the king of morality—to punish 'disgraceful' persons like us? Have you great sages become too degraded to know that you should criticize Lord Shiva's 'improper behavior'?"

The assembly members sympathized with Parvati's outrage.

"Chitraketu is the lowest of warriors," she continued, "for he has the audacity to find fault with Lord Shiva! Why, even Lord Brahma and other gods meditate on my husband's feet. Lord Shiva is religion personified and the guru of the whole world. But Chitraketu thinks himself *so* saintly that he can afford to teach him. How proud and impudent! I must therefore punish him!" Parvati gazed at him with flaming eyes. "You will soon take birth in a sinful, demon family! Perhaps then you will never again offend divine persons!"

Chitraketu landed his airplane, alighted from it, and bowed before Parvati with great humility. Although he was powerful enough to counter curse her, he considered it more noble to forbear, especially in view of Parvati's exalted status as Mother of the universe and Mistress of the material energy.

His devotion quickly pacified and pleased her.

Sitting on his knees with his palms folded, Chitraketu said, "My dear Mother, I fully accept your curse. I don't mind it at all, since I know it's God's will. Under His direction, the gods give one pleasure and pain according to one's past actions."

Parvati was touched by his detachment and understanding.

"You need not excuse or relieve me from your curse. But please pardon me for whatever you think I did wrong. I'm very sorry."

After pleasing Lord Shiva and his wife, the king boarded his airplane and soared into the sky as they watched. Surprised that

Chitraketu was unafraid of the curse, they smiled admiringly. Lord Shiva said to Parvati, "You have just seen the greatness of Lord Vishnu's devotees. They never fear any condition of life and are uninterested in material happiness. For them, the heavenly world, liberation, and the hellish world are all the same. Their only interest is to serve the Lord—wherever they may be. They know they are souls, they see everyone else as a soul, and thus they feel peace and oneness with all."

Even though Chitraketu would be born among the demons, by the Lord's special grace, he would not lose his transcendental knowledge nor its practical application in life.

But what were the circumstances that precipitated his demonic birth? And how would this birth result in his obtaining the greatest blessing God could ever award?

On one of the heavenly planets, Vishvarupa was a priest of the gods. Having three heads, he used one to drink *soma-rasa*, another to imbibe wine, and a third to ingest food. From his father's side, Vishvarupa was related to the gods, and from his mother's family, to the demons (the gods' enemies). When he performed sacrifices, he offered clarified butter in the fire and audibly distributed some of it to the gods. However, he also secretly allocated a portion of it to the demons. When the chief god, Indra, discovered this, he became very fearful. Since the offerings gave the recipients immense strength, Indra was afraid that the demons might defeat him. He therefore angrily decapitated Vishvarupa's three heads.

When Vishvarupa's father, Tvashta, learned about this, he conducted a ritualistic ceremony to destroy Indra. Feeding the sacrificial fire with oblations, Tvashta affirmed, "O enemy of Indra, kill your foe immediately!"

It was then that the monstrous demon, Vritra, arose from the fire. He was none other than the reincarnation of King Chitraketu, who had been cursed by Parvati.

Seeing this terrifying creature, the gods and their soldiers, led by Indra, attacked him furiously. They pierced him with their arrows and other weapons, but Vritra easily swallowed them. Noting the demon's vast power, the gods were amazed and became depressed, losing their strength and determination. They therefore left the battle area and assembled together to try to please Lord Vishnu by worshiping Him.

They knew that if they could somehow satisfy Him, He might help them conquer Vritra. They therefore expressed beautiful prayers of glorification and appreciation, citing His numerous incarnations wherein He provided His devotees with protection and victory.

Pleased by their sincere entreaties, Lord Vishnu appeared first within their hearts and then before them. He was surrounded by sixteen personal servants who closely resembled Him. Although on their chests they did not have the Shrivatsa mark [a white hair] and the Kaustubha jewel, as He did, they were decorated with similar attractive ornaments. When the gods saw the Lord's beautiful eyes and smile, they were flooded with felicity and prostrated themselves before Him. Then they rose slowly and satisfied Him with prayers that were both humble and transcendental. They entreated, "O Lord, we beg that You kill the big demon Vritra. Please free us from the anxiety he's causing us. We seek the shelter of Your lotus feet."

Satisfied by their prayers, Lord Vishnu said, "O Indra, all good fortune to you. My advice is that you approach the great saint Dadichi. Since his body is very strong, you should ask him for it." The Lord told him what to do with Dadichi's body, and then disappeared.

The gods went to Dadichi's residence and asked him if they could destroy his body and use it for their special purpose.

After some discussion, he said, "Although my body is very dear to me, I'll surrender it for your higher purpose."

The gods nodded gratefully.

"I'll have to give it up sometime," said Dadichi, "so what difference does it make whether I do so now or later? It is better that I give it up now for someone's benefit. Otherwise, in the future, I may have to suffer from some misery." Dadichi then controlled his senses, life force, mind, and intelligence. Fully entranced, he departed from his physical body.

From Dadichi's potent bones, the architect of the gods, Vishvakarma, fashioned a powerful thunderbolt weapon for Indra that was invested with Lord Vishnu's special power. Surrounded by the gods and praised by the sages, Indra mounted his elephant carrier, Airavata, and shone beautifully. He was now ready to confront Vritra.

But could he kill the monster? He could never be sure till the battle ended.

At the end of the Satya-yuga [Golden Age] and the start of the

Treta-yuga [Silver Age], the gods were engaged in a furious battle with the demons. It was happening on the bank of the Narmada River on one of the heavenly planets. When the demons, led by Vritra, rushed onto the battlefield, they saw Lord Indra carrying his deadly thunderbolt. Surrounded by many powerful gods, Indra glowed so brilliantly that his effulgence was unbearable to the demons. However, many hundreds and thousands of demons resisted Indra's army. Like lions, they roared thunderously and undauntedly. These invincible demons, decked in golden ornaments, attacked the gods from various directions with clubs, bludgeons, arrows, barbed darts, mallets, and lances.

Greatly pained, the leaders of the gods fled in all directions. Some of the gods were covered by so many arrows that they could not be seen. Others cut the countless weapons of the demons into thousands of pieces. After awhile, the demons exhausted their weapons. So they hurled mountain peaks, trees, and stones, which the expert gods similarly split into fragments. Seeing that the gods were uninjured, the demons felt that their efforts were futile. They thus became frightened and lost their pride. Feeling weak, they abandoned their leader, Vritra, and began fleeing from the battlefield.

When Vritra saw this, he smiled and shouted out their names. Then he urged them, "Please listen—and stop running! Everyone must die someday! No one can escape death. So why not die a *glorious* death— by staying and fighting, as recommended in the scriptures?"

However, the demon commanders were so overwhelmed by fear that they rejected Vritra's words. Seeing their weakness as an opportunity, the gods ran and attacked the demon army from the rear. Confused and terrified, the demons fled here and there, as if they had no leader.

This sorely aggrieved Vritra. Unable to tolerate such adversity, he halted and angrily shouted, "O gods, these demon soldiers are useless— like stool! What's the point of killing them from behind—while they're running away? A hero never kills an enemy who's afraid of death. Such killing is never praiseworthy, nor can it elevate you to the higher planets. O puny gods! If you really think you're heroes, if you're not ambitious for sense pleasure—then fight with me!" Vritra then roared so loudly—like an angry lion—that almost everyone there fainted, as if smashed by thunderbolts. Many of the gods fearfully closed their eyes and grimaced.

Vritra grabbed his trident and trampled over the gods, the way an elephant crushes hollow bamboo stalks in the forest.

Indra hurled a big club at the demon, but Vritra caught it in his left hand and vehemently smashed it across the head of Indra's elephant. It made a horrendous sound.

The demons, and even the gods, glorified Vritra's prowess.

The elephant felt excruciating pain, spit out blood, was pushed back about fourteen yards, and then collapsed with Indra on its back.

Noticing that Indra's elephant was exhausted and injured, and that Indra himself looked especially gloomy, Vritra observed the ethic of not striking a disinclined combatant.

Indra dismounted and touched his elephant mystically, relieving its distress and healing its injuries. The elephant then rose to its feet, and Indra, holding a thunderbolt in his hand, was again eager to fight.

But so was Vritra. He laughed mockingly at Indra and shouted, "You killed my brother, who was your priest and spiritual preceptor. You killed him out of fear that we demons might become more powerful than you—and take away your royal position. You mercilessly cut off his heads the way a butcher kills an animal. Oh abominable wretch! How shameful, inglorious, and unfortunate you are! Even the cannibals will condemn you. When I pierce your stone-like heart with my trident, I'll be freed from my debt to my sinless, self-realized brother. And after you die painfully, the vultures will feast on your sinful body!"

Glaring at Vritra, Indra anxiously mounted his elephant and desired to silence the demon forever.

Suddenly feeling pangs of separation from Lord Vishnu, Vritra mentally prayed, *O my Lord, will I again be able to serve Your eternal servants who take refuge only at Your lotuslike feet? May I once more become their servant—so that my mind may always meditate on Your transcendental qualities and my body always perform loving service to Your Lordship? I want no power or freedom that might cause me to stop thinking of You and serving You. Although I am still attached to my family members, I really desire to be attached to You only. O Lord, please make this happen.*

Vritra spiritedly seized his trident, the points of which were like deadly flames. Summoning all his power, he hurled the weapon at Indra and roared, "You sinful rascal—now die!"

As the weapon cruised across the sky, it looked like a glowing meteor.

Even though the trident was hard to look at, Indra fearlessly flung his thunderbolt, cutting the trident to pieces and also severing Vritra's right arm. As the warriors moved closer to each other, Vritra, with his iron club, furiously smote Indra on the jaw and also struck his elephant. The blow was so jarring that Indra dropped his thunderbolt.

The various celestials who were observing the battle from the sky glorified Vritra's skillful attack; nevertheless, when they saw that Indra was in serious trouble, they grieved, "Alas! How terrible!"

Having dropped his thunderbolt, Indra felt ashamed and almost defeated. He did not want to call attention to his blunder, so he dared not retrieve the weapon.

But Vritra bellowed, "Go get your thunderbolt, Indra, and try to kill me!"

Indra, however, looked too morose to continue.

So Vritra exhorted, "Give up your gloom and keep on fighting! Only providence knows which of us will win." Vritra then gave Indra excellent philosophical and spiritual advice, for which Indra felt quite grateful.

"Your counsel is wonderful," said Indra sincerely. He then retrieved his thunderbolt and continued to laud the demon. "I can see by your discernment, even though you're in danger, that you're a perfect devotee of God. Although you were born as a demon, you are free from illusion and are spiritually advanced. So you're obviously swimming in the ocean of nectar."

The two equally matched combatants continued talking about devotional service to God for awhile. Then, as a matter of duty, they resumed battling. Vritra whirled his iron club, aimed it at Indra, and hurled it fiercely. Indra flung his thunderbolt at it and not only split it into pieces, but also lopped off Vritra's other arm. In a strange way, Vritra looked quite beautiful, his bleeding shoulders resembling two waterfalls during a brilliant sunset.

The gigantic demon then placed his lower jaw on the ground and his upper jaw in the sky. His mouth was deep and his tongue was snake-like, and with his dreadful teeth, he appeared to be trying to swallow the whole universe. He then shook the mountains and crushed the earth with his feet, as if he were the Himalayas walking about. Seeing Indra and his elephant, he gobbled them up, just as a huge python might devour an elephant. Then he sat down, crossed his legs, stopped all his bodily activities, and entered a yogic trance, or *samadhi*. As far as he was concerned, he had nothing more to accomplish.

However, Indra was protected by the Lord's invincible armor and by his own mystic power, thus he did not die in the demon's stomach.

Using his thunderbolt, he ripped through Vritra's abdomen and emerged unscathed. Indra then hurled his thunderbolt at Vritra's neck. And although the weapon spun rapidly, his neck was so resistant that it took 360 days—nearly a complete year!—to decapitate him. At that final moment, Vritra's head tumbled lifelessly to the ground.

The Gandharvas and Siddhas in the celestial planets joyfully pounded kettledrums and showered down flowers, praising Indra with boundless joy.

Then the soul that had inhabited Vritra's body emerged from it, like a spark, and soared majestically up to the eternal world. There, he would become a perpetual companion of the Supreme Lord Vishnu.

But how could Vritra have been killed?

When his father, Tvashta, had first performed the ritualistic ceremony to invoke him from the fire, he had chanted, "O enemy of Indra, kill your foe immediately!" Therefore, Indra, and not Vritra, should have been killed. But why did the opposite occur? Simply because Tvashta had made a slight mistake in his pronunciation of the mantra. This changed it to mean, "O Indra, who is an enemy, kill your foe immediately!" Thus Vritra, and not Indra, was killed. But this entire scenario—from King Chitraketu insulting Lord Shiva to Parvati cursing him to become a demon—had all been secretly arranged by Lord Vishnu. This was done to burn away the last of the king's karmic reactions and then mercifully bring him to the eternal world, where he would joyfully reside forever.

After Indra killed Vritra, he was filled with the sin and the guilt of having killed a Brahmin. Thus he did not feel happy. Suddenly, he saw Punishment Personified before him in the form of an old, trembling woman wearing bloody garments and breathing a fishy odor. Although Indra hurried away from her, she hastened after him crying, "Wait! Wait!" Indra then fled to the sky, but the woman chased him even there. In fact, wherever he ran, she followed him. Finally, he went to the northeast and entered the Manasa-sarovera Lake. Invisible to everyone, he lived in the lake in the subtle fibers of the stem of a lotus for one thousand years. Indra's sins could not disturb him there, for he was protected by Lord Vishnu's wife, the goddess of fortune, who resided in the lotus clusters.

The celestial priests then summoned Indra back to the heavenly realm. When he arrived there, they reinstated him in his royal position.

The Brahmins then initiated him into a horse sacrifice meant to please Lord Vishnu, and Indra worshiped the Lord strictly during the entire performance. Consequently, his grave sin of killing a Brahmin was immediately nullified, and he was relieved of having to experience any future punishment for it. Once again, he was grandly honored by everyone in heaven.

By reading this story, we will be freed from all punishment normally awarded for immoral acts, will conquer our enemies, and will increase our duration of life. Moreover, we will have keen sense perception, will increase our wealth, and will expand our reputation. Because this story is auspicious in every way, learned scholars regularly listen to and repeat it on every festival day.

CHAPTER TWENTY-ONE

YOGI SAUBHARI'S DOWNFALL

After Yogi Saubhari offended one of God's illustrious devotees, he was too proud to apologize and repent: thus, he suffered greatly. If we offend anyone, we should be humble enough to apologize and repent; otherwise we may find great difficulty in trying to discover our true selves.

Seething with fury, Yogi Saubhari resolutely uttered a curse: "From this day on, if Garuda comes to this river to catch fish, then—and I say this with all my power—he will immediately be killed!"

Though Garuda looked like a giant eagle, he was actually a highly advanced devotee of Lord Vishnu. More intelligent and powerful than any god or yogi, he was entrusted with the service of carrying God on his back wherever the Lord wanted to travel.

But why was the yogi so enraged?

Yogi Saubhari, quite elderly, possessed many mystic powers. He exhibited one of them daily by submerging himself under the water of the Yamuna River and meditating there. Garuda would often go to that river to catch fish to eat. Sympathetic towards the fish, the yogi one day firmly said to Garuda, "You're disturbing the fish, so don't come here anymore."

"All right," said Garuda.

Although the Lord's devotee was not obliged to follow the yogi's order, he acquiesced out of respect for him. However, before leaving, he decided to have one more meal. Seeing a whopper of a fish—larger than any he had caught so far—he glided down to the water, opened his talons, and grabbed it firmly.

Seeing that Garuda had disobeyed him and had taken the leader of a school of fish, Saubhari was infuriated. He therefore cursed Garuda that if he took another fish, he would be killed.

Now if Garuda were just some ordinary eagle, such a curse might be

Yogi Saubhari is aroused by flirting fish

proper and effective. But since Garuda was the personal carrier of the Supreme Lord—an extremely lofty position—and was inordinately powerful, he was not subject to the yogi's order or curse. Moreover, whatever Garuda did, he did with God's approval, for he perfectly knew the Lord's will.

Although Garuda did not retaliate against the yogi, the Lord was deeply disturbed by this offense against His devotee. He therefore decided to punish the yogi and teach him a lesson. That day, while Saubhari was underwater, he opened his eyes and looked at his fish friends. As they swam about in front of him, he paternally thought, *You don't have to be afraid of Garuda anymore. He'll never touch you now.* The yogi felt very proud, considering himself their great benefactor.

Saubhari had been a celibate monk for many years, and he had planned to remain one. He had no need for sex now, for he regularly experienced the bliss of meditation. Nor did he care to have any children, for they would simply be a distraction from his joy. Moreover, becoming involved in family life might hinder him from acquiring more mystic powers. Thus, he felt quite satisfied in his life of abstinence and solitude. And he assumed that this would continue.

Suddenly he noticed two fish playing with one another. The yogi smiled. The fishes appeared to be exhibiting reproductive behavior. Saubhari closed his eyes and tried to return to his meditation. But he couldn't. Some uncontrollable force compelled him to keep watching the two fish. So he opened his eyes and gazed at their playful antics. Again he closed his eyes, determined to meditate. But his curiosity about the fish was now so strong that he had to open them again. As he watched the two fish playing, he wondered what they were feeling. "This is ridiculous!" he told himself. "I'm above all this. I don't need sex!"

Again and again, he opened and closed his eyes, each time more agitated by the fish playing with each other. And the more he suppressed his longing, the more stimulated he became. Finally, he could no longer restrain his desire—it was just too overwhelming! He wondered why he now felt so weak, conquered, and enslaved. Never before had he experienced such helplessness. Thus, he would have to do something about this.

The yogi emerged from the water and hastened to the palace of King Mandhata. The monarch happened to be emperor of the world and was now seated on his throne in the greeting chamber. Seeing the yogi, the king welcomed him respectfully and offered him hospitality. Saubhari then said, "If you don't mind, I would like to have one of your daughters for my wife."

"Your wife?" Mandhata was surprised.

"Yes. I'm sure, out of your fifty daughters, you can spare one."

Now if Saubhari were a strapping young prince, the king wouldn't have hesitated for a moment. But the ascetic was quite aged—his hair gray, his skin slack, and his head always trembling. To offer one of his daughters to the yogi would be like subjecting her to a curse. What kind of a future could she hope for with such an old man? And could he even give her a child? The proposition was absurd, so the king diplomatically replied, "O Brahmin, it is for my daughters to select their own husbands. I have no say in the matter."

The yogi nodded and returned to his thatched hut. He knew, by telepathy, that the king was opposed to offering him one of his daughters. Looking at himself in the mirror, Saubhari agreed, "Yes, I'm too old. Besides, I'm a yogi. So women don't particularly like me." But he would have to do something—and soon—for his sex desire was now driving him to distraction. However, as long as he continued to appear unsightly and decrepit, he knew he would never be able to satisfy his urge with a young wife. Thus, he wondered what to do.

After thoroughly considering the problem, Saubhari made a decision: he would use his mystic powers! Yes, he would transform himself into a young, handsome, vigorous man—one whom even a goddess could not resist, let alone a worldly princess. He therefore visualized the form he desired, meditated deeply on it, and then uttered a secret mantra. Next, he looked at his face in the mirror and could not help admiring his new, virile charm. "Let's see what the king has to say now," he said proudly.

When the ascetic again approached King Mandhata on his throne, he said, "I'm Yogi Saubhari."

At first glance, the king could hardly believe the yogi, for he looked too young. But on studying Saubhari's features closely, he stopped doubting. "How did you do it?" the king asked.

"I'm a yogi," said Saubhari, smiling.

"Is there something I can do for you?"

"I'm still interested in marrying one of your daughters."

"Oh?" The king was now delighted.

"Could I have a look at them?" the yogi eagerly asked.

"Of course."

The king had his personal messenger escort the yogi to the lounge of his daughters' quarters. The messenger then brought the fifty young, beautiful women before the suitor and asked them, "Which of you would like to marry Yogi Saubhari?"

Entranced by his manly beauty and heroic bearing, each of them shyly raised her hand.

The messenger looked at the yogi. "Which lady would you prefer?"

Saubhari studied each one of them carefully. All were paragons of exquisite beauty and virtue. Feeling that it would be shameful to disappoint any of them, he said, "If the king will allow, I'll take all of them."

"All? Are you sure?"

"Absolutely."

The messenger looked at the ladies. "Would all of you like to be his co-wives?"

They all nodded their heads eagerly. Each woman thought that even if she were to meet with him only once every fifty days it would be worth the wait—so charming and charismatic was he.

The messenger brought Saubhari back to the king and explained what had just happened. The king had no objection to the yogi marrying all his daughters, but he had one doubt. "Where were you thinking of living?"

"Living?"

"Yes.

"Well, I haven't thought about that yet."

The king wondered whether the yogi was planning to squeeze all fifty of his daughters into that one tiny thatched hut he dwelled in. "Until I know what kind of accommodations you'll offer my daughters, I'll have to withhold my approval of your marrying them."

"I quite understand." Saubhari closed his eyes for a few moments and chanted some mantras. Then he said to the king, "Come with me. I'll show you where your daughters and I will stay."

After a short drive on the king's chariot through the woods, Saubhari told the driver to halt. In front of them stood a huge magnificent palace—one that was more opulent than even the king's. Mandhata was astounded. "Where did this palace come from? Who built it?" he asked, for he had never seen it there before.

"A yogi," said Saubhari.

"What yogi?"

"Who do you think?" Saubhari said, smiling. "Now if you'll come with me, I'll show you around."

Stunned, Mandhata's eyes and mouth opened wide. The place beggared description.

As they passed through the golden gates, which were guarded by two dutiful sentinels, the king could scarcely believe his eyes. Stretching before them was a vast, scenic park. It contained tall trees, lush gardens, fragrant flowers, and fresh-water ponds. Birds chirped, bees hummed, and singers chorused. Inside the palace, there were opulent rooms, beds, seats, garments, ornaments, and baths, as well as attentive servants. There were also varieties of sandalwood creams, flower garlands, and scrumptious food and drink.

King Mandhata's head was reeling. Although he was emperor of the world, and although his own palace was certainly luxurious, compared to the yogi's, it paled into insignificance. Thus, his false prestige departed. Giving the yogi his highest respect, he said, "Yes, you may marry all my daughters!"

Shortly after, a grand wedding was held amid royal pomp and splendor. Everyone there happily celebrated the magnificent occasion with smiles and laughter. All the guests were impressed by the stunningly handsome groom and the fifty gorgeous ladies—and they gave them their heartfelt blessings. No one could stop talking about the yogi's splendid palace, which easily rivaled the palaces of the heavenly world.

In his household life, Saubhari engaged in sex frequently, making the transition from monk to "monkey" quite easily. Over a period of time, he gave each wife one hundred sons—who were now grown up—and which finally totaled five thousand. But after enjoying so much sense pleasure, he still was not satisfied. This was because he felt driven, badgered, and entangled by sex. The more he enjoyed it, the more he became addicted to it. Eventually, he had to conclude that he was a slave of it. Instead of his soul finding peace and freedom, it found only agitation and bondage. So many things easily upset him now. Thus, he wondered, what was the point of continuing like this? If he did, wouldn't his next lifetime be just as miserable?

Saubhari reflected on the simple life he had lived before he had been married. He used to regularly meditate on the beautiful form of God—in the quiet of the river. There were no screaming children and bickering wives, no ornate palaces and sparkling jewels. It had been just a humble life of transcendental peace and bliss. He had learned to depend not on sex for his happiness—but on the Lord alone. It had been such a fulfilling life, one that expanded and liberated him. But now— he felt contracted and imprisoned.

He wondered about how he had descended into this hell. Then he remembered—the two little fish! He had watched them playing with each other. Thus, his sexual drive had become aroused. He had known that he was not supposed to look at the fish. The scriptures clearly warned monastics against this. And although he had tried to stop himself from peeping, he had found himself helpless. Why? At other times, when he had seen birds or animals mating, he had been able to easily dismiss their activities from his mind. But why not *that* time?

Then he realized that the power of dispassion and detachment was a special gift given by the Lord. Thus, God must have withdrawn that power from him. The more he had tried to desist from looking at the fish, the more desirous he had become. Had he displeased the Lord in some way to warrant such disregard? If he had, he could not recall what he had done. But one thing he could remember—he had tried to overcome his strong sex desire by his own effort. He had totally for- gotten that this force was far more powerful than he—and that only with God's help could he overcome it. Then why had he not called on the Lord for help? Why had he tried to combat it by himself?

Pride, he concluded. *I was too proud to ask Him for help. I had acquired so many mystic powers that I had begun to think of myself as a god. I felt superior to everyone. So I felt no need to call on God.* He now understood that while he had been struggling with sex desire, had he begged the Lord for mercy, had he apologized for whatever offenses he might have committed, had he asked for forgiveness for those offenses, had he promised to try to rectify himself—the Lord might have bestowed His grace on him. But he hadn't done any of those things. Therefore, by his foolish pride, he had caused himself a life of suffering.

Thus, in a humble state of mind, Saubhari now prayed to the Lord for guidance. More than anything else, he wanted to be free of his worldly problems and stresses. He wanted to resume his devotional activities and ultimately enter the spiritual world. The Lord then informed him from within his heart exactly what he would have to do to achieve this. In response, Saubhari gathered his wives together in the sitting room and said, "I'm retiring from family life and going back to the forest."

The women began to sob, for they had become quite attached to, and dependent on, him. In fact, they could not live without him for a day, and they told him so.

"If you want to live as my sisters instead of as my wives, that will be all right. But our days of intimacy are over."

They all nodded, and one of them, speaking for all, said, "You're our only shelter."

In a short while, with only a few belongings, they left for the forest.

Saubhari then performed severe penances in a mood of devotional service to God. Day by day, as he prayed often and received the Lord's mercy, he purified himself of all materialistic desires and sensual interests. Experiencing the bliss of the Lord's holy company, he easily renounced sexual pleasure. After some time, he left his material body forever, assumed a spiritual body, and entered the eternal world.

But what about his wives?

Because they had been so devoted and faithful to him, and because they had assisted him in some of his spiritual practices, they also entered the divine realm. There, both husband and wives continued their service to the Lord forever.

Had the yogi not offended Lord Vishnu's great devotee Garuda, he would not have had to suffer as he had. Although the Lord can tolerate any number of offenses or blasphemies against Himself, He cannot tolerate even a fraction of offense against His pure devotees. This is because He loves them so dearly. Anyone who commits a wrong against them without offering a proper apology and without begging for forgiveness can expect to be seriously punished by the Lord—as Saubhari was. Nonetheless, after he had suffered enough, the Lord gave him the intelligence to understand the cause of his misery, as well as the means to overcome it. Accepting it gratefully, the yogi ultimately triumphed.

DAKSHA OFFENDS LORD SHIVA

*Because of his lofty position, King Daksha was exceedingly
proud; thus, he caused himself and others terrible chaos. We can
avoid creating such chaos in our lives by developing modesty
and simplicity. These qualities are extremely helpful to us in our
pursuit of self-discovery.*

A great sacrifice was about to be held by Lord Brahma's sons—the
forefathers who originally populated the world. All the great
sages, philosophers, and gods, along with their followers, had been
invited and were now seated in the arena. Several appointed Brahmins
sat around a sacrificial fire and chanted mantras, the smoke drifting
lazily into the clear sunny sky.

When King Daksha, the leader of the forefathers, entered the
assembly, he glowed like the shining sun, diminishing the splendor of
many of the other members. Seeing his luster, all the participants stood
up out of respect—all except Lord Brahma, the president of the
assembly, and his son Lord Shiva.

Noting that Lord Shiva had not risen, Daksha felt insulted. *Who
does he think he is? he* wondered angrily. *Has he forgotten that I'm his
father-in-law?*

Lord Brahma amicably welcomed Daksha, who in turn offered
proper respects to his father. But before sitting down, Daksha, seething
with indignation, shouted to the assembly, "O sages, Brahmins, and
gods—did you see what I just saw?"

Everyone wondered what he was referring to.

Pointing an accusing finger at Lord Shiva, he ranted, "Yes, my son-
in law—he refused to stand up and show me respect!"

Most of the participants glanced at Shiva and then turned back to
Daksha.

"Huh! He didn't even welcome me with pleasant words! Have any

Sati commits suicide

of you ever seen such shameless behavior?"

Some of the assembly members shook their heads regretfully. But the followers of Lord Shiva became incensed by this abuse.

"He has no manners whatsoever," Daksha continued, "so he's ruined all our reputations! And does he ever follow any rules or regulations? Never! And where does he spend most of his time? In filthy crematoriums, that's where! And who are his friends? Ghosts and goblins, that's who! I say he's a madman. Just look at him—he's practically naked. And look at his garland of skulls and bones, and the ashes of dead bodies smeared all over his skin. Is that *normal*? Why, he doesn't even bathe regularly! And sometimes he laughs or cries—without any reason."

Lord Shiva's followers were now enraged and could hardly restrain themselves.

"Yes, his name, Shiva, means 'auspicious'—but actually, he's the most inauspicious person around. That's why crazy people love him and follow him. And to think—I handed over my chaste daughter Sati to this monkey-faced madman. Why? Because Lord Brahma requested me to, that's why. It was only out of respect for my father; otherwise, I never would have. How dirty Shiva's heart is! Ehh! I've become impure just by looking at him!"

To emphasize his point, Daksha washed his hands and then his mouth. Next, he vengefully cursed Lord Shiva: "All the gods are eligible to share the oblations of this ceremony—all except Shiva. He's so low that he doesn't deserve to receive any. And he won't, either!" Daksha was so infuriated that he decided to leave the arena. As he proceeded, many members of the assembly tried to pacify and stop him, offering cogent reasons for him to stay. However, thinking that the place was greatly unfit for him, he shook his head disgustedly and returned home.

Lord Shiva's followers were furious. To them—as well as to all the great sages and saints there—Lord Shiva was the greatest devotee of the Lord. In fact, he was a partial incarnation of God and thus matchless in his spiritual splendor. And even though he associated with ghosts and goblins, this was solely for their benefit—to help elevate them spiritually from their gross state of ignorance. Though it was true that Shiva often acted unconventionally, he did this purposely to keep materialistic persons away from him so that he could fully absorb himself in devotional service to God.

Then why was Daksha so angry at Lord Shiva for not rising to greet him? Simply because Daksha's ego was hugely inflated and he wanted Shiva to inflate it even more by honoring him. Instead of regarding Lord Shiva as his superior—which he most certainly was—Daksha, because of his envy, referred to Shiva as his son-in-law (an inferior position). From a worldly viewpoint, that certainly was correct. But from a spiritual standpoint, Lord Shiva towered over Daksha—could even, in a sense, be considered his spiritual father. Thus, Lord Shiva was under no obligation to stand up and honor Daksha when he arrived, especially since Daksha envied and scorned him, being completely blind to Shiva's transcendental qualities.

Infuriated by Daksha's curse, Nandishwara, one of Shiva's chief followers, shouted out his own curse: "Whoever supports Daksha's envious views is not only stupid, but will soon lose his spiritual knowledge. Daksha has accepted bodily pleasure as everything. Since he's forgotten his knowledge about God and is attached only to sex, he will one day have the face of a goat. And those of you who support his insult to Lord Shiva will continue in the cycle of repeated birth and death—and remain attached to materialistic activities. You'll also lose your discrimination of what you should and should not eat, and you'll obtain money by begging from door to door just to please your body."

After this, the sage Bhrigu angrily counter-cursed Lord Shiva's followers: "Those of you who try to please Lord Shiva will definitely become atheists. You'll all be distracted from transcendental scriptural rules. How foolish you are—imitating him by growing long hair and subsisting on wine, meat, and other such things. You have blasphemed the Vedas and reviled the Brahmins—who abide by the Vedic principles—so you have already become atheists!"

Observing the unnecessary cursing and counter-cursing, Lord Shiva became very morose. He realized that the participants were not showing any concern for or interest in spiritual life. Thus, to stop them, he got up and left the sacrificial arena, his disciples following.

Nevertheless, as a way of worshiping Lord Vishnu, the forefathers continued the sacrifice for thousands of years. After its completion, all the gods who had been engaged in it took their baths at the confluence of the Ganges and Yamuna Rivers. Purified in heart, they then departed for their respective planets.

Years later, Lord Brahma designated Daksha as the chief of all the forefathers who had first populated the world. Daksha, in turn, became even more conceited than he had been. To increase his false prestige, he decided to perform a sacrifice called Vajapeya and to invite many illustrious sages, gods, goddesses, and celestials from various parts of the universe. Many of the invitees thus entered their spaceships and flew to Daksha's sacrificial grounds.

Lord Shiva's wife, Sati, was strolling near their ashram on Mount Kailash when she suddenly saw some white spaceships traveling nearby. She could see the celestial passengers—husbands and wives gorgeously attired and adorned—and hear them discussing various aspects of Daksha's forthcoming sacrifice. This was the first she had heard about it. As she thought about how beautiful those women looked—with their glittering earrings, necklaces, and bangles—she felt a strong urge to also dress up and travel with Lord Shiva to the sacrifice. But she wondered, *Would he be willing to go?*

Lord Shiva was sitting in their hut, chanting God's name. Sati entered it, sat down beside him, and anxiously expressed her desire. Then she wistfully added, "I'd like to wear some of the ornaments my father gave me when we were married."

"The ornaments?" he asked, wondering why this was so important, since she had fully adopted his ascetic lifestyle.

"Yes. How enjoyable it would be to see my sisters, my mother, and my other relatives at my birthplace."

"But—have we been invited?" He knew that they hadn't; thus, he implied that they were doubtlessly unwanted.

"Invited? Well, no, but—does it really matter?"

"Yes, I think so."

"Why? One doesn't need an invitation to go to a friend's, a husband's, a guru's, or a father's house."

Lord Shiva smiled affectionately and said, "Sati, what you have said is true. But that's only when the host *likes* having the guest and doesn't become angry towards him."

"What makes you think my father will be angry towards you?"

"Isn't that how he acted the last time he saw me?"

"Yes, but—that was a long time ago. Maybe he's changed."

"Then why didn't he send us an invitation?"

"It could have been an oversight."

"I really doubt that. I think it's best for us not to go where we're not wanted, because—"

"Because what?"

"Well, because it could become very painful for you."

"How?"

"Your father might insult you."

"But I'm his pet daughter, so why would he—"

"Doesn't matter."

"You really think he would?"

"Yes. Because you're married to me—and he hates me."

"Are you sure?"

"Absolutely. He envies me. That's why he hates me."

"But what does he envy?"

"My self-realization. He knows he can't reach that state—he's too identified with his body and too attached to sense pleasure."

"Hmm," Sati reflected.

After a few moments, Shiva gently said, "I don't think it's a good idea for us to go to the sacrifice."

Sati was now in a dilemma. She wanted to follow her husband's advice, but at the same time, she wanted to see her relatives. *What should I do?* she wondered. Unsure, she stood up and repeatedly walked in and out of the room. Feeling intense separation from her family, she began to weep. Afflicted and trembling, she looked angrily at her peerless husband. "I'm sorry, but—but—"

Lord Shiva stared at her. "Yes?"

"I can't stay here. I—I just have to see them!" Breathing heavily and reluctant to be checked by Shiva, Sati hastily walked into another room. She dressed and adorned herself in suitable clothes and jewelry, and then proceeded towards her father's domain. Seeing Sati leaving alone, thousands of Lord Shiva's Yaksha disciples quickly followed her, placing Nandi, the bull, in front. They arranged for her to be seated on a bull and gave her her pet bird. Covering her with a large canopy, they carried a lotus flower, a mirror, and other items for her pleasure. The whole procession, followed by a party of singers and musicians— playing drums, conch shells, and bugles—looked like a royal parade.

When Sati reached her father's place, the sacrifice had already begun. She entered the arena—which was surrounded by waving flags—and heard everyone chanting the Vedic hymns. Great sages, Brahmins, and gods were there, and there were also many required pots made of clay, stone, gold, grass, and skin. There were also animals which, after they would be killed, would be revived by priests who knew the secret mantras for giving them a new, young body.

Although everyone at the sacrifice recognized Sati, almost no one welcomed her. They knew King Daksha had practically disowned his daughter for being married to his supposed enemy Lord Shiva. Thus, afraid of displeasing Daksha, they deliberately ignored his daughter. However, her mother and sisters, being softhearted, gladly and tearfully greeted Sati. But Shiva's wife, keenly wounded by her father's indifference to her, did not answer them or accept the seat or the presents they offered her.

As the Brahmins offered oblations into the fire, Sati noticed that they did not utter the mantra "*namah shivaya svaha*," which meant that they were not offering any of the oblations to Lord Shiva.

Sati considered this neglect highly insulting. And so did Lord Shiva's followers. Therefore, they stood up and were ready to attack Daksha, but Sati ordered them to halt. Nonetheless, extremely angry and grievous, she cried out, "Father, of all beings, Lord Shiva is most dear! He's unrivaled and has no favorites or enemies. Yet you're envious of him—and are committing the greatest offense. Lord Shiva is pure, so he purifies the whole world. Though some of his adornments aren't auspicious, even great personalities like Lord Brahma honor him. Yes, they accept flowers that have been offered to his feet and respectfully place them on their heads."

As Sati railed, her anger grew hotter by the moment. "If somebody blasphemes the master and controller of religion, and if you're unable to punish him, then you should block your ears. But if you're able to kill the blasphemer, you should cut out his tongue and destroy him! Then you should give up your own life!"

Everyone looked at one another with astonishment. Was Sati serious—or was this her idea of a joke?

Fuming with rage, Sati yelled, "Father, you're an offender at Lord Shiva's lotus feet! Unfortunately, my body came from your body. And that makes my body contaminated. So I'm greatly ashamed to be your daughter. Yes, very much ashamed! Therefore, I have no choice but to destroy my body!"

Daksha glared at her with hatred.

Sati sat down on the ground and faced north. Dressed in saffron garments, she purified her body with water and closed her eyes. Then she carried her life force upward—from her abdomen to her heart to her throat to the point between her eyebrows.

Her father knew what she was doing. Yet, because he was so envious and hardhearted, he refused to intervene.

Due to fierce anger towards Daksha, Sati meditated on the fiery force within her body. Next, she meditated on her husband's sacred feet. Totally cleansed of all sin, she departed from her body, which suddenly burst into a blazing ball of fire.

Everyone was shocked.

"Oh, my God!" exclaimed one onlooker.

"How could she do that!" exclaimed another.

"I can't believe this!" remarked a third.

"Poor Sati!" affirmed a fourth.

Lord Shiva's disciples were enraged. They charged after Daksha, determined to kill him. But the sage Bhrigu, seeing this, immediately offered oblations into the southern side of the sacrificial fire. Then he uttered a powerful mantra from the Yajur Veda. And suddenly, from out of nowhere, thousands of mighty celestials, called Ribhus, appeared there. They grabbed the half-burned fuel from the fire and angrily attacked Lord Shiva's followers.

Seeing they were outnumbered, the devotees of Lord Shiva fled and disappeared in all directions.

Lord Shiva was sitting on the ground outside his ashram when one of his followers, who had been at the sacrifice, rushed over to him, bowed down, and wailed, "O lord, Sati is dead! Dead!"

"She's dead?" He was surprised and stunned.

"Yes! Because Daksha insulted her!"

"What?!"

The disciple described everything that had happened.

Lord Shiva became furious. Biting his lower lip, he twirled a lock of hair from his head around one of his index fingers. Then he yanked it out of his scalp and it blazed into a fire. Quickly standing up and laughing like a madman, he wrathfully hurled the strand of hair to the ground. When it hit, the fire transformed itself into a monstrous black demon named Virabhadra. He was as tall as the sky and he radiated light like three combined suns. His fangs were terrifying, and the hairs on his head resembled a blazing fire. He had thousands of arms—each hand holding a different weapon—and around his neck hung a grotesque garland of human heads. Carrying a huge, sharp trident, he wore ankle bells that, as he moved, seemed to roar.

The monster folded his palms and bowed his head to Lord Shiva. "What would you like me to do, my lord?"

"Since you have been born from my body, you are the chief among my followers." Shiva then told him exactly what he wanted him to do.

"Yes, my lord." The monster respectfully circled Lord Shiva and then led many raging soldiers to Daksha's sacrifice.

The arena suddenly became covered by an ominous darkness. Everyone wondered where it was coming from, but they soon realized it was from a dust storm. And yet—it was very mystical. One person said, "There's no wind blowing!"

Another added, "And there aren't any herds of cows passing!"

A third said, "It couldn't be from a band marauders—King Barhi would punish them!"

"Maybe the world is about to end!" said a fourth.

Suddenly Virabhadra appeared there, baring his dreadful fangs and roaring like thunder.

Many of the spectators were horrified. Amid the clamor and din, one of them exclaimed, "Oh, my God!"

"Who is he?" asked another.

"Looks like a monster!" cried a third.

"God save us!" prayed a fourth.

As the guests continued emoting anxiously, Daksha observed bad omens on the earth and in the sky.

Then Lord Shiva's followers besieged the sacrificial arena. Short in stature, they carried various weapons, such as swords and tridents. Their bodies appeared like yellowish and blackish sharks. Racing all around the grounds, they began to create numerous disturbances. Some of them threw down the pillars that were holding up the canopies, others went into the female quarters to frighten the women, some began destroying the sacrificial arena, and others entered the kitchen and residential quarters. They smashed the sacrificial pots, tore down the arena boundary line, and urinated on the arena itself. Some blocked the movements of the escaping sages, others threatened the ladies there, and some arrested the gods who were hastening from the canopied area.

Maniman, one of Lord Shiva's disciples, arrested Bhrigu; Virabhadra captured Daksha; and other assailants arrested some of Daksha's sympathizers. Then, as stones fell from the sky, the distressed priests and attendees, trying to save their lives, fled in all directions.

Bhrigu tried to offer an oblation into the sacrificial fire, but before he could, Virabhadra grabbed him and tore off his mustache. Then he seized Bhaga—who had joyfully moved his eyebrows as Daksha had cursed Lord Shiva—and threw him to the ground and plucked out his eyes.

Next, Virabhadra captured Pusha, who had smiled happily when Daksha had cursed Lord Shiva, and knocked out his teeth. Because Daksha had shown his teeth while cursing Shiva, Virabhadra bashed out Daksha's teeth. Then he sat on Daksha's chest and tried, with sharp weapons, to decapitate him. But Daksha's neck resisted the blades. Then Virabhadra tried to cut it with mantras. But that also failed. This puzzled the demon. Why couldn't he behead him?

Virabhadra noticed the wooden device used to kill the sacrificial animals. He dragged Daksha over to it, placed his head in it, and released the sharp, heavy blade. It tore right through Daksha's neck, lopping off his head. Virabhadra picked up the head and angrily tossed it into the sacrificial fire, offering it as an oblation.

Seeing this, Lord Shiva's followers cheered and applauded loudly. However, the few remaining Brahmins, who were in charge of the sacrifice, moaned and lamented. Lord Shiva's followers then devastated all the sacrificial arrangements and set fire to the entire arena. Their mission successful, they returned to Lord Shiva and brought him the good tidings.

Helpless and defeated, the gods and priests went to Lord Brahma's residence to obtain help. After offering him their respects, they related all the gory details of what had occurred. Lord Brahma replied, "Do you think you can be happy by offending a great soul like Lord Shiva?"

Ashamed, no one replied.

"If you do, you're greatly mistaken. Why did you exclude him from the sacrifice?"

"Daksha ordered it," said a priest.

"How foolish!" Lord Brahma exclaimed. "Do you have any idea of how powerful Lord Shiva is?"

Fearful, no one spoke.

"He is so powerful that just by his anger he can immediately destroy all the planets and their chief administrators! Yes, all of them!"

"So—what should we do?" asked one of the gods anxiously.

Brahma clearly advised them. "Do you all agree?" he asked.

"Yes, my lord," they answered.

"All right, then let's go."

When they arrived at Mount Kailash, they could not help admiring the attractive scenery. There were beautiful trees, flowers, forests, animals, birds, waterfalls, lakes, rivers, and bathing ghats.

Then they saw Lord Shiva. Sitting on a straw mat that was covering a deerskin—his left foot over his right thigh—he was shaded by a sacred tree. He wore a saffron loincloth, held prayer beads in his right hand, and was gesturing with his left hand. Surrounded by the celestials Kuvera, Narada, and the four Kumaras, he was discussing spiritual matters with them.

All the visitors approached Shiva, offered him their respectful obeisances with clasped hands, and then rose.

When Lord Shiva, Narada, Kuvera, and the sages saw Lord Brahma, they stood up and then bowed down and touched Brahma's feet reverently. Brahma then offered Shiva prayers of glorification, appreciation, and devotion.

Lord Shiva said, "Thank you, my lord," and offered seats to all the guests.

Having pacified Lord Shiva somewhat, Brahma said, "The gods and the priests are very sorry for the offensive way they treated you."

Lord Shiva nodded gravely.

"They promise not to let that happen again."

Shiva glanced at them and then back to Brahma.

"Without a doubt, you should have been offered a share of the oblations—even though the bad priests didn't offer you any."

Lord Shiva nodded indifferently.

All the gods and priests accompanying Brahma anxiously wondered whether Shiva would forgive them. Suppose he wouldn't. Suppose he demanded that they be punished further. And what punishments would he demand? These and other misgivings haunted them now.

Lord Brahma prayed, "I beg your mercy, Lord Shiva—that you may revive Daksha's life; that you may restore Bhaga's eyes, Pusha's teeth, Bhrigu's mustache, and the gods' and priests' broken limbs; and that you may please accept your portion of the sacrificial oblations—and allow the sacrifice to be finished; that is, if you no longer feel offended."

Lord Shiva replied, "My dear father, I don't really mind the offenses the gods committed. Since they are sometimes childish, I don't take their wrongs very seriously."

The gods and priests sighed with relief.

"But their punishment—why did you—?"

"I punished them to correct them," Lord Shiva interrupted.

"And quite well, I must say. But are you ready to answer the prayers I just offered you?"

Lord Shiva considered them for a few moments.

The gods and priests nervously awaited his decision. Would he resuscitate Daksha and the others—or would he just allow them to rot in hell? The suspense was overwhelming.

"Lord Brahma," said Shiva slowly, "here's what I will do."

Everyone leaned forward, listening intently to Shiva's every word.

"Daksha's head was burned to ashes, so he will have a goat's head."

Everyone's eyes opened wide with surprise.

"Bhaga will be able to see his share of the sacrifice through Mitra's eyes. Pusha will be able to chew only through his disciples' teeth; but if he's alone, he'll have to eat dough made of chickpea flour. The gods who agreed to give me my share of the sacrifice will recover from their injuries."

The injured gods present smiled gratefully.

"Those whose arms were cut off," Shiva continued, "will have to work with the Ashwini-kumara's arms, and those who lost their hands will have to work with Pusha's hands. And Bhrigu—he'll receive the beard from the goat's head."

All the culprits, knowing that Lord Shiva could have burned them to ashes with his glance, were relieved and satisfied by his merciful blessings.

"Would—would you—" Bhrigu began hesitantly, "go with us now back to the sacrificial arena?"

"Yes, of course," Lord Shiva smiled.

So the gods, accompanied by the sages, Shiva, and Brahma, went to the grounds where the sacrifice had been started. Lord Shiva gave specific instructions regarding the ceremony, and they were all carefully followed. The neck of Daksha's dead body was then joined to the head of one of the goats meant to be slain in the sacrifice. As if awakening from a deep sleep, Daksha then opened his eyes and immediately became conscious of Lord Shiva standing before him.

As Daksha looked at Shiva and felt his merciful glance, he immediately became aware of his offenses towards him. Realizing how powerful and pure Lord Shiva was, notwithstanding his unconventional appearance, Daksha felt deep regret for the way he had treated him. He had imagined that he was superior to Lord Shiva, but now he understood how foolish and wrong he had been. He realized that his transgressions had been caused by his burning envy of Shiva and his selfish love of himself. Thus, he felt not only sorry for having committed those offenses, but also determined to prevent them from ever occurring again.

As Daksha remembered his deceased daughter, Sati, who had committed suicide because of his neglect, his eyes flooded with tears. He wanted to pray to Lord Shiva for forgiveness, but his voice was now too choked up. After Daksha finally quieted his mind and composed his feelings, he entreated, "My dear Lord Shiva, I committed a great offense against you. But you have given me your mercy by punishing me. You and Lord Vishnu never neglect even unqualified Brahmins like myself. I had no idea of your glories, and therefore I offended you with my words in the open assembly. Yet you saved me by punishing me. Thank you, my lord. I can never repay you with words. So please be satisfied with your own mercy, which I'm sure fills you with constant joy."

After Lord Shiva forgave Daksha, the latter, with Lord Brahma's permission, restarted the sacrifice along with the sages, priests, and others. The Brahmins then purified the arena that had been polluted by Virabhadra and his companions. Next, the Brahmins offered oblations into the fire. When Daksha offered clarified butter into it, along with appropriate mantras, Lord Vishnu suddenly appeared there. He had eight arms and was seated on the shoulder of his eagle carrier, Garuda. His handsome body resembled a blossoming tree, and the goddess of fortune, along with a colorful flower garland, rested against His broad chest. Consequently, the whole atmosphere became so illuminated that everyone else's luster was diminished. Indeed, He captivated everyone's attention.

All who were there prostrated themselves before the Lord and then rose to their feet. After the Lord accepted the oblations offered to Him, Daksha prayed, "My dear Lord, You are transcendental and omniscient. You are fearless and in control of the material energy. Though You appear in this energy, You are definitely above and beyond it. Since you are fully self-sufficient, You are free from all materialistic contamination."

Then all the important personalities there offered their prayers to Lord Vishnu. And the Brahmins concluded, "Simply by chanting Your holy name, one can surpass all obstacles. Please accept our respectful obeisances."

Daksha then worshiped Lord Vishnu, Lord Brahma, and Lord Shiva. And of course, he did not forget to offer Lord Shiva his share of the sacrificial offerings. Completing all his duties with the priests, he bathed himself and felt fully satisfied. Thus, by this sacrifice, Daksha became solidly situated on the religious path. The gods there blessed him to increase in virtue, and then departed.

Sati was soon reborn in the Himalayan kingdom and again accepted Lord Shiva as her husband.

If one hears or recites with faith and devotion this story of Daksha's sacrifice as it was conducted by Lord Vishnu, one's life is surely washed of all materialistic contamination.

CHAPTER TWENTY-THREE

URVAŞHI ENCHANTS KING PURURAVA

When Pururava became obsessed by his wife's beauty and addicted to having sex with her, he never knew a moment of real peace. Therefore, if we desire to discover ourselves, it is helpful to develop some detachment from sex; otherwise, we may often become agitated and then diverted from our goal.

One day, in King Indra's celestial palace, the sage Narada described King Pururava's beauty, personal qualities, magnanimity, behavior, wealth, and power. On hearing the enticing description, the nymph and Apsara Urvashi was smitten by strong affection for him. Since she had been cursed by the gods Mitra and Varuna to live on Earth for some time, she left the heavenly world with her two pet lambs and journeyed to the Earth. There, she hoped to meet and marry Pururava, the son of Budha and Sudyumna.

With her lambs in tow, Urvashi entered the king's fragrant garden, where he was strolling leisurely and glancing at the flowers. When he turned towards the path, he was surprised to see her standing about twenty feet away. Instantly, he was mesmerized by her exquisite beauty. She had full lips, a raised nose, lotuslike eyes, and black shiny hair, strewn with flowers, that flowed over her shoulders and down her back. Her form-fitting gown emphasized her shapely breasts, small waist, and rounded hips. And on her neck, wrists, ankles, and ears she wore sparkling adornments.

When Pururava saw her strolling towards him and smiling alluringly, his eyes widened and his body hairs stood up. He was wearing only a dhoti and a *chaddar,* so his muscled chest, arms, and waist looked highly attractive. Never having seen a woman so lovely, he wondered who she was, what she wanted, and how she had gotten past the guards. As she approached him, he smiled and said, "Excuse me, but—do we know each other?"

King Pururava considers Urvashi's proposal

"I don't think so. My name is Urvashi."

"Urvashi?

"Yes."

"The Urvashi from—King Indra's court?"

"That's right.

"Well, welcome to my palace."

"Thank you."

"Is there—something I can do for you?"

She glanced at him romantically. "What do you think?"

"I'm not sure."

"Well, to be quite frank, I'd like to marry you."

The king smiled. "Any particular reason?"

"Yes. I heard about your nice qualities. And now I see them myself."

He smiled modestly, intoxicated by her fragrance and beauty.

"Are you interested?" Urvashi asked.

"Yes. Yes, I am."

"Good. But before we become intimate, I'd like you to promise me something."

"Such as?"

"These two lambs here—they're not only my pets; they're like sons to me."

"They certainly look very lovable."

"They are. But promise that you'll fully protect them."

"I'll be glad to."

"And my food—promise that all of it will be cooked in ghee."

"Sure. I'll tell the cook personally."

"And promise that you'll never show yourself to me naked—except when we're having sex."

"But—why would that bother you?"

"Because—quite frankly, I find it very uncivilized."

"Oh. Well, all right. I promise."

They didn't know it, but hiding behind a bush and listening to their conversation was a Gandharva named Vishvasu. He was certain that the information he had just gathered would be very useful in the future...

From that day on, Pururava intensely enjoyed Urvashi's company. By her mystic power, she transported him to many celestial pleasure grounds. Sporting sexually, they lived in the charming Chaitraratha Garden for ten years, in Alaka City for five years, in the Vadari Forest for six, in the Nandana Gardens for seven, at Uttara Kuru province for eight, at the foot of Gandhamadana Mountain for ten, and on the summit of north Sumeru for eight. Fifty-nine years of sensual delight!

One day King Indra was in his assembly hall with some Gandharvas. Noting that the curse under which Urvashi was living on earth was just about to expire, he said to them, "Without Urvashi here, my assembly is no longer beautiful. So think of some way to bring her back."

"I know a way," said Vishvasu, the Gandharva who, many years ago, had eavesdropped on the couple.

"Good. Then do it immediately."

Vishvasu left with a companion for Pratishthana City, where Urvashi and Pururava were now staying. Arriving at the palace at midnight, the Gandharvas secretly entered the royal bedroom and saw the couple sleeping. Urvashi's pet lambs were asleep at the foot of the bed. Each Gandharva grabbed the collar of one lamb and began dragging the animal out of the room towards the garden. As they did, the lambs began bleating fearfully. This awakened Urvashi. Observing the Gandharvas in the moonlight, she was both surprised and angry to see them kidnapping her pets.

"Stop!" she shouted.

But they ignored her.

"I said stop!"

"*Baaaaa! Baaaaa!*" cried her lambs.

The Gandharvas hastened into the garden.

Urvashi turned to Pururava and shouted, "They've kidnapped my sons!" Seeing that he was too steeped in slumber to hear her, she shook him forcefully. "Wake up! They've kidnapped my sons!"

The king opened his eyes drowsily. "Who? Wha—?"

"The Gandharvas!"

"G'dharvas?"

"Yes, you coward!"

This brought the king to his senses.

"Coward! Eunuch!"

"What's wrong? What's—"

"You said you would protect my lambs, but the Gandharvas just kidnapped them!"

"What?!" He could hardly believe it.

"Look at you—lying there in fear, like a woman!"

"Stop it," he declared.

"No, you stop it—pretending to be a man during the day but acting like a woman at night!"

His heart pierced by Urvashi's words, he scrambled to his feet, grabbed his sword, and, wearing no clothes, rushed out to stop the Gandharvas.

"*Baaaaa! Baaaaa!*" cried the animals in the distance.

Following the sounds of the lambs, Pururava raced through the vast garden. When he saw their outline, he hastened faster till he caught up with the kidnappers. The Gandharvas then released the lambs and quickly disappeared.

"*Baaaaaa! Baaaaaa!*"

Breathing rapidly, the king grabbed the lambs by their collars and walked them back towards the door. "I've got the lambs," he said proudly, releasing them to Urvashi, who was waiting in the doorway.

Just then the Gandharvas, who shone like lightning, flew over Pururava. Their illumination made his naked body clearly visible to Urvashi. Seeing him in that "uncivilized" state, she turned away. Since Pururava had broken his promise, she and her lambs instantly vanished.

The king looked in the bedroom for her. "Urvashi? Where are you? Urvashi?" He could not find her—in the bedroom or anywhere in the palace. This disturbed him greatly. Thus, like a madman, he began traveling all over and searching desperately for her. Not too long after, on the bank of the Saraswati River at Kurukshetra, the king saw her playing in the water with five other Apsaras. Pururava brightened, for he felt as if he had regained his life.

When Urvashi saw him coming, she began to swim away.

"My dear wife, please stay. Stay."

"Why should I? You broke your promise."

"But I couldn't help it."

"You could have thrown something over your body."

"I was too concerned about getting back your lambs."

"You should have thought about—"

"How was I to know the Gandharvas would illuminate my body?"

"Still, you should have—"

"Please stay! I'm your husband. I'm devoted to you. I can't live without you. If you leave me—I'll die here."

"Die?"

"Yes. Since my body is unfit for your pleasure, let it be eaten by foxes and vultures."

"No, that's not right."

"Why not?"

"Because you're a king, a hero. And a hero controls himself."

"Controls? Ha!"

"Don't let your senses conquer and eat you."

"I can't help it."

Then she tried to discourage him by revealing her own worst qualities and generalizing them, as if they belonged to all women.

"Don't you know that a woman's heart is like a sly fox's?"

"Yes, I'm learning."

"A woman is merciless and cunning," Urvashi emphasized. "She can't tolerate the slightest offense. For her own pleasure, she can do anything irreligious. She doesn't fear killing even a faithful husband or a brother."

"Stop it. Please."

"Women are easily seduced by men. Such women renounce the friendship of a man who is their helper and develop false friendship with fools."

"Stop!"

"Indeed, they continue seeking new lovers again and again."

"I can't believe you're like those women."

"How can you be so sure?"

"Because I know you too well. Please—don't leave me."

There was a long pause. "I think there's something you should know," she said seriously.

"And what's that?"

"That I'm pregnant."

"Pregnant?"

"Yes, with your child."

The king was overjoyed. Yet his joy was quickly eclipsed by the thought of Urvashi leaving him, which he considered intolerably painful.

Seeing how he was suffering, she offered him a concession. "All right. Here's what I can do. At the end of every year, we can meet—and you can have sex with me for one night only."

"One night? Only one night?"

"Yes. But on that night you'll conceive a child in me."

Urvashi then disappeared and the king returned to his palace.

Throughout the year Pururava pined for the delightful company of his lovely wife. He counted the days and hours, wishing that they would pass faster. But each day felt like many years, so he grieved in separation from her. And when the time came for them to finally meet, he became extremely joyful—like a dead man reborn. However, after he had enjoyed sex with Urvashi and they were about to separate for another year, he felt extremely sorrowful.

Seeing this, Urvashi suggested, "O King, try to please the Gandharvas. If you do, they may let me live with you as before."

The king then began to pray unceasingly to the Gandharvas—until they were fully satisfied. They then returned Urvashi to Pururava, making him exceedingly happy. He therefore went with her into the forest to enjoy sex. However, during the act, something did not feel right. Although the woman looked exactly like Urvashi and smelled like her, spoke like her, smiled like her, and dressed like her—she did not *love* like her! He noted distinct differences in her mannerisms. He therefore concluded that the Gandharvas had tricked him by creating an illusion [or *agnishthali*] of Urvashi. And he was right—they had.

Pururava therefore left the illusory Urvashi in the forest and returned to his palace. There, he meditated on Urvashi all night. During his meditation, the Treta, or silver, age began. Thus, the principles of the three Vedas—including the way to perform sacrifices to fulfill materialistic desires—were revealed within his heart.

The king then returned to the spot where he had left the illusory Urvashi. At that place he noticed that a fig tree had grown from the womb of a *shami* tree [*acacia suma*]. He then took a piece of wood from that tree and broke it into two pieces. Since he desired to go to the heavenly planet where Urvashi now resided, he chanted special mantras for this purpose. He also meditated on the lower piece of wood as Urvashi, the upper piece as himself, and on an ordinary piece of wood between the two as a son. In other words, his only ambition was to have sex with Urvashi and thereby produce more children.

As the king rubbed the sticks together, a fire was ignited in the middle stick, which would enable him to attain complete success in sense pleasure and which he also symbolically considered to be the son that he desired. Pururava then used the fire to perform a sacrifice wherein he satisfied Lord Vishnu. As a result, the king was able to, as he wished, reach the Gandharva planet. There, with Urvashi, he produced five more celestial sons.

Because the king was so strongly afflicted by lust, he was unable to either think of or pursue the true goal of human life—self-realization. Instead of continuously thinking of offering pleasure to the Lord, he constantly dwelled on obtaining pleasure for his own senses. This inevitably caused him anxiety, anger, and misery. And even though he was able to quell these feelings momentarily, as long as he remained attached to Urvashi—and was always afraid of losing her—these feelings haunted his consciousness continually. Thus, his illusion and ignorance of who he was and why he was here were simply intensified. Such foolishness does not liberate the soul but instead enslaves it, preventing it from ever knowing real or transcendental happiness.

CHAPTER TWENTY-FOUR

KING AMBARISHA PROTECTED

Believing that he could harm one of God's self-surrendered devotees with his mystic powers, Yogi Durvasa painfully learned how the Lord protects such devotees from harmful attacks. When we surrender our body, mind, and speech to the Lord, we not only gain His protection but also His help in discovering ourselves.

King Ambarisha was really in a dilemma. To eat or not to eat—that was the question!

If he ate, he would evoke the wrath of one of the most powerful yogis in the world. And if he didn't eat, he would lose the spiritual merit he had acquired by fulfilling an arduous vow. The king was certainly in a quandary.

It had all started a year ago.

King Ambarisha, along with his queen, had decided to worship Lord Krishna in a special way. He observed the vows of Ekadashi and Dvadashi for a complete year. This means that he ate no grains or beans for a year except on the Dvadashi days (usually the twelfth day from the full or new moon of each month). However, on the last three days and nights of that year, the king undertook a complete fast. And on the next day, Dvadashi, he was expected to end the fast. Before doing so, he washed himself in the holy Yamuna River and then bathed and worshiped the Deity of the Lord in Madhuvana Forest (in Vrndavana). Moreover, he gave numerous cows in charity to the Brahmins, whom he also fed sumptuously and satisfied completely.

The specific time period had now arrived for the king to break his fast. If he did not break it within this interval, there would be a flaw in the observance of his vow. Such a defect would result in his not earning all the spiritual merit he was entitled to.

Just as he was about to break his fast, the famous Yogi Durvasa unexpectedly arrived in the king's dining chamber. This mighty yogi

Yogi Durvasa tries to kill King Ambarisha

was known to be easily pleased and displeased. When pleased, he would graciously bestow blessings on those who satisfied him; and when displeased, he would harshly pronounce curses on those who offended him.

Greeting Durvasa, the king respectfully stood up, offered the yogi a seat, and worshiped him with various paraphernalia. Ambarisha then humbly sat at the yogi's feet and said, "May I serve you a meal now?"

Durvasa smiled appreciatively and said, "Not at the moment. I have some rituals to perform in the river now. But when I return, you can do so."

"It will be my pleasure," said the king.

Durvasa went to the Yamuna, dipped into the spiritually charged water, and meditated deeply on the Brahman effulgence.

Meanwhile Ambarisha was in a predicament, for only a few moments remained for him to break his fast. However, if he did so, the yogi would deem it an act of disrespect, for Vedic etiquette demanded that the king not eat until his guest had first eaten. If the king ate, Durvasa might become displeased and curse him. And if Ambarisha didn't eat, he would surely forfeit some of his earned spiritual merit. Thus, he asked the Brahmins there what he should do.

"I'm not sure," answered one Brahmin.

"Neither am I," said another.

"I've never encountered a problem like this," replied a third.

None of the Brahmins could give the king a definite answer.

So Ambarisha considered the matter carefully and, searching his memory, arrived at a possibility. He said to the learned men, "I somehow recall the scripture saying that drinking water may be accepted as eating as well as not eating. Do any of you remember that?"

The Brahmins reflected on the statement for a few moments, discussed the matter among themselves, and concluded that there indeed was such a statement in the Vedas.

"All right, then I will drink water now."

"Please do," urged the Brahmins.

So the king drank, meditated on God within his heart, and felt satisfied that he had completed his vow successfully. Certain that the yogi would not be offended, he waited for Durvasa to return.

When the yogi entered the dining hall, his fists were clenched and he looked incensed.

Ambarisha wondered what was bothering him. "My lord, is there something wrong?"

"Yes, very wrong!" he boomed.

Ambarisha folded his palms and asked, "Oh? Can I do something to remedy it?"

"You pretender!"

"What?"

"You pose yourself as a great devotee of Lord Vishnu. But you're anything but that."

"I don't understand."

"Stop lying! By my clairvoyant power, I saw you eat. And you know it's improper to eat before I do."

"But—"

"Don't you?"

"Yes, but I only drank water and—"

"You violated the etiquette!"

Ambarisha was stunned.

"You're an offender!"

"But I—"

"That's because you've become so proud of your wealth and position!"

"My lord, please—"

"You think you're God, don't you?"

Realizing how angry Durvasa was, Ambarisha stopped speaking.

"Therefore, you deserve to be punished!"

Although the yogi was wrong, Ambarisha knew that he would only further inflame him by trying to vindicate himself. Therefore, he mentally took shelter of Lord Vishnu.

"And that's exactly what I will do—punish you!" The yogi grabbed a bunch of hair on his head, pulled it out, and gazed at it furiously, silently uttering an incantation. The batch of hair suddenly transformed into a blazing titan. Holding a deadly trident, the demon roared and raised his weapon belligerently.

But Ambarisha neither moved from his position nor tried to challenge the demon, for he knew he could not defeat him. Nor did he pray to the Lord to protect his life. He simply accepted this situation as the will of God and surrendered to it. He also mentally prayed, *O Lord, if You feel I deserve to be killed by this monster—because I'm an offender—then I welcome this, for You know what is best for Me and what will help me to become a better devotee.*

The Lord, in the king's heart, heard His devotee's prayer and instantly responded to it.

As the demon was about to pierce the king with the sharp points of his trident, Lord Vishnu's blazing, whirling disk weapon—the Sudarshana-*chakra*, the most powerful weapon in existence—suddenly appeared there. Filled with the Lord's personal potency and intelligence, the effulgent disc whirled towards the demon with amazing speed and force. And within a second, the disc's devastating heat burned the demon to ashes!

The yogi was astonished. How could this happen? Was the king more powerful than he? Impossible! And yet—the disc had destroyed the demon.

The disc now changed course. It began whirling towards Durvasa.

Seeing it coming, Durvasa was perplexed and frightened. What could he do?

The disc whirled closer...

The yogi began running around the dining hall.

The disc chased him closely.

The yogi ran out of the palace—so fast he could not even be seen.

But the disc stayed right behind him, almost touching his back.

Durvasa was astonished and bewildered. Wherever he ran—all over the earth, in dark caves, over the ocean—the disc continued trailing him. The yogi then used his mystic power to fly in the sky and travel to the heavenly planets. There, he tried to find some shelter from the disc. But he couldn't, for wherever he went, the disc pursued him with fierce resolve. The yogi then flew up to Lord Brahma's planet, the highest one in the material world. As he saw Brahma, he cried, "Save me, lord! Save me!"

When Lord Brahma saw Lord Vishnu's disc, he said, "I'm sorry, Yogi. I have no power to defeat Lord Vishnu's weapon. Better approach Lord Shiva and ask him for help."

With the flaming disk still dogging him, Durvasa flew to the snowy recesses known as Mount Kailash. Seeing Lord Shiva there, he begged, "Please save me from this disc!"

But Shiva just shook his head and said, "Sorry, but I can't stop Lord Vishnu's weapon."

"Why?"

"Because He's supreme. And so is His weapon. Better ask Him for help."

Frustrated and frightened, with the disc sizzling behind him, Durvasa zoomed up to the spiritual world of Vaikuntha. There, he reached Lord Vishnu's opulent marble palace and hastened into His jewel-studded chamber. The four-armed, handsome-faced, blue-complexioned Lord was sitting on His throne, surrounded by happy, devoted servants. The yogi prostrated himself before the Lord's lotus-like feet and cried, "O Lord, save me!"

"Save you?"

"Your disc wants to kill me!"

The disc whooshed into the chamber and hovered near Durvasa. Since the Lord was talking to the yogi, the disc respectfully waited for the conversation to end.

"Well, you committed an offense against My great devotee."

"But he committed an offense first—by eating before I did," said Durvasa, rising to his knees.

"That was no offense—for drinking water *is* and *isn't* considered eating."

The yogi was surprised.

"He was only trying to fulfill his vow to Me—breaking his fast at the proper time."

Feeling ashamed, Durvasa realized he had attempted to harm an innocent man.

"By trying to hurt him with your mystic power, you have actually hurt yourself."

Durvasa nodded anxiously.

"But at least you now know—that I protect My devotees from unjustifiable harm."

Realizing his mistake, the yogi submissively asked, "Then what can I do to save myself?"

"You should immediately return to King Ambarisha. If you can somehow satisfy him, you'll be saved."

With the disc whirling behind him, the yogi quickly but apprehensively flew down to earth into Ambarisha's dining hall.

Due to the relative time difference in the higher planetary region, one year had elapsed on earth. The king, who was awaiting the yogi's return, had been fasting, drinking only water during the entire time.

Seeing Ambarisha, the aggrieved Durvasa prostrated himself before the king and clasped his feet. "I'm sorry for my offense against you. Please—forgive me!" he pleaded.

When the king saw the great yogi holding his feet, due to humility, he felt embarrassed. And when he saw Durvasa trying to offer him prayers, he felt even more embarrassed. Thus, to calm the yogi and to restrain the disc, he offered beautiful prayers of glorification to it. He venerated the disc as if it were nondifferent from the Lord Himself. Then he concluded, "For the benefit of my entire dynasty, please favor this poor yogi. And if my family has satisfied the Lord by its devotional service, then I beg that you please not burn the yogi."

The disc then became peaceful and vanished. Noting this and feeling greatly relieved, Durvasa rose to his feet and said, "My dear king, today I have experienced the greatness of God's devotees. Although I committed a grave offense against you, you have prayed for my good fortune. And by overlooking my offense, you have saved my life. You are so merciful, therefore I feel very much obliged to you."

The king bowed down to the yogi's feet. He then stood up and served Durvasa a sumptuous meal.

After eating a variety of delicious foods, the yogi was so satisfied that he affectionately urged the king, "Please take your meal now." When Ambarisha sat down, the yogi said, "My dear king, I'm very pleased with you. Initially, I thought you were just an ordinary human being. But now I realize you're a great devotee of the Lord. Just by seeing you, touching your feet, and talking with you, I've become obliged to you. All the people of this world and of the heavenly planets will always sing about your spotless character and glorious deeds."

The yogi then took his leave. Continuously praising Ambarisha, he soared into the sky and headed for Lord Brahma's planet.

The king fully realized that he was far more powerful than the most powerful yogi—simply because he always depended on, and received the mercy of, the Supreme Lord. In other words, Ambarisha was extremely dear to, and always protected by, God.

But how had he obtained this amazing grace? By simply remembering the Lord continuously—whether he was working, playing, eating, worshiping, or even sleeping. Whatever he did, he related to Lord Krishna and tried his best to always serve the Lord's pleasure. By such devotional service, he developed attachment to God and became free from all materialistic desires, despite his royal and wealthy position. Moreover, many of his subjects followed his fine example and thus became extremely happy.

After some time, the king retired from active family life and retreated to the forest, where he centered his attention exclusively on God.

Whoever recites, or even thinks about, this story of King Ambarisha certainly becomes a pure devotee of the Lord and becomes liberated from the thralldom of materialistic miseries.

CHAPTER TWENTY-FIVE

KING SUDYUMNA'S SEX CHANGE

Although the king reluctantly became a woman, he learned to tolerate the change. Similarly, to discover ourselves, it is useful to tolerate changes in our lives that we may not be able to reverse. This helps us to stay peaceful while persevering towards our goals.

"I must have a son!" said the childless King Manu. To make certain that his wife Shraddha would give birth to a son—and not to a daughter—the king approached the great saint Vasishtha. "O sage, I would appreciate if you would perform a sacrifice for me."

"What kind?" asked the elderly Brahmin.

"One that would assure me of getting a son."

"Very well. We will do it in a few days."

A sacrificial arena was prepared and Vasishtha, as well as several assistant priests, sat around a fire chanting specific mantras. The king and queen, along with many well-wishing guests, sat near the fire and watched. Queen Shraddha, who had been observing the vow of subsisting only on milk, rose from her seat and approached the priest who was about to offer oblations into the fire. She offered her obeisances and then leaned towards him.

He glanced at her curiously, as did everyone else.

"Please give me a daughter," she whispered emphatically.

"A daughter?" he asked, puzzled. "But—"

"Yes, a daughter!"

Before he could say anything more, the chief priest ordered him, "Now offer the oblations."

As the priest ladled ghee into the sacrificial fire—which sprang up and crackled—and chanted mystical mantras, he uncontrollably remembered Shraddha's request. Consequently, when the child was later born, it was not a boy—as Manu had wanted—but a girl. She was named Ila.

King Sudyumna becomes a woman

Although Manu was pleased to have a child, he was displeased that it was a girl. *How could this have happened?* he wondered. *A sacrifice conducted by the great Brahmin Vasishtha could never go amiss. And yet—it had. Something must have gone wrong.* Manu therefore traveled to Vasistha's home and then approached him, saying, "My lord, I'm disappointed."

"About the sex of your child?"

"Yes. I thought the mantras were infallible."

"They are," Vasishtha assured.

"Then why did a different result occur?"

Vasishtha explained why.

"My wife caused this?" asked the king angrily.

"Yes, but you need not be upset."

"How can I *not* be upset? I wanted a son! Not a—"

"Then you will have a son!" interrupted Vasishtha.

"I will?" Manu was surprised.

"Yes."

"But—how?"

"Leave that to me."

The king felt relieved. But—could Vasishtha really do it?

The sage dropped to his knees and began to pray. After glorifying Lord Vishnu in many ways, he begged, "My dear Lord, by your grace and power, please transform Ila into a male."

Since God was highly pleased with Vasishtha, He answered his prayer immediately. Thus, Ila was changed into an excellent male and was re-named Sudyumna.

One day when Sudyumna was a young man, he and his companions, riding on swift horses, went hunting. He was decorated with armor, outfitted with a bow and arrows, and looked extremely handsome. The group chased various animals till they reached the northern part of Sukumara Forest. There, at the base of Mount Meru, they entered the wooded area. And when they did, something very strange happened.

When the prince shouted to his companions, "Let's go this way!" he noted that his voice had changed. It had become high pitched—like a woman's. He wondered why. Then he noticed another change: his chest—it was no longer manly. For he had sprouted two female breasts! *What is happening?* he wondered. And when he focused his attention on his crotch, he realized that his male genitals were now gone and had been replaced by female organs! Feeling extremely embarrassed, she stopped her horse. How could she face her male friends now with this feminine persona? They would all laugh at her.

Sudyumna dismounted from her horse, but remained facing away from the warriors. Then, summoning her courage, she anxiously turned around and looked at them. "Oh, my God!" she exclaimed. She couldn't believe what she saw. They, too, had turned into women! They were all women now! Even their male horses had turned into mares! "Why is this happening?" shouted Sudyumna. "What did we do to deserve this?"

But everyone there either shook her head or shrugged her shoulders. They really felt morose and ashamed now. How could they return to their kingdom, to their wives, and to their children? They would be the laughingstock of the citizens. Their wives would feel cheated, and their children would probably start calling them "Mother." It was the most embarrassing situation they had ever encountered.

They walked away from Sukumara Forest and meandered through other forests. Then one day, during their wanderings, they saw an ashram nearby. They wondered who it belonged to. As Sudyumna sauntered towards it, she noted the reflection of her face in a small pond. She could not help marveling over how beautiful she was. Any man would love to marry her now. She then approached the ashram and knocked on the door. A handsome young man opened it. "Yes?" he said, smiling and enjoying Sudyumna's beauty. "Can I help you?"

"Not really. I was just wondering who was living here."

"My name is Budha and I happen to be the son of the moon god."

"Oh?"

"And who are you, lovely one?"

"My name is Sudyumna. I'm King Manu's—eh, daughter."

"Daughter? I didn't know he had a daughter."

"Yes, he—he does."

"Well, please come in."

When Sudyumna entered, she could not help feeling instant affection for Budha. And he, also, felt intense attraction to Sudyumna. In fact, it was love at first sight. Thus, he immediately asked her to marry him. After she agreed, they enjoyed conjugal pleasure together. And after some time, she delivered a son to him, who was named Pururava.

One day Sudyumna wondered whether she would ever become a male again. Who could tell her except her family spiritual master, Vasishtha? As she mentally called him, the great sage suddenly appeared before her. Seeing Sudyumna's anomalous condition, the saint was greatly aggrieved. "When did this happen?" he asked, astonished.

"When my friends and I rode into the Sukumara Forest."

"The Sukumara?"

"Yes."

"Well, that explains it. You never should have gone there."

"Why?"

"Because it's cursed."

"Cursed? By whom?"

"Lord Shiva."

"But—why?"

"It happens to be the pleasure grove where he sports with his wife."

"I don't understand."

"Well, one day some sages entered it to see Lord Shiva. And when they approached him, his wife, Ambika, happened to be there."

"So?"

"Well, she was naked and sitting on his lap."

"Naked?"

"Totally. So she naturally felt embarrassed. In fact, she jumped up and covered her breasts with her hands."

"And what did the sages do?"

"Well, they turned around and went the other way—to Nara-Narayana's ashram."

"That makes sense."

"But Lord Shiva wanted to please Ambika—so that if anything like that ever happened again, she wouldn't have to feel so embarrassed."

"So he cursed the forest?"

"Exactly. He said that if any male entered it, he would immediately become a female."

"Oh. So that's why I'm a woman now."

Vasishtha nodded.

"Well, is there any possibility of me becoming a man again?"

"I'll let you know shortly."

Vasishtha then worshiped and prayed to Lord Shiva. When Shiva appeared, the sage explained what had accidentally happened to Sudyumna. Then he asked, "Do you think you could lift the curse from my disciple?"

Lord Shiva considered the matter for a few moments. He loved the sage and he also loved his wife. Therefore, he wanted to please both. Then he arrived at a solution. "To satisfy you and to keep my word to my wife, your disciple Sudyumna may remain a male for one month and a female for the next. In this way, he may rule as he likes."

Thus, Sudyumna regained his maleness every other month and ruled his kingdom accordingly. However, his subjects were not particularly pleased by this arrangement. This was because they knew that on the month he would be a female, the Vedic tradition would prevent him from discharging certain royal duties reserved for men—such as fighting enemies, protecting citizens, and punishing criminals.

After some time, when King Sudyumna became elderly, he bestowed his entire kingdom on his son Pururava and retired to the forest for the purpose of discovering his real self and realizing the Supreme Lord.

CHAPTER TWENTY-SIX

KING RANTIDEVA'S MERCY

This amazing king teaches us, by an extreme example, the value of sacrificing our personal comfort to relieve others of suffering. This quality of mercy is greatly desirable as we strive to discover the real self within.

King Rantideva looked as though he were about to starve to death. Grave and trembling, he was so thin that his cheeks and eye sockets were deeply hollowed, and his rib cage and shoulder bones showed through his leaf-thin skin. And why not? He hadn't eaten even a morsel of food or drunk even a drop of water in the past forty-eight days!

But this morning, all that would change. Because he was now ready to break his fast.

Surrounded by a few servants, the frail monarch doddered towards the dining hall. Wearing only a white dhoti, a green sash, and a thin white shawl, Rantideva shuffled to a small platform, where he sat down on a soft, thin, bluish cushion. Before him was a large table over which hung a smooth maroon cloth. Two servants then flanked and fanned him with yak-tail whisks, while another carried a tray of food and a goblet of water to the table, setting them down before the king. The meal consisted of hot vegetables and grains that had been carefully cooked in milk and ghee.

Rantideva closed his eyes, folded his palms, and thanked God for providing him with this splendid repast. "My Lord, You are so merciful!" he said. Then he opened his eyes and gazed at the scrumptious-looking food for a few moments, allowing his digestive juices to begin secreting.

As all the servants watched the king, they eagerly yearned for him to begin. Since he looked so emaciated, they wondered if he would

King Rantideva feeds his guests

even have the strength to lift the food to his mouth. *Why was he now waiting?* they wondered. *Did he not have any appetite?* They believed that if the monarch did not eat soon, he would surely die. And since they all loved him immensely, they greatly feared for his life. *Please begin*, they mentally begged. *Begin!*

At that moment, the outside guard entered and began walking towards the king. However, one of the servants stepped in front of him and said, "What do you want?"

"I have a message for the king."

"It will have to wait. Our lord is about to break his fast."

"But it's urgent."

"What could be more urgent than the king eating? Can't you see that he's almost dead?"

"Yes, but—an offense may be committed."

"An offense? What are you talking about?"

As the king reached his hand out to take a morsel from the plate, the guard called, "My Lord, there's a Brahmin outside the door. He said he has to see you—now."

"Now?" asked Rantideva.

"Yes. He said it was urgent."

"Oh. Then please bring him in."

The guard exited and quickly re-entered, leading the Brahmin to the king. On seeing him, Rantideva stepped down from his seat and bowed before him. Straining to rise, the king asked, "O Brahmin, how may I serve you?"

"I'm very hungry," he said anxiously.

"Hungry? Well, you've come at the right time." The king asked one of the servants to bring another plate, which he did. Rantideva then seated the Brahmin on a comfortable maroon floor pillow and had a small table placed before him. The king then slowly scooped up half the food from his own plate, transferred it to the other plate, and gladly set it down on the Brahmin's table. "Please relax and enjoy your meal," Rantideva said warmly.

The Brahmin began eating with obvious satisfaction.

Standing nearby with his palms folded, the king felt more pleasure watching the Brahmin relish his food than if he himself had been eating it. This pleasure enabled him to forget his own gnawing hunger.

Several minutes later the Brahmin finished. He then arose from his seat, thanked the king for his hospitality, and happily departed.

Rantideva then cheerfully divided the remaining food in half and sent one part of it to his family members, who also had been fasting. The other half, he reserved for himself. The king returned to his seat and gazed for a few moments at the food.

At that moment, the guard re-entered the room. Again the servant confronted him, "What is it now?"

"Another urgency," the guard whispered.

"Who?"

"Some laborer."

"What laborer?"

"I've never seen him before."

"Tell him to wait till the king finishes eating."

"All right."

As he turned, the king called out to the guard, "Is there a problem?"

"Just a laborer—he wants to see you."

"Oh? Then bring him in!"

"My lord," protested the servant, "the laborer can wait till you're finished."

"Maybe he can't. Please bring him in. "

"Are you sure?"

"Yes."

The disappointed servant nodded to the guard and, in a few moments, the latter brought the scruffy laborer in.

"Welcome," said Rantideva. "How may I serve you?" The king, being a spiritually advanced soul, did not see the laborer as a low-class man. Rather, he saw him as a spiritual soul, a particle of God, and thus equal to himself, also a particle.

The laborer bowed to the king and then stood up. "My Lord," he said anxiously, "I'm very hungry. Can you help me?"

Although the king's hunger was obviously greater than the laborer's, the monarch considered the laborer's more important. "Yes, I can," he said. "Please come here."

The king seated the laborer on the floor pillow and had the servant cleanse the small table in front of it. After the servant brought the king another empty plate, the latter divided the remaining food into two portions—one for the workman and one for himself. He next set the laborer's share of food on the table and then stood to the side. Watching him eat voraciously, the king was ecstatic to see relief and pleasure come into the laborer's face.

When the workman finished eating, the king asked, "Are you fully satisfied?"

"Very. And thank you, my lord." He stood up, joined his palms, bowed his head, and then departed.

Although Rantideva's stomach was growling and his hands were trembling, the weakened king felt extremely happy. He was now ready to eat the small remaining portion of the food and drink the water. He sat down, smiled at his meal and, just as he reached out his hand, heard an unfamiliar sound. It was the barking of dogs in the outer hallway. Rantideva wondered why they were there and what they wanted. Then he heard the door guard shout, "You can't come in!"

"Please!" entreated an unknown voice.

"No! Now take your dirty dogs out of here!"

"I must talk to the king!" insisted the man.

"The king is eating. Now leave!" warned the guard.

Rantideva called to one of his servants, "Who is that?"

"Just a man and his dogs. Don't worry, we'll get rid of him."

"What does he want?"

"My lord, it's not important. Please—eat."

"Maybe it is important. Let him in."

"In?"

"Yes."

"But—"

"Now!"

"With or without the dogs?"

"With."

The aggrieved servant signaled the guard to usher them in. The two dogs stopped barking, but they began pulling their master by their leashes towards the king. They smelled the delicious food on the plate and began panting, their drooling tongues flopping about outside their mouths. The dog's master looked like a vagabond—his hair and clothes disheveled, his face and hands covered with road dust. But the king saw them as God's children and as his own brothers.

The dog-owner offered the king an obeisance, then rose to his feet.

"How can I serve you?" Rantideva smiled.

"My dogs and I—we're very hungry. We haven't eaten for awhile."

"I'm sorry to hear that."

"Can you help us?"

"Certainly."

The king had the man sit down on the pillow and had the table before him thoroughly cleansed. Rantideva then picked up his plate of food and set it on the small table in front of the man, adding, "May you and your dogs be happy."

The dog-owner placed some of the food on the marble floor, and the dogs began gobbling it up with gusto. Then he himself began devouring the rest of the eatables.

Standing to the side and empathizing with the man's and the dogs' relief and enjoyment, Rantideva could scarcely contain his ecstasy. He had now completely forgotten that he was even hungry and that his body desperately needed nourishment.

But the servants there had not forgotten. Indeed, they were extremely sad. The last thing they wanted was for their king to collapse and die due to his charitable nature. Just looking at the monarch—so feeble, gaunt, and fragile—was more than they could bear. True, more food was being prepared for him now, but they wondered whether he would remain alive until it was delivered. Of course, there was still the goblet/ of water on the tray. Hopefully, that would sustain him in the meanwhile.

Several minutes later, the man and the dogs finished their meal. "Thank you very much," said the dog owner. "You are very kind."

"No, only God is kind," Rantideva replied. "And through me, He has fed you and your animals."

The man nodded humbly, grabbed the dogs' leashes, and led them out of the dining hall, their tails wagging spiritedly.

A few moments later, another man in the hallway shouted to the guard, "But I must see the king! I must!"

"Later!" insisted the guard. "The king can't see *anyone* now!"

"But I have to!" exclaimed the man, in a rough, uncultured voice.

Hearing the loud pleading words, the king ordered, "Let the man in!"

But when the guard did, the servants were aghast. By the man's primitive looks and shabby dress, they could discern that he was of the lowest class—an untouchable dog-eater! They did not want to subject the king to such lowly company, especially now, while he was so weak and famished. "My lord," said one servant, "you can see him later—after you've eaten and refreshed yourself. Please."

But the king disregarded the advice and asked the dog-eater, "Why have you come to me?"

"Because I'm tired and thirsty! *Very* thirsty. I must have some water now." He glanced at the king's filled goblet.

Rantideva folded his palms, closed his eyes, and raised his head. "O Lord," he prayed, "I don't pray to you for the eight mystic powers of the yogis nor for salvation from repeated birth and death. I only ask that You let me stay among living beings and bear difficulties for them, so that they may be freed from all suffering."

Then something amazing happened: the king stood up straight, appeared strong and energetic, and smiled joyfully. Opening his eyes, he turned to the servants and the guard and added, "Simply because I desire to give my water to this poor man—who is struggling to live— the Lord has freed me from all hunger, thirst, trembling, dejection, sadness, and illusion!"

Rantideva clutched the goblet of water and handed it to the man, who gulped it down quickly.

Then something even more astonishing occurred: the dog-eater suddenly vanished and in his place stood Lord Brahma and Lord Shiva! In fact, it was they who had appeared as the Brahmin, the laborer, the dog-owner, and the dog-eater—to ascertain how great the king's quality of mercy was. The king respectfully clasped his palms and bowed down before them. When he rose, he could have asked them for any benediction he desired—and received it—but he didn't. This was because he knew he already had the greatest benediction, namely, attachment and devotion to Lord Vishnu. This blessing had freed him from all materialistic desires and from the illusion that real happiness can be acquired from temporary, limited pleasures.

Thus, although the king, while performing his daily duties, had dealt with countless materialistic matters, he had never been affected or disturbed by them because he was constantly conscious of the Lord's transcendental, peace-giving presence. And anyone in the kingdom who emulated Rantideva's glorious example was blessed by his mercy to become a pure devotee of the Lord and live up to the highest ideals. Hence, many persons became truly happy, self-realized persons.

But why had the monarch fasted for forty-eight days?

The king was aware that he and many of his subjects, either in their past or present lifetimes, may have committed sins for which they had not yet atoned. This meant that they would eventually have to suffer for those wrongs. To stave off such future distresses, Rantideva voluntarily accepted various kinds of suffering to pay for them. Knowing he was freeing his subjects from future misery and enabling them to become more absorbed in self-discovery and God-realization, the king felt great happiness and satisfaction. And so did the Lord.

GLOSSARY

Aditi—The mother of the gods.

Agastya—A sage with great mystic powers. He hosted the divine incarnation Rama and Sita during their exile in the forest.

Agni—The god of fire.

Agnishthali—A girl produced from fire.

Airavata—An elephant produced from the churning of the ocean of milk.

Ajamila—A lapsed Brahmin who was saved from going to hell by chanting Lord Narayana's name as he was dying.

Ajita—A name of Lord Vishnu that means invincible.

Alaka—The god Kuvera's capital.

Amaravati—The god Indra's capital.

Amarka—One of Prince Prahlada's teachers and a son of the sage Shukracharya.

Ambarisha—A king of the Ikshvaku dynasty known for his great devotional qualities and service. Even Yogi Durvasa was amazed by him.

Ambika—Lord Shiva's wife.

Angira—A great sage who was the mind-born son of Lord Brahma.

Anima—The mystic power of making oneself as small as one desires.

Apsara—The wives of the heavenly Gandharvas who sing and dance.

Arjuna—The third-oldest Pandu prince, born of the god Indra. Lord Krishna spoke the *Bhagavad-gita* to him.

Ashvatthama—The son of Drona and Kripi, and a Kaurava general in the Kurukshetra battle.

Ashram—A residence where spiritual disciplines are practiced.

Ashwini-kumaras—Twin gods who are physicians of heaven.

Asuras—Demons (atheists) who are enemies of the gods.

B

Badarikashram—A place sacred to Lord Vishnu, especially in His Nara-Narayana form; it is near the Ganges River in the Himalaya Mountains.

Bahvrcha **scripture**—The name of a Vedic scripture, which is a collection of mantras from the Rg Veda.

Bala—A demon warrior who served under King Bali.

Bali—A virtuous Daitya king who was Virochana's son and Prahlada's grandson.

Bhaga—A god who bestows wealth and presides over marriages.

Bhagavad-gita—Literally, the "song of God" spoken by Krishna on the battlefield of Kurukshetra.

Bhagavat Purana—Another name of the *Shrimad Bhagavatam.*

Bhakti—Devotion to the Lord, particularly manifested as loving service to Him.

Bharata—An ancient king devoted to Lord Vishnu. He renounced his kingdom and became attached to a fawn, leading to his spiritual downfall.

Bhavani—One of the names of Lord Shiva's wife.

Bhima—The second of the five Pandava brothers known for his great strength. The wind god, Vayu, is his father and Kunti is his mother.

Bhrigu—A Vedic sage and son of Lord Brahma.

Bhrigukaccha—A field on the northern bank of the Narmada River where sacrifices were held.

Bhumi—A name of Mother Earth (who appeared as a cow).

Brahma—The creator of this universe and of all its creatures. He is born from a lotus sprung from the navel of Lord Vishnu.

Brahman—The Supreme Lord; the impersonal all-pervasive aspect of God; the individual soul.

Brahmaloka—The planet on which Lord Brahma resides. It is the highest in this universe.

Brahmin—The first of the four castes or divisions of society: a priest and/ or educator.

Brahmastra—One of the most powerful fiery weapons in existence. It is released by mantra.

Brihaspati—A sage who is the son of Angira and father of Bharadwaja.

Budha—The son of the moon-god.

C

Chaitraratha—The celestial gardens of the god Kuvera, treasurer of the gods.

Chandra—The moon or god of the moon.

Chitraketu—A famous emperor who realized God but who was later cursed by Parvati to become a demon monster when he insulted her husband, Lord Shiva.

D

Dadichi—A famous sage who donated his bones to the gods, who used them to create a thunderbolt weapon to defeat the demons.

Daitya—A descendent of Goddess Diti and the sage Kashyapa. They are demons who fight against the gods and interfere with sacrifices.

Daksha—A son of Lord Brahma who had many daughters.

Danava—Descendants from Danu and the sage Kashyapa. Often referred to as demons, they warred against the gods.

Danu—The mother of the Danavas, who were asuras (demons).

Devala—A Vedic sage to whom some Vedic hymns are attributed.

Dhanvantari—An incarnation of God acting as a god. He is the physician of the gods.

Dharma—Righteousness or duty. Also the name of the god of the departed souls.

Dhoti—An Indian garment worn by men. It is a large piece of cloth that is folded to form pants.

Dhrishtadyumna—King Drupada's son and Draupadi's brother. He commanded the Pandava army in the battle of Kurukshetra.

Dhruva—The son of King Uttanapada and Suniti. He achieved the post of chief of the polar star.

Diti—A goddess married to the sage Kashyapa. She gave birth to the Daityas or demons.

Draupadi—The daughter of King Drupada and wife of the five Pandava princes.

Drona—A Brahmin generated in a bucket by his sage father Bharadraj. Married to Kripi, he fathered Ashvatthama. He was a great military teacher.

Durvasa—A sage known for his irascible temper, curses, and blessings.

Dvadashi—Generally, the twelfth day after the new or full moon, or the day following Ekadashi.

Dwaraka—Lord Krishna's capital, in Gujarat, which was submerged by the ocean after He disappeared from the earth.

E

Ekadashi—Generally, the eleventh day after new or full moon. On this day, one fasts from grains and beans and increases one's spiritual activities.

G

Gajendra—An elephant who achieved salvation by Lord Vishnu's special mercy.

Gandaki—A river in northern India that falls into the Ganges.

Gandhamadana—A famous mountain lying to the east of the Himalayas.

Gandharvas—Celestial singers and musicians who perform for the gods. They descended from the sage Kashyapa and his wife Arishta.

Ganges—A sacred river that flows down to Earth from the toe of Lord Vishnu in the spiritual world.

Garbhodaka—The ocean on which Lord Vishnu rests and which exists at the bottom of the universe.

Garuda—A devotee eagle who acts as the carrier of Lord Vishnu.

Gauri—A name of Lord Shiva's wife.

Gayatri—A sacred prayer recited morning, noon, and evening by those who have been spiritually initiated.

Gods—The administrators of the universe who act under the directions of the Supreme Lord. They reside in the planets above the earth.

H

Halahala—A deadly poison produced from the churning of the ocean of milk.

Hastinapura—The capital city of the Kauravas, presently near New Delhi.

Hiranyakashipu—The son of the sage Kashyapa and Diti. He persecuted his son Prahlada for the boy's religious beliefs.

Hiranyaksha—The son of the sage Kashyapa and Diti. He exploited and terrorized the universe and made the Earth fall into the Garbhodaka ocean.

Holy Names—Names of God like Vishnu, Krishna, Govinda, Rama.

Huhu—A male Gandharva who was cursed by the sage Devala to become a crocodile.

I

Ikshumati—A river that flows near Kurukshetra, a plain near today's Delhi.

Ila—King Manu's and Shraddha's daughter, who was turned into a boy named Sudyumna.

Indra—The king of heaven and the god of rain.

Indradyumna—A king whom the sage Agastya cursed to become an elephant.

J

Jada Bharata—The reincarnation of King Bharata who, after being diverted from his spiritual goal, finally achieved a high level of self-realization.

Jambhasura—A demon slain by Indra.

Janamejaya—The son of King Parikshit who succeeded him on the throne.

Jaya—A gatekeeper at the entrance of Vaikuntha, the spiritual world.

Jaya Kali Ma—A prayer that means "Victory to Goddess Kali!" which is recited by her votaries.

K

Kailash—A mountain in the Himalayas, north of the Manasa Lake, where Lord Shiva resides.

Kalanemi—A great demon. The son of Virochana and grandson of Hiranyakashipu, he was killed by Lord Vishnu. However, he reincarnated as King Kamsa and was killed by Lord Krishna.

Kalanjara—A famous mountain at Medhavika Tirtha (a pilgrimage spot) and a part of Mount Mahameru.

Kali—The fourth age, personified by the spirit of evil, during which only one quarter of righteousness remains.

Kali—A great goddess who is Lord Shiva's wife and who destroys demons.

Kali-yuga—The iron age, characterized by quarrel and hypocrisy. It lasts 240,000 years and began about five thousand years ago.

Kanyakubja—A famous city on the banks of the Ganges River. It is now known as Kanauj.

Karma—(1) Action performed according to scriptural regulations; (2) action pertaining to the development of the physical body; (3) any materialistic action that will incur a subsequent reaction; (4) the materialistic reaction one incurs from materialistic activities.

Kashyapa—A great sage who was the son of Marichi, Lord Brahma's son.

Kaushika—A river, also known as the Gomati. The great sage Vishvamitra's hermitage stood on the bank of this river. Today it is called Kosi.

Kaustubha—A celebrated jewel produced by the churning of the ocean of milk by the gods and demons and worn on Lord Vishnu's chest.

Krishna—The Supreme Lord, who lived in Vrndavana as a cowherd, in Mathura as a prince, and in Dwarka as a king. He spoke the famous *Bhagavad-gita*, the Song of God, on the battlefield of Kurukshetra.

Kritadyuti—The queen of King Chitraketu.

Kumaras—Four great sages who are Lord Brahma's mind-born sons and who appear like five-year-old children. Their names are Sanaka, Sanatana, Sanandana, and Sanat-kumara.

Kurma—The Lord's tortoise incarnation in which He acted as a base for the Mandara Mountain when the ocean of milk was churned by the gods and demons.

Kurus—The descendants of Kuru, especially the sons of King Dhritarashtra, who were enemies of the Pandavas.

Kurukshetra—A plain near Delhi where the great battle between the Kauravas and the Pandavas was fought. It lies southeast of Thanesar near Panipat and is a place of pilgrimage.

Kusha grass—A sacred grass used for ceremonies. It has long stalks and pointed leaves like rushes.

L

Lakshmi—The goddess of fortune and Lord Vishnu's wife.

M

Madhuvana—A forest in the Vrndavana region where Prince Dhruva practiced harsh disciplines along with devotional meditation.

Mahabharata—Vyasa's epic history of greater India, which includes the events of the Kurukshetra war and the narration of the *Bhagavad-gita*.

Manasa-sarovara—A lake on the peak of the Himalayas in which Indra hid for one thousand years.

Mandara—A mountain that was used as a churning rod to churn the ocean of milk.

Mandhata—A famous king of the Ikshvaku dynasty. He gave his fifty daughters in marriage to Yogi Saubhari.

Maniman—A disciple of Lord Shiva who arrested the sage Bhrigu.

Manu—A son of Lord Brahma who is the forefather and lawgiver of the human race. There is a succession of fourteen Manus during each day of Brahma.

Marut—The wind god and regent of the north-west quarter.

Maruts—Forty-nine sons of Diti known as the storm gods.

Matali—The charioteer of Indra.

Maya—The energy of the Supreme Lord that illusions the inhabitants of the material world and makes them forget they have a relationship with God.

Mitra—The god who rules the day, guarding the world, encouraging religion, and chastising sin.

Mohini-murti—Lord Vishnu's gorgeous female incarnation.

N

Nakula—The fourth of the Pandava princes and one of the twin sons of Madri, the second wife of King Pandu.

Namah Shivaya Svaha—This mantra means, "I respectfully offer these oblations to Lord Shiva."

Namuchi—A demon warrior who fought for King Bali.

Nanda—A personal servant of Lord Vishnu.

Nandana—The grove of Indra, lying to the north of Mount Meru.

Narada—A great devotee sage born from Lord Brahma. He travels throughout the universe glorifying devotional service to God.

Nara-Narayana—Two incarnations of God, the name is sometimes applied to Krishna alone and sometimes to Krishna and Arjuna. They performed austerities for one thousand years at Badarikashram in the Himalayas.

Narasingha—The half-man, half-lion incarnation of the Supreme

Lord, who protected Prahlada and killed the demon Hiranyakashipu.

Narayana—An incarnation of God who has four arms. He presides over the Vaikuntha planets.

Narmada—An esteemed holy river.

Nivatakavacha(s)—A class of Daityas who descended from King Prahlada.

O

Ocean of milk—The ocean surrounding the island known as Shvetadvipa, where Lord Vishnu resides. It is located in the area of the Polar Star.

Om Namo Bhagavate Tasmai—This mantra means, "I offer my respectful obeisances to the Supreme Lord Vishnu."

Om Namo Bhagavate Vasudevaya—This mantra means, "I offer my respectful obeisances to the Supreme Lord Vishnu."

P

Padmaraga—Coral.

Paka—A mighty asura who once fought against Indra.

Pandavas—The descendants of King Pandu, whose mothers were Kunti and Madri and whose actual fathers were the gods Yama, Vayu, Indra, and the Ashwini.Kumaras. The Pandavas were Yudhishthira, Bhima, Arjuna, Nakula, and Sahadeva, all intimate friends of Lord Krishna.

Parijata—The tree produced by the churning of the ocean of milk and which is kept in the heavenly garden of the god Indra. Its fragrance is delightfully intoxicating.

Parikshit—The son of Abhimanyu by his wife Uttara, the grandson of Arjuna, and the successor to Yudhishthira's throne. He became the emperor of the world, and heard the *Shrimad Bhagavatam* from Shukadeva Goswami.

Parvati—A name of Lord Shiva's wife.

Payo-vrata—A twelve-day ritualistic ceremony consisting of certain foods, mantras, prayers, worship, donations, etc.

Pingala—A prostitute who realized the futility of materialistic living.

Polestar—The North Star or polar star.

Prahlada—A great devotee of God whom Lord Vishnu (in His

Narasingha incarnation) protected from being killed by his demon father, Hiranyakashipu.

Prasadam—Food that has been offered to and accepted by the Supreme Lord, and which is generally eaten by His devotee to honor Him. Such food is specially blessed and helps a devotee advance spiritually.

Pratishthana—A sacred place in the city of Prayaga, presently called Jhusi.

Pulaha-ashrama—The residence of one of the forefathers named Pulaha.

Pumsavana—A rite that purifies one's heart and inspires one to become a devotee of Lord Vishnu.

Pururava—The son of Ila from King Budha who became exceedingly attached to the Apsara Urvashi.

Pusha—He is a brother of the sun-god and is identified with the sun.

R

Rakshasa—Generally, a demon who disturbs sacrifices, harasses devout persons, devours human beings, and vexes and afflicts people in many ways.

Rantideva—A pious and benevolent king of the Lunar race. He was very rich, religious, and charitable.

Ribhus—Spiritually advanced beings who live in the region of Lord Brahma.

Rudraksha—The seeds of the Rudraksha tree. They are strung on a rosary and used by the devotees of Lord Shiva for the purpose of repetitiously chanting his name.

S

Sahadeva—The fifth Pandava brother. His mother was Madri and his actual father was one of the twin Ashwins (physicians of heaven).

Samadhi—Total absorption of the soul with the Supreme Lord.

Sanaka—One of the four Kumaras.

Sanandana—One of the four Kumaras.

Sanatana—One of the four Kumaras,

Sanat-kumara—One of the four Kumaras.

Sanda—One of Prince Prahlada's schoolteachers. His father was Shukracharya.

Sanjivani—A mantra for reviving a dead person, used by the Brahmin Shukracharya.

Saraswati—A sacred river that falls from the Himalayas and is now lost in the sands of the desert. But in ancient times it flowed on to the sea. It is also a name of Lord Brahma's wife.

Sati—A name of Lord Shiva's wife.

Satya-yuga—The golden age, or the age of truth. It lasts 1,728,000 years.

Saubhari—A yogi with great mystic powers who fell from his spiritual path but who later realized his unfortunate mistake.

Sauvira—An ancient country near the Sindhu River.

Self-Discovery—The discovery that one is an eternal soul instead of a temporary material body—and to perform one's actions in this understanding.

Self-realization—The state of experiencing and knowing that one is not one's material body but is the spiritual soul within one's body.

Shakti weapon—A weapon infused with the power of Shakti, or Lord Shiva's wife.

Shamika—He was a sage and the father of Shringi, the boy who cursed king Parikshit.

Shiva—The god who destroys this world at the designated time.

Shraddha—Faith in God and the scripture. Also, a ceremony performed yearly for one's deceased ancestors, for their spiritual advancement.

Shraddha—A daughter born to Daksha by his wife Prasuti.

Shrimad Bhagavatam—The *Bhagavata Purana* written by Krishna Dwaipayana Vyasa. It is considered a Vedic scripture and was written to give one a deep understanding of Lord Krishna, His devotees, and devotional service.

Shringi—The young ascetic who cursed King Parikshit to die in seven days.

Shudra—A laborer or artisan who is in the lowest of the four castes.

Shukadeva Goswami—The son of Vyasa, who narrated the Bhagavatam to King Parikshit just prior to his death.

Shukracharya—A son of the sage Bhrigu and a priest of King Bali and the Daityas.

Shurasena—A king whose kingdom was Mathura. His kingdom was also called Shurasena.

Shvetadvipa—An island in the ocean of milk where Lord Vishnu lives.

This ocean is located in the Polestar region, or King Dhruva's planet.

Siddha—A semi-divine being of great purity and holiness. Such beings usually have many mystic powers. They live in regions between the earth and the sun.

Sindhu—The Indus River. Also, the country along that river and the people dwelling in it.

Soma-rasa—The juice extracted from the soma creeper. This juice is fondly accepted by the gods in sacrifices.

Soul—The living entity or spark of light that exists in the heart of all living beings. It gives life to the material body and survives death, generally reincarnating in another physical form according to its previous karma.

Sudyumna—The son of Vaivasvata Manu who was born as a female but later became a male.

Sukumara—A forest that Lord Shiva cursed so that any male who entered it would become a female.

Sumeru—Also known as Mahameru. It is the golden-colored peak of the Himalaya Mountains. Frequented by many gods, sinners cannot approach it.

Sunanda—A personal servant of Lord Vishnu.

Suniti—Prince Dhruva's mother and the less favored of King Uttanapada's two wives.

Suruchi—Prince Dhruva's stepmother and the more favored of King Uttanapada's two wives.

Svayambhuva Manu—The name of the first Manu. He was a progenitor of mankind and a ruler of the Earth. He wrote the original law book for the human race.

T

Takshaka—The chief of snakes. He bit King Parikshit and killed him.

Treta-yuga—The silver or second age of the world. It lasts 1,296,000 years.

Trikuta—A mountain with three peaks that rises from the ocean of milk.

Tulasi Devi—One of Lord Vishnu's wives, who dwells in the Tulasi (Holy Basil) plant. Considered to be highly important by devotees of Lord Vishnu, she is thus worshiped daily.

Tvashta—He was both a god and a demon. He invoked the monster Vritrasura to kill the god Indra in reprisal for Indra's killing of his son Vishvarupa.

U

Urvashi—An extremely beautiful Apsara who was cursed to live on earth for some time. She married King Pururava.

Uttama—Son of King Uttanapada and Suruchi and half-brother of Prince Dhruva.

Uttanapada—A son of Svayambhuva Manu who became a king.

V

Vaikuntha—The spiritual or eternal world known as "the place of no anxiety," where Lord Vishnu resides.

Vajapeya sacrifice—The name of a sacrifice performed by King Daksha, one of the original ancestors of the world.

Vamana—The dwarf incarnation of Lord Vishnu, who helped the god Indra recover his position and property in heaven from King Bali.

Varuna—The god of the waters (oceans, rivers, etc.)

Vasishtha—A mind-born son of Lord Brahma and great sage who taught Lord Ramachandra Vedic knowledge.

Vasuki—The serpent king.

Vayu—The god of wind.

Vedas—The holy scriptures revealed by God (the *Rg, Sama, Atharva, and Yajur*).

Vedic—Pertaining to a culture in which all aspects of life are under the guidance of the Vedas.

Vibhavari—The watery home of the god Varuna.

Videha—An ancient country whose capital was Mithila. Today, it is called Tirhut or North Bihar.

Vijaya—A gatekeeper at the entrance of Vaikuntha, the spiritual world.

Virabhadra—A monster created by Lord Shiva to avenge the death of his wife, Sati.

Varaha—An incarnation of Lord Vishnu who assumed a boar form.

Vishnu—The Supreme Lord.

Vishnuduta—A servant of Lord Vishnu.

Vishvakarma—A god who is the architect of the gods.

Vishvarupa—A three-headed priest of the gods, who was killed by Indra.

Vishvasu—The chief of the Gandharvas in Lord Indra's heaven.

Vrika—A demon who tried to kill Lord Shiva, who had blessed him with a special power.

Vritra—The reincarnation of King Chitraketu, who tried to kill the god Indra.

Vyasa—The incarnation of Lord Krishna who compiled the Vedas and wrote the *Puranas, Vedanta-sutra* and *Mahabharata*.

Y

Yajur Veda—One of the four Vedas containing hymns and chants.

Yaksha—A class of supernatural beings who serve Kuvera, the god of wealth.

Yamaduta—A servant of the lord of death.

Yamuna—A sacred river in India that rises in a mountain called Kalinda. It is closely associated with Lord Krishna's activities.

Yudhishthira—The eldest of the five Pandu princes and the son of Dharma (or righteousness) and Kunti.

APPENDIX 1

Shrimad Bhagavatam Story References

ŚRĪMAD BHĀGAVATAM

Eighth Canto

His Divine Grace
A.C. Bhaktivedanta Swami Prabhupāda
Founder-Ācārya of the International Society for Krishna Consciousness

ŚRĪMAD BHĀGAVATAM

With translations and elaborate purports by

His Divine Grace A.C. Bhaktivedanta Swami Prabhupāda

Śrīmad-Bhāgavatam (*Bhāgavata Purāṇa*) is a virtual encyclopedia of yoga, meditation, and the mystic arts. It brings together in one complete source information that previously took hundreds of books to explain.

This edition of the *Bhāgavatam,* with elaborate commentary, is the most widely read and authoritative translation available to the English-speaking world. Cantos One through Nine, as well as Chapters One through Thirteen of the Tenth Canto, are the products of the scholarly and devotional effort of His Divine Grace A.C. Bhaktivedanta Swami Prabhupāda. After Srila Prabhupada departed from this world in 1977, his disciples completed the work by translating the balance of the Tenth Canto, along with the entire Eleventh and Twelfth Cantos.

"This Bhāgavata Purāṇa is as brilliant as the sun, and it has arisen just after the departure of Lord Krsna to His own abode, accompanied by religion, knowledge, etc. Persons who have lost their vision due to the dense darkness of ignorance in the Age of Kali shall get light from this Purāṇa."

Śrīmad-Bhāgavatam 1.3.4

SPECIAL FEATURES

- ◆ *Original Sanskrit text*
- ◆ *English equivalents*
- ◆ *Elaborate commentary*
- ◆ *Complete glossary*
- ◆ *Complete subject index*

- ◆ *Several appendices*
- ◆ *High readability*
- ◆ *288 full-color illustrations*
- ◆ *Dust jackets*
- ◆ *Silk bookmarks*

Hardbound ◆ 18 volumes ◆ 17,900 pages ◆ ISBN 0-89213-624-7 ◆ $360.00

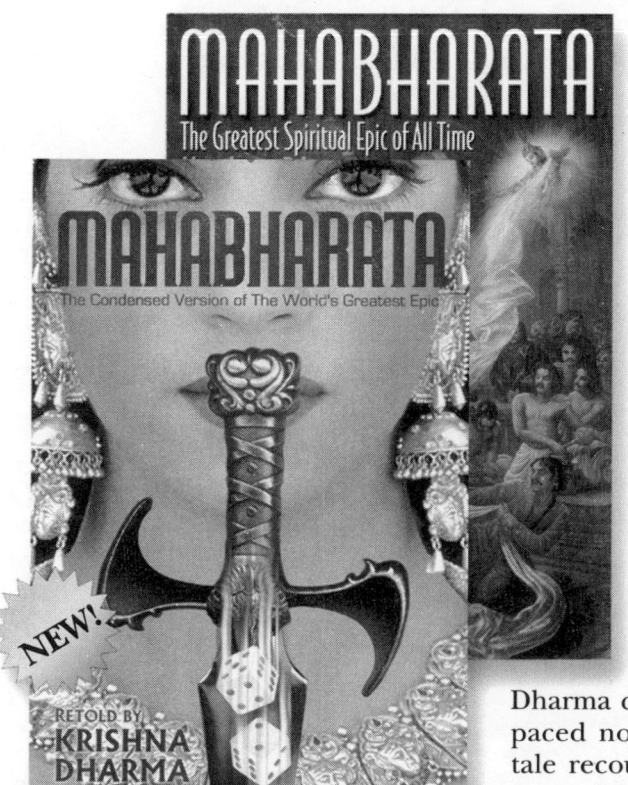

BHAGAVAD-GITA
THE SONG DIVINE
A New, Easy-to-Understand Edition of India's Timeless Masterpiece of Spiritual Wisdom

The *Bhagavad-gita*, India's greatest spiritual treatise, contains far too much drama to remain the exclusive property of philosophers and religionists. Woodham presents the timeless wisdom of the *Gita* in contemporary English poetry, bringing to life its ancient yet perennially applicable message. It recounts in metered stanzas the historic conversation between Krishna, the Supreme Mystic, and the mighty warrior Arjuna as they survey the battlefield preparations for the greatest world war of all time. This reader-friendly edition will attract the minds and hearts of not only spiritualists and philosophers, but of dramatists, musicians, children, poetry-lovers, and all who seek inspiration in their daily lives.

$15.00 ♦ ISBN 1-887089-26-8
5" x 7" ♦ Hardcover ♦ 118 pgs.

BHAGAVAD-GITA AS IT IS

By
His Divine Grace
A.C. Bhaktivedanta
Swami Prabhupada

The *Bhagavad-gita* is the concise summary of India's spiritual teachings. Remarkably, the setting for this classic is a battlefield. Just before the battle, the great warrior Arjuna begins to inquire from Lord Krishna about the meaning of life. The *Gita* systematically guides one along the path of self-realization. It is the main sourcebook for information on karma, reincarnation, yoga, devotion, the soul, Lord Krishna, and spiritual enlightenment.

Bhagavad-gita As It Is is the best-selling edition in the world!

INTERACTIVE CD

Interactive Multi-media CD-Rom version, over 30 hours of Audio, 275 full-color illustrations, video clips, and nearly 1000 pages of text.
$19.95
ISBN 91-7149-415-4.

"*Bhagavad-gita As It Is* is a deeply felt, powerfully conceived, and beautifully explained work. I have never seen any other work on the *Gita* with such an important voice and style. It is a work of undoubted integrity. It will occupy a significant place in the intellectual and ethical life of modern man for a long time to come."
—Dr. Shaligram Shukla, assistant Professor of Linguistics, Georgetown University

"When doubts haunt me, when disappointments stare me in the face, and I see not one ray of hope on the horizon, I turn to *Bhagavad-gita* and find a verse to comfort me; and I immediately begin to smile in the midst of overwhelming sorrow. Those who meditate on the *Gita* will derive fresh joy and new meanings from it every day."
—Mohandas K. Gandhi

Deluxe edition with translations and elaborate purports:

$24.95 ♦ ISBN 0-89213-285-X ♦ 6.5" x 9.5"
Hardbound ♦ 1068 pgs. ♦ 29 full-color plates
Standard edition, including translation and elaborate purports:
$12.95 ♦ ISBN 0-89213-123-3 ♦ 5.5" x 8.5"
Hardbound ♦ 924 pgs. ♦ 14 full-color plates

BOOK ORDER FORM

◆ Telephone orders: Call 1-888-TORCHLT (1-888-867-2458)
  (Please have your credit card ready.)
◆ Fax orders: 559-337-2354
◆ Postal Orders: Torchlight Publishing, P O Box 52, Badger, CA 93603, USA
🕉 **World Wide Web: www.torchlight.com**

PLEASE SEND THE FOLLOWING:	QUANTITY	AMOUNT
☐Bhagavad-gita As It Is		
Deluxe (1,068 pages)—$24.95	x_____	= $_____
Standard (924 pages)—$12.95	x_____	= $_____
☐Bhagavad-gita Interactive CD—$19.95	x_____	= $_____
☐**Śrīmad-Bhāgavatam**—$360.00	x_____	= $_____
☐Bhagavad-gita, The Song Divine—$15.00	x_____	= $_____
☐Mystical Stories from the **Bhāgavatam**—$19.95	x_____	= $_____
☐Mystical Stories from **Mahabharata**—$17.95	x_____	= $_____
☐Mahabharata, unabridged—$39.95	x_____	= $_____
☐Mahabharata, condensed—$19.95	x_____	= $_____

Shipping/handling (see below) . . . . $_____
Sales tax 7% (California only) . . . . $_____
TOTAL . . . . $_____

(I understand that I may return any book for a full refund—no questions asked.)

☐PLEASE SEND ME YOUR CATALOG AND INFO ON OTHER BOOKS BY TORCHLIGHT PUBLISHING

Company _____

Name _____

Address _____

City _____ State _____ Zip _____

PAYMENT:

☐ Check/money order enclosed ☐ VISA ☐ MasterCard ☐ American Express

Card number _____

Name on card _____ Exp. date _____

Signature _____

SHIPPING AND HANDLING:

USA: $4.00 for the first book and $3.00 for each additional book. Air mail per book (USA only)—$7.00.
Canada: $6.00 for the first book and $3.50 for each additional book. (NOTE: Surface shipping may take 3 to 4 weeks in North America.)
Foreign countries: $8.00 for the first book and $5.00 for each additional book. Please allow 6 to 8 weeks for delivery.